Contents

For Laureen
—once missed but never forgotten—
who makes it possible

Introduction

As WHITE SETTLERS SURGED RELENTLESSLY westward across the North American continent in the 19th century, they encountered the Native tribes that had occupied the land for centuries. The traditional Native way of life became impossible to maintain in the face of changes that were dramatic, rapid and unlike any the Native people had ever experienced. The Great Spirit saw the people's struggle and provided them with a handful of leaders with wisdom, bravery and strength. These leaders were relied upon to negotiate treaties, and when those failed, to help the people withstand the inevitable armed forces that were sent to eliminate them or relocate them to distant reservations.

As I understand it, Native leaders had special powers—beyond wisdom and bravery—usually associated with a spirit helper that gave assistance, often through visions. But having spirit helpers and visions were not enough for a man to become a leader. An individual had to travel a path worthy of respect. The choices he made, especially as those choices conformed to band values, demonstrated leadership potential. Power and behavior made a chief, who then shouldered

GREAT CHIEFS

VOLUME I

BY TONY HOLLIHAN

FOLK LORE PUBLISHING

The Publisher: Folklore Publishing
Website: www.folklorepublishing.com

Distributed by Lone Pine Publishing
10145–81 Ave
Edmonton, AB Canada T6E 1W9
Toll Free: 800-661-9017

National Library of Canada Cataloguing in Publication Data
Hollihan, K. Tony (Kelvin Tony), 1964–
Great chiefs / K. Tony Hollihan.

(Legends series)
Includes bibliographical references.
ISBN 1-894864-03-4 (v. 1)

1. Indians of North America—Kings and rulers—Biography. I. Title. II. Series: Legends series (Edmonton, Alta.)
E89.H64 2002   970'.00497'00922   C2002-911043-2

Editorial Director: Faye Boer
Cover Image: Pretty Blue Blanket Man; artwork by Dale Auger, with special thanks to Duval House Publishing
Photography credits: Every effort has been made to accurately credit the sources of photographs. Any errors or omissions should be directed to the publisher for changes in future editions. *Photographs courtesy of* American Museum of Natural History Library (p. 237, 124781); Denver Public Library, Western History Dept. (p. 122, X-32238; p. 139, X-32234); Glenbow Archives, Calgary, Canada (p. 10, NA-1151-1; p. 45, NA-1183-2; p.51, NA-3665-30; title page & p. 60, NA-3665-36, p. 190, NA-1193-4, p. 288, NA-1406-214; p. 315, NA-1081-3); Institute of Texan Cultures (p. 144, ITC-68-140); Library of Congress, Prints & Photographs Division p. 108, USZ62-98166; p. 154, USZ62-91032; p. 183, USZ62-107774); Montana Historical Society, Helena (p. 73, 955-976; p. 99, 955-969); National Anthropological Archives, Smithsonian Institution (p. 18, Ms. 1929A, 08584300; p. 230, NAA-999; p. 233, NAA-44654); National Archives, Still Pictures Branch, College Park, MD (p. 32, 999-ANSCO-CA-10; p. 180, 111-SC-95986); Provincial Archives of Manitoba (p. 253, N5733); Saskatchewan Archives Board (p. 276, R-A533); Woolaroc Museum (p.194; p.244).

PC: P6

great responsibility because his only concern was the welfare of his people. Volume I of *Great Chiefs* explores the lives of six such men.

Sitting Bull, a Hunkpapa Sioux, was ranked as the most feared Native on the mid-western Plains. His power as a war leader and medicine man gave him the previously unheard-of responsibility of leading the western Sioux during the Plains wars of the 1870s. His part in the defeats of General Crook on the Rosebud River and General Custer on the Little Bighorn River gained him an unrivalled notoriety among Americans.

Chief Joseph, a Nez Perce, was so committed to principle and to peace that he almost defeated the United States government without firing a single bullet. When Chief Joseph's band was forced to abandon their territory, he and his people fled rather than be placed on a distant reservation. For months the army chased the Nez Perce. Americans marveled as they read the news that Chief Joseph would not resort to violence. Even when Chief Joseph was faced with defeat, he would not allow a rifle to be raised in defense.

Quanah Parker, a Quahadi Comanche, was unique as a leader. Throughout the late 1860s and early 1870s he led his warriors on violent raids in what would soon become New Mexico and Texas. His commitment to the traditional way of Comanche life was legendary, but when it became clear that following such a path would result in the death of his people, he surrendered. Quanah Parker refused to let defeat be the end. By example he showed his people how they could adopt the ways of the white man without sacrificing what it meant to be Comanche.

Red Cloud, an Oglala Sioux, was the only Native to force the United States into making treaty on dictated terms. Angry that white settlers traveling along the Bozeman Trail were killing the buffalo that were so important to his people's way of life, Red Cloud initiated a series of campaigns in the mid-1860s. Red Cloud's War ended only when the United States agreed to close its forts along the Bozeman Trail and to abandon the route.

Sequoyah, a Cherokee, invented a written language for his people in the early 1800s, the only person known to have achieved such a feat. Sequoyan, as the written form of Cherokee was called, allowed the Cherokee to resist cultural erosion by enabling them to avoid the white man's education and to communicate over distance and time in their own words. Today Sequoyan remains the Cherokee's written language.

Louis Riel, a Métis, was a politician who led his people to victory against the Canadian government in the Red River Rebellion of 1869–70. The result of the rebellion was the creation of the province of Manitoba and the protection of Métis rights. Riel gained such a reputation among his people that he was asked to organize a second campaign to protect Métis rights. Although comfortable in Montana, Riel returned to western Canada, where he led his people in the North-West Rebellion of 1885.

Finally, some notes of explanation. Natives called white people, including government officials and the British monarchy, by different names so terms will vary from chapter to chapter. Usually, a Native's name changed over his lifetime, so the same individual may have different names. Often, when a young Native performed some notable feat, he was given his father's name whereupon his father took another name.

CHAPTER ONE

Sitting Bull

~~~

Hunkpapa Sioux, 1834–1890

THERE HAD LONG BEEN RUMORS in the East of gold in the Black Hills, mountains that straddled the Dakota and Wyoming Territories. Unfortunately, the presence of the Sioux made the persistent rumors difficult to prove. After the Fort Laramie Treaty of 1868, the United States government recognized the Black Hills as part of the Great Sioux Reservation. The Sioux link with *Paha Sapa*, as they called the Black Hills, was first forged in some distant, misty past. Their legends identified it as the Sioux's place of creation and experience revealed it to be the home of powerful spirits. The mountains were abundant with wildlife and trees, and fresh streams coursed through the valleys. *Paha Sapa* provided for the Sioux's every spiritual and physical need.

By the mid-1870s the rumors of gold were confirmed, and the United States government was determined to take control of the Black Hills. When some Sioux resisted,

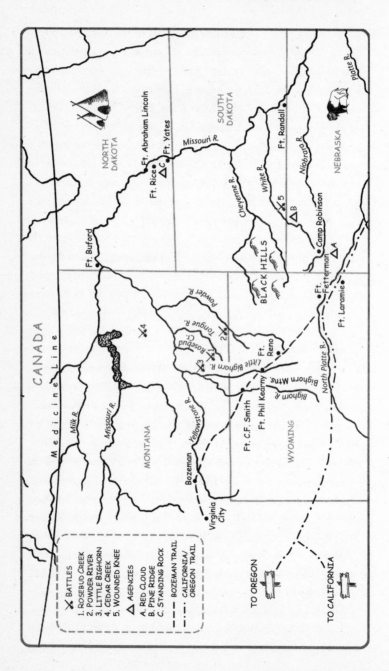

they were labeled hostile and enemies of the United States. In early 1876 the American offensive to rein them in began. The first encounter between the U.S. army and the Plains Natives of the area was with a small band of off-reservation, but peaceful, Sioux and Cheyenne. The Battle of Powder River was indecisive, but when news of it reached another who had resisted the government's demands—Sitting Bull, the chief of the Hunkpapa Sioux— it was to have far-reaching consequences. Sitting Bull was a man whose countenance suggested good humor but, on this occasion, his face was darkened with rage.

"Who are these Long Knives! They agree that the Black Hills are ours forever and then they demand to own it!" he ranted. "It is known that I accept no price for them. And when they learn of this? They attack! They are not to be trusted. My brothers, we are patient and put up with much. Well, now the Long Knives have come shooting. They have brought war. War they will have."

Throughout the spring, Sitting Bull's camp sent runners to Natives across the Plains. All had a similar request to deliver: come to the war council. More than 1000 warriors came, including those from different tribes and many who had settled on reserves. At the war council, Sitting Bull was chosen to lead the Sioux. To appoint a single leader was an unusual course of action for these independent people, but the times demanded a new approach. It was a great responsibility for Sitting Bull. Only one thing was certain: Sitting Bull would not be rushed. He would not be pressured into choosing a rash course of action. After he had visualized all the possibilities, he settled on an ingenious solution. He would unite his Native brothers and sisters so that they might act as one single, strong arrow. He would do this in the traditional way, by seeking a vision from Wakan Tanka (the Great Mystery), a vision that would serve all. Sitting

Sitting Bull, taken in 1877 while he was exiled in Canada, likely at the North-West Mounted Police post at Fort Walsh.

Bull called for a Sun Dance, perhaps the greatest of all Plains Native ceremonies.

The singers fell silent and the dancers stood still when they saw Sitting Bull emerge from the small willow dwelling covered in buffalo robes. His damp body, marked with deep red rashes and scars from previous dances, had a reddish glow, and the smell of sweet grass and tobacco drifted from him as he made his way to the Sun Dance pole in the middle of the dance circle. Fasting and sweating had purified him, and he was ready to ask Wakan Tanka for a vision. He sat, his back against the pole. His brother, Jumping Bull, soon joined him. He took Sitting Bull's left arm in his hand and inserted an awl beneath his skin. He pierced the flesh 50 times before he let it fall. He took the right arm and did the same. Satisfied that Wakan Tanka had his sacrificial bloodred blanket, Sitting Bull rose to dance.

The blood dripped from his arms and painted a dark circle on the ground around the pole. By the time the blood on his arms had finally congealed, the gravel scattered within the dance circle had rubbed his feet raw and his path was soon a deep red once again. He danced throughout the day, his eyes never leaving the sun, his songs never interrupted. When the sun went to its lodge, Sitting Bull did not rest. He continued as he had all day, and the next morning he greeted the sun with his dance and song. When it reached its midday peak, Sitting Bull stopped, his arms hanging limp by his side. Black Moon, a close friend, ran to his side and gently lowered him to the ground. He put his ear close to Sitting Bull's mouth and listened as the hoarse voice whispered. When others came to their chief's assistance, Black Moon rose and spoke.

"My brothers, Sitting Bull has had a vision. Wakan Tanka has answered his prayers! Sitting Bull wishes me to tell you that he heard a voice. 'Look below the sun,' it commanded. As he did he saw many soldiers falling to the ground in our camp, their heads below their feet. Under them were some Natives, also upside down. Again the voice spoke to him. 'These Long Knives do not have ears. They will die, but do not take their belongings.'"

The vision was well received because it was easily understood. The Long Knives would not listen to the Sioux; they would not hear their words of peace. Instead, the Long Knives would attack and they would die. So Wakan Tanka had told Sitting Bull.

~~~~~

In a Hunkpapa camp on a summer's morning, the sun not long departed from its lodge, a crowd of boys gathered outside the tipi of Village Center, the band's foremost arrow maker. They babbled excitedly because rumor had it that he was going to announce a competition, and there was little more to quicken the blood of a Sioux, young or old, than a contest. Finally Village Center appeared.

"My fellow Sioux," he formally declared, "I have spent many, many days making this bow and set of arrows." He held them high for all to see. It was not the small set that the boys were used to, but an adult's and full sized. "I am going to give them to one of you." The declaration was met with a hushed silence, a mark of the respect in which the boys held the arrow maker. "They will go to he who brings me the prettiest bird. I will decide tonight."

The boys rushed to their lodges to retrieve their bows and arrows. Soon, they were scampering into the woods, arrows notched against the sinew of their bows, eyes fixed on the high branches of trees. One boy, however, did not ready his weapon for firing. Rather, he sat in a shady grove with the bow and arrows on his lap. It was Jumping Badger, whom everyone called Slow (Sitting Bull's name as a child). The boy was living up to his name. A challenge like this one required some reflection; it was not to be rushed into.

Slow thought about the birds that lodged around his camp. Which one would be the worthiest prize? He quickly eliminated many. The crow was too bland. The magpie's tail feathers shimmered blue and green in the light, but it was no test to kill. The cardinal, however, might be suitable. The bloodred of its feathers was a color respected by the Sioux. As Slow thought about the birds, his eyes caught sight of something orange and yellow darting through the trees above his head. An oriole, of course! Only the sun matched its bright colors; its speed made it a challenge to strike with an arrow. Slow plotted his strategy and imagined carrying it through. Only when he felt comfortable did he set off after his prey.

The day slipped by and with it Slow's supply of arrows. By mid-afternoon he was still hunting the oriole. He was patient. What would come would come, and all he could do was be prepared for it. As he searched for the oriole, he came upon a group of fellow competitors. All were silent, save Crossed Rabbit. He was angry because his prized arrow had missed its mark and was lodged in a tree.

"I can't win the contest without it," he moaned. Then he called, "He who retrieves my arrow will be given one of my best arrows!"

Slow notched one of his arrows, let it fly and hit the mark. Unfortunately, Crossed Rabbit's arrow shattered when it landed.

"You've broken it, Slow! My best arrow!" His voice became cold and measured. "You will pay for it."

An argument ensued, with the boys taking opposing sides. When it became apparent to Slow that a fight involving them all might erupt, he intervened.

"Crossed Rabbit, take my best arrow and let us be done with this."

That night the boys gathered around Village Center, anxious for his decision. Before he spoke, one of the boys asked if he might first say something. His request granted, he explained the events of the afternoon. The boy concluded by suggesting that Slow's sacrifice had prevented a great fight.

Village Center was quiet for a moment.

"There are many ways to measure victory. Sometimes it is to be found in compromise. Today Slow has demonstrated something of what it is to be wise. The bow and arrows go to him," he declared.

Village Center's words were high praise for one so young. Time would demonstrate that they were not misplaced. During a period in which nothing was as it had been, Wakan Tanka had delivered to the Sioux a leader as unique as his era.

Slow was born a Hunkpapa (meaning "the Campers at the Entrance of the Circle"). The Hunkpapa was one of the seven tribes of the western Sioux known as the Teton. Farther to the east were the other divisions of the Sioux: the Yankton, the Yanktonai and the Santee. They called themselves Lakota; the more popular term Sioux was an Ojibwa word meaning "enemy." Throughout many decades the Hunkpapa had migrated from the northeast and, by Slow's time, they lived west of the Missouri River and south of the Yellowstone River (primarily in present-day South Dakota and Wyoming) close to the Black Hills. Although wooded plateaus and green valleys occasionally marked the territory, vast rolling plains dominated the area. Slow was born in 1834, and in his youth there was little challenge to Sioux authority in the region. There were few white men, mostly traders, and enemy tribes knew enough of Sioux skill and bravery to limit their incursions to the occasional raid.

The Sioux depended on the great resource that Wakan Tanka had furnished—the buffalo. Hunted skillfully on horseback, the shaggy beast provided for the Sioux's every need. They ate its flesh, used hides for clothing and shelter and turned sinew into bindings and bones into utensils. But the importance of the buffalo to the Sioux cannot be measured in purely physical terms. It figured prominently in their social and cultural lives, the hunt providing opportunities for boys to become men and for girls to learn the skills of women. And it was the much-respected center of their spiritual life, a creature of myth and great power.

Slow was only 10 years old when his Uncle Four Horns, who as tradition dictated had been responsible for his education for the past few years, took him on his first buffalo hunt. The boy had accompanied hunters before, but he was allowed to do little more than observe. Slow had watched carefully and he was ready to put to use what he had seen. Slow took the lead as soon as he mounted his gray cayuse. The herd was close to camp and quickly reached. Slow slipped downwind of the animals, selected a likely position of attack and waited. As the sun rose in the sky, Four Horns wondered whether the test was too great for the young boy. The herd was tightly gathered, and the tough bulls, bigger in size than both the boy and his cayuse together, roamed along its border. Perhaps Slow was afraid or maybe just patient. Four Horns decided to let the boy deal with it as he chose. A choice was soon made.

A few buffalo broke from the main herd. As they grazed towards the pair, Slow notched his arrow and tightened his legs around the midsection of his horse. Suddenly his heels jabbed and he shouted as his horse sped towards the animals. Unwilling to risk an arrow that was off the mark, he rode closer to the herd only pulling the bow string taut when he could feel the heat of the beasts. The arrow struck true, and Slow brought down his first buffalo. Four Horns did not congratulate his nephew because that was not the way of things, but he did ask why Slow had targeted a bull and not the easier cow.

"There was a calf, uncle. To kill the mother was to kill it also. Both will return."

Upon returning to camp, Slow informed his mother, Her-Holy-Door, of the kill. She gathered the tools needed to dress it and, as she left, Slow directed her to give the hump, the best piece of meat, to a recently widowed Sioux. Those who knew of his act reflected on his generosity, a leadership trait respected by the Sioux.

Glimpses of leadership were suggestive, but Slow was still a young boy. A first buffalo hunt was important, but it was merely one step towards becoming a man. Slow was 14 when he took the second, accompanying Hunkpapa warriors on a raid. He was determined to count his first coup, to strike his opponent in battle with his coup stick while his opponent was still alive and fighting. Natives considered it an act of bravery that defined the warrior.

Slow's opportunity came unexpectedly. He was traveling with a war party, performing the duties of an errand boy, as was usual for boys. The warriors were on the trail of some Crows, a traditional enemy whom the Sioux had come to hate even more since they had made treaty with the rapacious Long Knives. When they were not far from the Crow camp, Slow's father, Sitting Bull, approached him.

"Slow, Four Horns tells me that you have learned well. Today you have a fast horse. Show me that you are brave." With those words, he gave his son a coup stick.

The Sioux war party caught the Crow by surprise. Slow was among those who rushed down the hillside into the coulee where the enemy camped. The Crow were outnumbered and, sensing defeat, some of them sought to escape. Slow saw one on horseback break for the open end of the coulee, and he set off in pursuit. Perhaps the Crow smiled when he glanced over his shoulder to see the yellow-painted, naked boy following him. He took the time to

notch an arrow and shoot it. It missed its mark, and the
Crow urged his horse on with greater concern. Slow
pushed his horse and gained on the enemy. When the
Crow next looked behind him, the boy was almost abreast.
The Crow closed his eyes as he felt the whack of the coup
stick. Slow then lifted the tomahawk that he held in his
other hand and brought it thundering down on the Crow's
head. The Crow fell from his horse, stunned. Before Slow
could dismount, another Hunkpapa pounced on the Crow.
He pulled the hair of his enemy tight and, with a quick
pull of his arm, dragged his knife across the forehead. With
a tug, the scalp was his along with second coup.

Later that evening, his father spoke to him, "Son, today
you are a warrior. Today you are a man."

The war party had been successful, which was cause for
great celebration when it returned to the camp at Powder
River. There was feasting, singing, dancing and stories of past
coups. Those who had counted first coup were finally able to
realize dreams long held and speak of their courage. Slow,
however, did not speak because his father desired to introduce
the new warrior to the band. When his father Sitting Bull
stood, a silence embraced the camp. While he was a respected
warrior and chief, he was also a dreamer, one to whom powerful spirits often revealed their messages. In one particularly
memorable vision, a great white buffalo, understood by all to
be the Buffalo God, had visited Sitting Bull. It was that being
who had given him permission to use the name Sitting Bull.

"In recognition of my son's bravery, I give these horses
away," he declared, as he walked through camp distributing
horses to those in need. One he kept, a magnificent bay. He
took it to his son.

"Slow, I place this white eagle feather in your hair as
a symbol of your first coup. I give you this bay. It is a warrior's
horse that has served me well."

Sitting Bull's own drawing of his first coup at age 14 in a battle with a band of Crow.

Sitting Bull reached into a pot that lay by his feet. When he pulled out his hands they were black. He rubbed them over his son until he was so painted.

"This is my son, a warrior of the Hunkpapa Sioux. He is no longer naked. From this day on, my name is Jumping Bull. This warrior's name is Sitting Bull."

All present recognized the strength of the name. It implied a powerful connection with the spirit world. The name also identified the young man with the animal that was so important to the Hunkpapa. Murmurs throughout the camp suggested that the people agreed that the name suited the one formerly known as Slow. A sitting bull would not be moved until it was ready to do so.

Before the ceremony was complete, Jumping Bull gave his son a shield. "May it protect you in battle."

Its component parts, buffalo hide and willow, were not of themselves strong enough to deflect arrows or coup sticks. The potency of the shield lay in its sacred powers. Painted on the intensely colorful background was a figure that had visited Jumping Bull in one of his dreams. From the frame extended four eagle feathers, each one representing a virtue to which all Sioux aspired: bravery, fortitude, generosity and wisdom.

"My people, I give you the warrior Sitting Bull!" exclaimed Jumping Bull. The announcement was met with a roar of approval.

In the months that followed, Sitting Bull was anxious to prove his courage, and he participated in many Sioux raids and war parties. Like other fiery young braves, he was rarely content to fire arrows or to bide his time and wait for a promising opportunity to count coup. A popular manner of demonstrating heightened courage was to "run the daring line" where a warrior rode his horse through the middle ground between opposing forces. While the exercise was not a tactical ploy, it was known to strengthen the resolve of braves who watched their courageous brother. Because it provided the enemy with a good target, it involved considerable risk so it was not attempted by all. Sitting Bull rode the daring line more than once, and usually his strong medicine protected him. On one occasion, however, a Flathead arrow found his foot. The wound permitted him to wear a second eagle feather. This one was bloodred, telling all that he had been injured in battle.

Sitting Bull's courage was beyond question and his tribe took notice. He was invited to join the Strong Hearts Society, the most prestigious of the Hunkpapa war societies.

Membership was limited to 50 of the tribe's bravest. Even among that number, Sitting Bull was one of the elite because he was chosen to be one of two sash bearers. As one of these, Sitting Bull donned a headdress of blackened buffalo horns (still attached to the fur from the animal's head), erect crow feathers and long strips of dark ermine, and he pledged to ride first into battle and stake his red sash to the ground. It would remain fixed until a fellow Sioux tore it loose. There was no retreat for the sash bearer; he would fight until there was victory or death. While wearing the sash in an encounter with the Crow, a bullet shattered Sitting Bull's heel. It never mended properly, and it forced Sitting Bull to walk with a limp for the rest of his life. The limp proved an asset rather than an impediment because when the Hunkpapa saw him shuffle along, they were reminded of his great bravery. He was soon chosen leader of the Strong Hearts, a great tribute to one in his 20s. It proved a good choice—Sitting Bull led many raids that expanded Hunkpapa hunting territory.

While a brave warrior had the respect of his people, a *wichasha wakan* (a holy man) had their reverence. Some Hunkpapa believed that Sitting Bull might be such a man. Visions had been revealed to him, he communicated with animals and, like his father before him, he had the gift of prophecy. However, one could not be a *wichasha wakan* until he had been the central participant in the Sun Dance, an act that demonstrated to the community both his willingness and readiness. The Sun Dance was not just any Sioux ceremony. It honored Wi (the sun), the great spirit that watched over the world of the living and the dead. Lasting 8 to 12 days, the Sun Dance consisted of ritualized ceremonies that reinforced tribal ideals and mores and unified the community. Central to the event was the dance itself and the self-torture endured by the dancer. The belief was that Wakan Tanka would look favorably upon the sacrifice and grant a vision that could aid the tribe.

Sitting Bull was in his early 20s when he decided that it was his time to dance. The first few days of preparation were lighthearted, marked by feasting, excitement and great anticipation. The spiritual leader assigned roles and directed the dance. Special care was taken in choosing those responsible for the sacred tree that served as the Sun Dance pole—the hunter who would select it, the one who would dig the hole in which to place it and the women who would cut it down. Once the preparations were completed, the dance circle was selected. Warriors battled evil spirits and counted coup where the Sun Dance pole was to be erected. When the pole stood firm, it was colored and decorated with human and buffalo representations. The men were not ready to dance until a final day of reflection, full of special dances and sweat lodge rituals. Finally, the central participants stepped forward to offer their bodies as sacrifices for their people.

The sun was approaching its lodge; Sitting Bull had watched it journey across the sky. He stretched at an angle from the sacred pole, supported by bow-tight sinews attached to the buffalo bones that skewered his chest. Blood seeped slowly from the incisions. His red, welted arms, hanging limply at his sides, no longer bled as the blood from his many wounds had congealed. His mind drifted to memories of childhood, foggy experiences that became as startlingly clear as the prairie sky. He remembered the woodpecker that had saved him from a grizzly. He had composed a song for the bird (he loved to make songs and to sing them), and he heard it again.

"Pretty bird, you saw me and took pity on me; you wish me to survive among the people. Oh Bird People, from this day you shall be my relatives!"

On that day long ago he had realized that he had a special connection with the animals. Other memories were revisited, other experiences that reminded him of his communion with the animals. He was in the woods when a wolf appeared, two arrows dangling from its bloodied flank.

"Boy!" called the wolf. "Help me and all will know your name."

He removed the arrows and, as the wolf disappeared into the trees, the boy sang a song to the wolf tribe.

"Alone in the wilderness I roam; with much hardships in the wilderness I roam. A wolf said this to me." Perhaps the wolf spoke of his own journey.

As the tail of the wolf slipped into the darkness, Sitting Bull found himself next to the dying embers of a fire. The light it cast was weak, but enough for Sitting Bull to see the *wichasha wakan* who sat next to him. This was no memory. He told the old man of his vision. When he was finished, the night was eerily quiet. Finally, the *wichasha wakan* spoke, his voice a whisper carried on the cooling heat of the fire.

"You have dreamed of much. You have seen the buffalo. The thunderbird has visited. You are blessed by Wakan Tanka."

He reached out a frail but steady hand to Sitting Bull's face and painted it with streaks of lightning. "Your honor is great. But your responsibilities are greater."

As he heard those words, the buffalo bones ripped free from his chest and Sitting Bull fell to the ground. He was exhausted and he drifted off into unconsciousness, but he did it with the knowledge that he was a *wichasha wakan*. In providing such a leader, Wakan Tanka had truly smiled upon the tribe. It came none too soon because a series of rapidly unfolding events were to challenge Sioux life.

Trouble rumbled in the northeast. In the early 1850s the Santee Sioux, who lived in what would be known as Minnesota, had made treaty with the American government. In return for their land, they were to be given food, equipment and money. The government's treaty obligations were poorly met, leaving the Santee hungry and demoralized. In the years that followed, uprisings occurred. In 1862, the violence crested when the Santee went on the warpath. Joined by Sioux tribes west to the Dakotas and south to Iowa, they killed some 800 whites, 700 of whom were civilians. By year's end, the American army had reined in the Santee. Anxious to send a message to other potentially hostile Plains Natives, 300 Santee were sentenced to hang. President Abraham Lincoln subsequently reduced that number to 38. The army continued pushing west. By the mid-1860s, it had reached the territory of the Teton Sioux.

The government exerted great pressure on the Teton to make treaty, and many wished to comply. Mostly they were bands who lived close to trading posts and forts, Natives who had become dependent on the white man's goods. Sitting Bull was not among their number. As leader of the Strong Hearts' society, few were surprised at his militant attitude: the Sioux should stand firm against the encroaching Long Knives. He did not, however, advocate war. He believed war was an option, but one only appropriate following Long Knife aggression. Of course, he was not naive. He knew what the soldiers and settlers had done to the Santee, and he fully expected that armed resistance would be necessary. When that day came, Sitting Bull was introduced to the treachery that came to characterize his people's dealings with the whites, or so he believed.

His tribe was camped just north of Fort Rice. The Hunkpapa were there with several other Sioux tribes. They had come at the request of American officials who wanted to talk of peace. While they were in camp, a runner appeared bringing news that 300 Sioux camped around Fort Rice had been slaughtered. Unknown to Sitting Bull, the news was false. He acted quickly. He tore his clothes, slashed his arms and walked through the Sioux camps calling all braves to avenge their brothers. Soon he had 300 warriors ready to ride with him. Painted in red and wearing only his eagle feathered headband and a loincloth, Sitting Bull led the charge. More Sioux than soldiers died on that day, but they effectively derailed the peace talks. Sitting Bull counted coup, but his actions after that called his bravery into doubt. It was noticed that he pulled out of the fight. Sitting Bull never explained his reasons, but he was whipped and the two horses he had stolen were taken because it was an act that many considered cowardly.

In the years that followed, Sitting Bull worked hard to restore his reputation. Concentrating on the Dakota territory surrounding the northern forts, he led his warriors with unwavering purpose in raids against army communication and supply lines—he rode to maintain a way of life. He was ready to cease hostilities when the Long Knives met the conditions he deemed necessary. They had to close all roads in Native territory, stop the steamboats, remove the forts and expel all white settlers except the traders. The conditions were no more than the American government had pledged to do in treaties signed in Minnesota and Wyoming. Should such a treaty be offered to his people, Sitting Bull would lay down his weapons—weapons that he never wanted to raise in battle against the white man.

As Sitting Bull engaged the Long Knives, his uncle Four Horns was working to bring about a change that would forever alter his nephew's life. Four Horns envisioned a radically new approach to fighting the Long Knives. For generations, the Sioux had operated mostly as autonomous tribes, their efforts rarely unified. Four Horns saw that the ways of the past were inadequate in addressing the new problem of the white man's arrival. Scattered and isolated attacks won occasional victories, but they were not effective in achieving the main Sioux goal of driving the white men out of Native territory. By 1867 Four Horns was ready to put his plan into action. He called for a meeting of all Teton Sioux. Eventually, representatives of six of the tribes were camped along the lower Powder River. At council he announced his proposal: Sitting Bull should be the chief of all Teton Sioux.

Only a minority of those gathered approved of Sitting Bull's hard-line position with regards to the white man. But, like the respected Four Horns, all realized that without better organization they could not effectively counter the white man's presence. As important chiefs like Crazy Horse and Gall voiced their support for the plan, others fell into line. Only the Brulés and the southern Oglala, who were not present and who were led by their own strong chiefs, Spotted Tail and Red Cloud respectively, refused to recognize Sitting Bull as supreme chief. With the decision settled, Four Horns spoke for all those in the camp.

"Today we have a new chief and renewed hope. It is his responsibility to ensure that the Teton are well fed, that the miseries of want do not throw their long shadows across our lodges. When you say fight, we will; when you say make peace, we will lay down our bows and arrows. We will smoke the Sacred Calf Pipe so that Wakan Tanka may bless our decision."

All were quiet during the solemn pipe-smoking ceremony. Four Horns took the pipe from its tripod, lit it and made offerings to the earth, wind and sun before passing the pipe around the circle, from left to right as the sun journeys. As the smoke drifted skyward, all prayed that

Wakan Tanka would look favorably upon their decision. Sitting Bull was the last to take the sacred pipe, and he held it as he listened to the Sioux warriors, chiefs and elders count coup and offer advice. Some say that the Ogala war chief Crazy Horse was appointed his second in command. Sitting Bull was given a bow, 10 arrows and a flintlock rifle, but these items paled in comparison to the great war bonnet he was asked to wear. It was made of a beaded headband, ermine pendants, a crown and a tail of double eagle feathers that flowed to the ground, each one representing a coup of the man who had contributed it. Finally, Sitting Bull was led to a magnificent white stallion. When he mounted it, those that surrounded him began to chant. They fell silent when Sitting Bull indicated he was prepared to speak. Characteristically, his words came in the form of a song.

"Ye tribes, behold me. The chiefs of old are gone. Myself, I shall take courage."

Soon after Sitting Bull donned the war bonnet, the Teton had an opportunity to see their leader in action. In early 1868, the well-respected missionary, Father Pierre Jean De Smet, visited Sitting Bull's camp. He traveled with a message from the President Andrew Johnson: the Great Father wanted to make peace and to ensure that the Sioux could live on their own lands as free men. Sitting Bull was pleased to hear it.

"The soldiers of the Great Father have waged war upon us. I have killed many of them," Sitting Bull conceded to the priest. "But as bad as I have been towards them, I am willing to be just as good."

When De Smet added that the president was also willing to provide rations to the Sioux, Sitting Bull's face darkened.

"I have my own plans for my people," he growled. "If they follow what I say, they will never be hungry. Wakan Tanka has bestowed the bountiful land that provides for us. All that is wanted from the white strangers are their traders, no soldiers, no settlers."

Nevertheless, he invited De Smet to deliver the president's message to a peace council. De Smet suggested the president's motivation for seeking peace was in the best interests of the Sioux. In reality the government was concerned about the mounting cost of fighting the Sioux. The president's representatives were waiting at Fort Rice. When De Smet finished, council members voiced their opinions and finally, Sitting Bull addressed the gathering.

"Black Robe, I thank you for praying to the Great Spirit for us. When I first saw you coming, my heart was filled with hatred, as I remembered the past. I commanded it to be silent and it was. When I shook hands with you, I was glad.

"I have always been a fighting fool," admitted Sitting Bull. "My people have made me so. When the wars with the white men started, they were confused. They believed that the whites caused their problems and became crazy. They pushed me forward and I have done many bad things to the whites. They are responsible. Now, before them all, I say welcome to the messenger of peace.

"I have said what can be said. My people will return with you to Fort Rice and meet with the chiefs. We will make peace. If the Great Father wishes to be my friend, I will be a friend to the whites. I will not sell any of our land. And the forts of the white men must be abandoned," he concluded, stating his long-held position.

Sitting Bull sent Gall to Fort Rice, instructing him to take no gifts and to hold fast to the demand that American forts be closed. Some, along the Bozeman Trail were abandoned (owing mostly to the efforts of the Oglala chief Red Cloud). Gall signed the Fort Laramie Treaty of 1868 in July. The treaty established the Great Sioux Reservation—all of what would be the state of South Dakota west of the Missouri River, including the Black Hills—and promised that it would be "set apart for the absolute and undisturbed use of the Indians...." Save those connected with the government who needed access to the reserve to discharge their duties, white men could neither pass through, nor settle there without prior Sioux consent. Additionally, the land north of the Platte River near the Powder River was identified as unceded territory and open to the Sioux for hunting as long as there were enough buffalo to justify it. For their part, the Sioux agreed to keep the peace. Although Sitting Bull had not actually signed the treaty, he pledged to abide by its terms.

In the years following 1868, Sitting Bull kept his word for the most part. Although he sometimes raided the cattle herds of the northern forts, his battles were waged against other tribes, usually in an effort to extend Sioux hunting territory. On one such occasion, when he prepared to lead his warriors on a raid against the Crow south of the Yellowstone River, he discovered a surveying party for the Northern Pacific Railroad and a 500-strong military escort. Sitting Bull called a council to address the issue. There was fear that the white man's presence was but a precursor to a continued southerly movement. Sitting Bull was convinced that such an intrusion would mean an end to the buffalo. He was prepared to fight, but he first counseled that the Sioux should meet with the surveyors to determine their intent. Sitting Bull led 500 warriors to the Long Knives' camp at Arrow Creek, but before they could parley, warriors attacked.

The rash actions of young Sioux braves were an ongoing problem for Sitting Bull. They were always too ready to fight and too often unwilling to abide by his orders to keep the peace. Incensed, Sitting Bull rode to the scene of the battle. He saw braves running the daring line. One was killed;

another injured. The braves were being foolhardy. Sitting Bull rode down to the skirmish.

"Enough, brothers!" he called. "Your courage is no longer in doubt. No longer run the daring line. The shedding of your blood does us no good."

Instead of listening and obeying, the braves challenged Sitting Bull and accused him of losing his stomach for fighting. They alleged that he had become soft and cowardly. It proved too much for Sitting Bull. The courage of the head chief of the Teton could not be called into question. The courage of the man could not be doubted. Sitting Bull dismounted and, with his tobacco pouch and weapons, walked to the open space between the opposing forces and sat down.

"Other Sioux who wish to smoke, join me," he invited.

Four others accepted the invitation. They trembled as Sitting Bull filled the bowl of the pipe and lit the tobacco. He inhaled with strong, confident puffs; theirs were somewhat ragged. Finished, he carefully cleaned out the bowl and placed it back in his pouch. He rose and limped back to his warriors, followed by his companions who soon rushed past him. His critics were silenced. No coup was greater, no running of the daring line more courageous. His position intact, Sitting Bull again called for an end to the fighting, and this time the warriors listened. The Battle of Arrow Creek was indecisive, although it did cause the railroad to temporarily suspend its operations.

For his part, Sitting Bull decided that he would no longer wage battle on the white man.

"Let the white man come," he confided to Crazy Horse. "If he comes shooting, I will shoot back. If not, I will leave them be."

They continued to come, determined to build the Northern Pacific Railroad. Throughout 1873, there was more violence around the Yellowstone River. Sitting Bull's name became well known among the American people, and by the end of that year, there was no longer talk of making peace with the man seen as responsible for terrorizing the northwestern plains. And his greatest victories were yet to come.

White men had only known the Black Hills for a few decades. The La Verendrye brothers, who explored the region in the 1740s, were likely the first to see the range. The first accounts of white men actually penetrating the Black Hills date from the 1820s. In subsequent decades, a handful of others followed. Most were drawn by rumors of gold, and the price of their curiosity was death at Native hands. In the mid-1860s, the government finally organized its own military expeditions into the region. Although the Sioux prevented a thorough exploration, each expedition reported discovering gold deposits. With the signing of the Fort Laramie Treaty in 1868, the government found itself in the uncomfortable position of protecting the Black Hills against white incursions. The army never more than half-heartedly enforced the regulations designed to do that, and they allowed more prospectors into the Black Hills than were kept out. As reports of Sioux attacks on the arrivals filtered back to Washington, officials decided that they would break the spirit of the Laramie Treaty and take advantage of the clause that allowed them to send into the Black Hills officers of the government discharging lawful duties.

The U.S. government sent in the Black Hills Expedition, which consisted of 10 companies of the Seventh Cavalry and a full roster of civilian aides, all under the command of General George Armstrong Custer. His orders were simple: to conduct reconnaissance and to determine the best location for a fort. Clearly, it was a violation of the Laramie

Treaty, but government officials rationalized it by pointing to Sioux aggressions that had first broken the treaty. And although Custer often denied that the expedition was also searching for gold, the fact that miners and a scientist accompanied him undermined his assertion. While it's possible that government officials hoped there would be no gold discovered—news that would stem the tide of prospectors—it's likely that they knew the ore was there. By the mid-1870s, the American government wanted the Black Hills; they just wanted to be certain as to what they would get.

Custer made his report in the late summer of 1874. Although he was cautious in his wording, "until further examination is made regarding the richness of gold, no opinion should be formed," the message was clear: there was gold in the Black Hills.

Newspaper reporters also accompanied the expedition, and by the time editors finished revising their copy, folks were reading about the great gold deposits of the Black Hills. The *St. Paul Daily Press* suggested that gold and silver lay scattered on the ground and declared, "From indications this is the Eldorado of America." Such reports were more than enough to open the flow of prospectors into the region, regardless of the Sioux and warnings that they were the most aggressive of Plains Natives. There was gold to be mined, and prospectors found no room to pack sober thought along with their picks, shovels and pans.

The government wanted to avoid bloodshed, so it offered to buy the Black Hills. When the Sioux wouldn't sell, President Ulysses S. Grant became determined to take control by stealth: they would allow prospectors into the mountains and take control by sheer force of numbers. To limit the violence, the Sioux were ordered to return to their reserves. Those Sioux who resisted were labeled hostile and targeted as enemies of the American government.

George Armstrong Custer (1839–1876) graduated—barely—
from the prestigious military academy at West Point. He
distinguished himself during the Civil War after which he was
posted on the Plains. Custer was pleased to be given
command of the Seventh Cavalry because he was certain that
the subjugation of the Natives would deliver the glory he so
desperately sought. In 1874, Custer led an expedition to
explore the Black Hills, where he discovered gold. The
American army's questionable incursion into the Dakota
Territory and the subsequent unlawful rush of miners into the
region raised the ire of the Sioux and resulted in many deaths,
both Native and white. But none was more famous than
Custer's last stand at the Battle of the Little Bighorn in 1876.

Sitting Bull resisted, and when he received reports of an American attack on a Sioux and Cheyenne camp in March of 1876, he sent word to other Natives to join him in his cause. At the subsequent war council, his leadership of the Sioux was reaffirmed. He called for a Sun Dance to seek guidance and to unify the Natives. The message he received from Wakan Tanka invigorated the Sioux and their Cheyenne allies. They were confident that they could defend their rights. Their first opportunity came against General "Three Stars" Crook at the Rosebud Creek in June 1876.

The Sioux, under the leadership of Sitting Bull and Crazy Horse, prepared well. But, as good as the Sioux strategy was, it is certain that Sitting Bull's vision inspired the warriors to be courageous and contributed significantly to their victory. Crook marched his troops into the vicinity of the Rosebud Creek in mid-June in search of Crazy Horse's band. He commanded close to 1500 men, including some 250 Natives. Crook's Crow and Shoshone scouts informed him that the Sioux were in the area. It was no surprise because the region was close to the Sioux hunting grounds. What was unexpected was the number of Sioux, estimated at more than 1000. Never had they gathered in such numbers to wage battle. When the Sioux attacked, Crook's soldiers were caught totally unawares. The Native scouts saw the approaching enemy just in time to mount a defense, giving the soldiers time to prepare. Unlike previous battles, where the Sioux fought as they had traditionally—seeking to count coup, riding the daring line—many of the warriors held back. As the Long Knives pursued the first wave of retreating Sioux, they were outflanked and ambushed. The resulting hand-to-hand style of combat favored the Sioux for a time. Eventually the Sioux were forced to retreat when a column of soldiers circled them and attacked from the rear. By then, many of the soldiers were also in retreat. Crook claimed victory, but even his Crow scouts conceded that the Sioux had won the day. To military and government officials, it was inconceivable that the Sioux could be outnumbered and still best the army. The next thing that happened was even more shocking.

In the third week of June, army officers prepared for a major assault on the Sioux. Generals Alfred Terry and George Custer marched the Seventh Cavalry out of Fort Abraham Lincoln to the mouth of the Rosebud Creek, where he met up with General Gibbon. They decided that Custer would attack Sitting Bull's village, approaching from Rosebud Creek. Terry and Gibbon would march their men up the Yellowstone River to the mouth of the Little Bighorn River and thereby cut off the Sioux's northern escape route. The offensive would take place on June 26, although Custer was given leeway to change the date if he saw an opportunity. When he arrived at the Little Bighorn, he settled on a strategy for attacking the village. He divided his forces. Major Reno was to strike the southern end of the camp; Captain Benteen was to scout the western bluffs and provide support for Reno; and Custer was to circle around and attack the camp at its northern end. Custer also decided that the offensive would take place on June 25, even though his Ree (Native) scouts suggested that the Sioux were amassed in greater numbers than anticipated. Nothing would deter Custer because his judgment was clouded by visions of glory.

As Custer outlined the strategy to his officers, Sitting Bull spent time alone. He knew an attack was forthcoming; the Sioux victory on the Rosebud would not be enough to deter the Long Knives, and his vision foretold of an attack on the Sioux camp. He could do no more to prepare his people, to bring greater courage. Instead, he smoked the pipe and offered prayers.

"Wakan Tanka, take pity on me. In the name of the Sioux and their allies, I offer you this pipe. Where there is the sun, moon, four winds, there are you also. Wakan Tanka, save my people, I beg you. We wish to live. Guard against misfortune and calamity. Take pity on us."

What happened next suggested that Wakan Tanka heard his prayers and responded. Reno first attacked the Hunkpapa camp. Although he had the element of surprise, Sitting Bull and Gall quickly mounted a counterattack. When Reno realized that the Sioux warriors numbered at least 1000 and saw that they were advancing, he directed his men to make for the trees. As they waited for Benteen's reinforcements, Custer initiated his attack at the northern end of the camp. No longer concerned about Reno, Gall led some 300 warriors to the north end. He met Custer's forces full on, while Crazy Horse attacked Custer's flank and Two Moons (leader of the Cheyenne) struck at the rear of the column. For awhile Custer's superior firepower held the Natives at bay, but as the soldiers' ammunition ran low and because they had no retreat route, they were forced into hand-to-hand combat. The soldiers were determined, but their ability did not approach Native skill, and soon all 225 of Custer's men and Custer himself lay dead. The Natives then turned back to Reno, who had been finally joined by Benteen. They fought until sundown and began again with renewed vigor the next morning. Eventually Sitting Bull called an end to the fighting, but not before another 50 soldiers were dead.

It was a great victory for the Sioux and their Cheyenne allies. They had defeated the brash Long Hair (as the Sioux called Custer), had killed many Long Knives and had lost fewer than 50 braves. For most of the battle, Sitting Bull stayed near Reno, preventing him from supporting Custer. While he didn't take a visible role in the battle, all agreed that a demonstration of his courage was not needed on this day. Nonetheless, dazed Americans blamed him for the defeat of the Seventh Cavalry. Americans were mostly ignorant about Native warfare, which was founded on the courage of individual braves rather than the unquestioned direction of an officer. However, Sitting Bull did play a prominent role; he had unified the Sioux and their allies, and he had inspired courage through his vision. All Sioux knew that what he provided was much more profound than orders on a battlefield.

The period of mourning that followed any skirmish in which braves were lost soon gave way to celebration. It would have been difficult to find a Sioux in the Valley of the Greasy Grass who realized that the Battle of the Little Bighorn was the victory that ushered in their ultimate defeat. Sitting Bull had a sense of it. He did not join in the celebrations because he was troubled. He saw braves taking trophies, weapons and horses from the fallen Long Knives, and his vision had clearly revealed that such plunder should be avoided. He shared his concern with his nephew One Bull.

"The young braves have taken the spoils of victory....From this time on they will covet his goods. They will be at his mercy; they will starve at his hands. The soldiers will crush them."

Sitting Bull's words proved prophetic. Americans did not take the killing of their own lightly, and they struck back without mercy, using the force of their law and the might of their army as necessary. They sent a commission west to "renegotiate" the Laramie Treaty of 1868, demanding both the Black Hills and the unceded territory to the west. The Sioux pointed out that the treaty stipulated any new settlement required the assent of three-quarters of their people, but the commissioners weren't there to listen. They declared that hostile Sioux, which included Sitting Bull, were not to be counted among that number. Those already on the reserves were persuaded by threats of withheld rations. It was a weighty threat; the buffalo herds were rapidly decreasing, as white hunters cashed in on the government bounty on the animals.

The large contingent of Sioux that had fought along the Yellowstone River during the summer was equally affected by the decimation of the buffalo. There were no herds large enough to feed the entire group, so they split up for the fall. Aware of their dispersal, the army renewed its pursuit, but only a few encounters occurred before winter set in, none of which were decisive. One such skirmish occurred at Cedar Creek in October. In retrospect, the encounter is enlightening because it demonstrates Sitting Bull's contin- ued, though surely naive, desire for peace and his misread- ing of the army's hostility towards him.

Sitting Bull saw the Long Knives before they made camp. He knew they were aware of the Sioux presence because they soon arranged themselves into attack forma- tion. Sitting Bull decided to send two emissaries to arrange for a parley. The officer in charge, Colonel "Bear Coat" Miles, agreed. The two met alone, although each had at his back a force of men designed to give the other cause for concern. When Sitting Bull offered his pipe, Miles first declined but eventually accepted. He was first to speak.

"Sitting Bull, you have long been an enemy of the whites," he declared.

"No. I am not against the white man, although I admit I am not for him," replied Sitting Bull.

"You are ready to fight the white man. You do it all the time. You like to."

"Your words are not true! I do not wish to fight. I only fight when I have to. I want to be friendly. I like the traders."

"There are no traders here," countered Miles. "They are to be found at the reserve. Why are you not there?"

"I look out for my people and find meat for them. We search for buffalo. You try to stop us."

"It was you, Sitting Bull, who attacked our wagon train," accused Miles. Sitting Bull had indeed attacked an army supply line some weeks earlier. "Where are the mules that you stole?"

"Where are the buffalo that you have scared away?" asked Sitting Bull.

Miles had had about enough of talking. Sitting Bull was evasive and, in Miles' opinion, clearly a liar.

"There will be no more buffalo, Sitting Bull. You and your people must surrender unconditionally and accompany me to the Tongue River post, where we will await further instructions from the Great Father," proclaimed Miles.

"No," countered Sitting Bull. "It is best that you withdraw your soldiers from the Yellowstone and close the post at Tongue River and the fort at Buford. That will allow the buffalo to return so that my people may hunt them in peace as we have always done."

Miles abruptly stood. "This is going nowhere. We should think through the night and talk again tomorrow."

Sitting Bull agreed and the two parties left. The meeting the following day was no less rancorous. Miles concluded it by issuing an ultimatum.

"The Great Father demands that you surrender immediately and unconditionally. Fail to do so and we will attack."

They did attack, and the Sioux were forced into retreat. For the rest of the winter, Sitting Bull led his people through the country south of the Yellowstone River in search of food and safety. It was a long, cold winter, and Sitting Bull knew that it was no life for his people. The mantle of chieftainship weighed heavily upon his shoulders. He was responsible for his people; he had pledged to provide for them, to keep them safe. He was convinced that they could not live as Sioux on the reserves, but he also knew that a life on the run was no more satisfactory. Over the winter he spent much time praying to Wakan Tanka in search of guidance. In the spring, he announced his decision. The Sioux would cross the Medicine Line and go to the land of the Grandmother (the British Queen).

Sitting Bull knew something of Canada. He had medals from George III that seemed to prove his grandfather had fought with the British, had probably hunted buffalo across the Medicine Line and had perhaps even raided Blackfoot there. For awhile he even claimed that he had been born in British territory, which was a dubious assertion designed to improve his chances of remaining in the country. Certainly he had encountered many Natives who lived in Canada. The stories they told him were encouraging; the Canadians did not wage war against the Natives. To the contrary, the Grandmother had sent Red Coats, the North-West Mounted Police, to the West to protect Natives from the whisky traders. And had she not given a reserve to those Sioux who had fled north during the Minnesota troubles in the 1860s? Perhaps she would do the same for Sitting Bull.

Being a cautious man, Sitting Bull tested the northern waters by sending two advance groups to Canada. When the news returned that they were well received, he followed. He wasn't camped long when a Red Coat arrived at his camp. It was Major James Walsh, the Mountie in charge of nearby Fort Walsh. Accompanied by only four other Mounties and two scouts, Walsh rode by heavily armed Sioux scouts directly to the fringe of the camp where he was escorted to Sitting Bull's lodge. The chief smiled when he saw him coming; he appreciated such courage. Walsh was not one to waste time, and he got right to the purpose of his visit.

"Sitting Bull, I speak for the Grandmother. You need to know that we've got laws here that must be obeyed by whites and Indians alike. There's no killing and no stealing. And that includes horses. Women and children are not to be harmed. Most importantly, you are not to go back to the United States and wage war upon the Americans and then return to Canada. Should that happen, the Americans would not be your only enemies. Do you agree?"

"In the land below the Medicine Line, I fought because I had to. I had no wish to fight," declared Sitting Bull. "But my wishes were as smoke in the wind. I buried my weapons before I crossed the Medicine Line. My heart is no longer bad."

"I am glad to hear it. Obey the laws and no harm will come to you," advised Walsh.

Sitting Bull then asked Walsh for ammunition so that his people might hunt buffalo. Walsh could see the impoverished state of the Sioux. He was not an unfeeling man, but it was more than compassion that made him agree to Sitting Bull's request. If the Sioux could hunt, they would not be a burden on the Canadian government. After extracting a pledge that the bullets would not be used in fighting, he gave them what amounted to two rounds apiece.

"My heart is full with feeling for the Red Coats," replied Sitting Bull, his fist on his chest. "I will do no wrong in the land of the Grandmother. If I go south to fight the Long Knives, I will not return to her land. White Forehead, know that my heart is good…except when I come into contact with the Long Knives."

"That won't be a problem as long as you remain in the land of the Grandmother. The Americans will not come here," noted Walsh. "Obey Canada's laws and you will be treated as any other who lives in her territory."

"This is the greatest experience of my life," declared Sitting Bull. "Truly a change has come over me. This is a world different from the one I have left. The white men are brave and fearless. Chief White Forehead walks into my camp and takes my hand in friendship and peace. He treats me as a man, not as an enemy to hunt. Have I fallen? Is this the end, my brothers?"

Silently, he wondered if the Grandmother's land was truly a Medicine House where his people could be safe and live without fear. He measured the man in the scarlet jacket. Scarlet was a powerful color for the Sioux, a good omen. Perhaps he could finally rest. However, it didn't quite turn out that way. Major Walsh was correct when he pledged to Sitting Bull that his people would be safe in Canada as long as they obeyed the law. However, Sitting Bull took that to mean that his people could live north of the Medicine Line as long as they kept the peace. Perhaps even Walsh believed that. His superiors, however, had their own plans for the refugee Sioux, and they did not include Sitting Bull remaining in Canada.

Top ranking officials in the Canadian government and the North-West Mounted Police saw Sitting Bull's presence largely as a financial problem. As in the United States, buffalo were drastically declining in number. Without that resource, it was clear that the Sioux would have to be fed and that meant a drain on government coffers. Officials believed that more than enough money was already being spent on Canada's own western Natives. Without government support, it was anticipated that the Sioux would raid western settlements for supplies. Not only would that hamper immigration, but it would also require the hiring of more Mounties, another expense that the government was

unprepared to meet. From the very beginning then, the
Canadian government was determined to have Sitting Bull
and his followers leave Canada. However, given Walsh's initial message and his subsequent relations with Sitting Bull,
the intent of the Grandmother was confusing at best.

Canadian diplomats worked to persuade the American
government to take Sitting Bull back. It was not an easy
task because many in the United States were happy to be
rid of him. Nevertheless, in September 1877, the Terry
Commission was dispatched to Canada to try to come to
terms with Sitting Bull, although they were determined
not to make any concessions. The Sioux Chief was hardly
anxious to meet with the Long Knives. Despite Sitting
Bull's assertion that he could not trust the Americans, Walsh
convinced him to meet with the commission. Predictably,
the meeting solved nothing.

General Alfred Terry, who was a long-time Sioux opponent, outlined his government's position.

"The president makes an offer to you. Should you
return to your country and hereafter refrain from hostility
against its government and people, you will be granted
a full pardon for all acts previously committed. Let me be
clear: you will not be punished for any such acts. They will
be forgotten. You shall be received with the same friendly
spirit that has welcomed other surrendered Indians once
hostile. As the last band of Indians yet to surrender, you
should look to your red brothers," advised Terry. "Like
them, you will not want for either food or clothes as long
as you remain peaceably at your agencies.

"It is true that those Indians who have surrendered were
required to give up their horses and arms," he continued.
"But most of those goods have been sold to aid them. The
money so obtained has been used to buy cows and farming
implements so that they can make an easy transition to an

agricultural lifestyle. Eventually the proceeds of all such goods will serve that purpose," assured Terry. "Under no circumstances will the president allow you to return to the United States mounted, armed and ready to fight. The violence of years past is not an option."

Sitting Bull spoke for his people.

"For 64 years you have kept me and my people and treated us bad. What have we done that you should want us to stop living as we do? We have done nothing. Long Knives have committed the hostile acts. We had nowhere to go but to the land of the Grandmother. We did not give you the country," Sitting Bull declared. "You followed us all over, so we came to this country."

Sitting Bull rose from his seated position and walked to the Mounties. He shook hands with each of them, then continued to speak.

"You have ears and you have eyes and you see how I live with these people. Here I am! If you think me a fool you are a bigger fool than me. This is a Medicine House," he continued. "You come here with lies, lies to tell in the Grandmother's House! I do not wish to hear them. Go back to where you came from. This country is mine and I intend on staying and raising my people here. We were raised with these British," restated Sitting Bull, shaking hands with the officers. "That is enough. No more," he concluded.

Before the American commissioners left, Red Coat officers made a last attempt to get Sitting Bull to change his mind, but they failed. All they could report to the commissioners was that Sitting Bull would not cross the border. It was enough for the commissioners. Over the next couple of years, Sitting Bull mostly remained true to his pledge. He did occasionally cross the Medicine Line, but only to hunt buffalo. Although his braves sometimes broke the law, he pleaded the rashness of youth and made compensation where possible. He did try to form an alliance with Crowfoot, the powerful Blackfoot chief, possibly with a mind to mounting a challenge to government authority in the West. Crowfoot rejected his overtures. However, it's likely that Sitting Bull was not very serious about challenging the Canadian government. When the Métis leader Louis Riel called on him in the late 1870s or early 1880s to support his planned Native rebellion, Sitting Bull declined to participate.

By 1880 it was clear that the Canadian government was not going to grant Sitting Bull's Sioux a reservation. The sympathetic Walsh had been removed, and those who replaced him were single-minded in their determination to evict the refugees. Sitting Bull was feeling pressure, most of it self-imposed, to resolve the matter. The winter of 1879 had been particularly cold and they could find few buffalo. He knew that his people could not continue on as they had. Once he received word from Walsh assuring him that no harm would come to him if he returned to the United States (Walsh had received assurances from high-ranking American military officials), he made his decision. In July 1880, he led 230 of his followers to the Standing Rock Agency on the Missouri River in central Dakota Territory.

When he arrived in the United States, he declared, "Today I am home. The land under my feet is mine again. I never sold it; never gave it away. I left it only to raise my family in peace. I always wanted to come back."

The wily old chief then tried to negotiate with the military officials who were to escort him to his new home. But he was not the feared Sitting Bull of five years before so terms were dictated to him.

Much had changed in the years he had been gone. The buffalo no longer roamed. The white population had

Sitting Bull, taken at age 49 while he was being transported to the Standing Rock Agency.

exploded. When Sitting Bull had left for Canada, only about 5000 lived around the Great Sioux Reservation. He returned to more than 120,000. There were new pressures on the Sioux to renegotiate once more the Laramie Treaty of 1868 because the government wanted to reduce the size of Sioux holdings. While Sitting Bull could no longer lead his people freely across the Plains, he continued to hold dearly his responsibility to take care of them. To that end he even began farming. He did it without enthusiasm, although he realized that his people's future lay in adjusting to the new economic reality brought by the white man and he wanted to set an example. There were, however, those Sioux who believed that his time had passed. Nevertheless, he still possessed enough authority to derail the treaty negotiations. The local Indian agent figured his influence was mostly malignant and decided that it was best to get him off the reserve. Thus began Sitting Bull's tour of North America.

Ironically, he found himself in great demand. White men from the Midwest to the East Coast in both the United States and Canada were anxious to see him. At first, he simply made public appearances at special events. When he realized that the public was willing to pay to see him and to buy his autographed pictures, he agreed to join traveling shows. He believed it was a good way to bring much-needed money to his people. In 1884, he signed on with Alvaren Allen's "Sitting Bull's Combination." Occasionally, he was given the opportunity to address audiences. He regularly spoke of peace and the need for young Natives to become educated in the ways of the white men. Interpreters, however, read prepared stories detailing the slaying of Custer and brutal scalpings.

In 1885 he joined up with Buffalo Bill Cody's "Wild West Show." Although Cody was an entrepreneur, he also had a holster full of experiences on the frontier and a good understanding of the plight of the Natives. He developed a good relationship with Sitting Bull, sometimes defending the actions of the Sioux during the Plains wars (a position he more readily expressed in Canada than in the United States). Cody wanted Sitting Bull to travel to Europe with the show, but he declined. The government was trying to resurrect its failed attempt at taking control of Sioux land, and Sitting

Bull believed that he could be of more help to his people back on the reserve. The Sioux were no longer united as they had once been, however, and government officials found it relatively easy to divide and conquer. Sitting Bull was kept in the dark for most of the negotiations. Meetings were held and votes were taken without his being informed, and the Great Sioux Reservation was dismantled against his wishes. By the late 1880s, he no longer held the position of authority he once had. But he still commanded respect and it was that which brought the Miniconjou Sioux, Kicking Bear, to his lodge.

Kicking Bear told Sitting Bull of Wovoka, a Paiute from Nevada who had been granted a vision. It foretold of the imminent arrival of a happy, bountiful and peaceful land, peopled by all the Natives who had died. There would be no white man. Sitting Bull was skeptical. He believed it impossible for a man to die and live again. But Kicking Bear was insistent; all one had to do was to accept the teachings of Wovoka and perform the Ghost Dance. As a *wichasha wakan*, Sitting Bull knew the power of visions, so he was not prepared to reject Kicking Bear's words out of hand. Instead he allowed Kicking Bear to organize a Ghost Dance among the Hunkpapa. For five days they danced. Some claimed to have had visions of Plains full of buffalo, but Sitting Bull was not one of them.

Disappointed, Sitting Bull left the dancers and retreated to the forest, so that he might reflect and pray to Wakan Tanka. There he was granted a vision, and as he considered it, he grasped the potency of the Ghost Dance. Perhaps a land of peace full of his people did await the Sioux. Who knew the limits of Wakan Tanka's power? But the real value of the Ghost Dance was that it served to unite his people, unite all Natives. Decimated by disease and hunger, their cultures under attack by the white man, the Ghost Dance offered Natives a spiritual bond, an opportunity to regain pride. It could serve as a foundation on which to resist the white man's ways.

When Sitting Bull subsequently heard word of a great Sioux gathering at a nearby reservation and the Ghost Dance they would perform, he decided to travel there to further investigate the phenomenon. The local Indian agent feared that Sitting Bull would stir up unrest and he gave orders to the agency policemen to have him arrested. When Sitting Bull resisted, chaos ensued. Shots were fired. One struck Sitting Bull in the chest, and another in the back of the head.

Sitting Bull had foreseen his end. In the spring of that year, while walking through the woods, a meadowlark had called to him.

"Lakotas will kill you."

The agency policemen were his own people. Sitting Bull was buried in an unmarked grave outside Fort Yates.

CHAPTER TWO

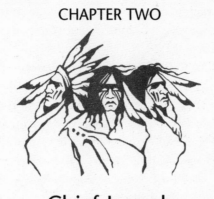

Chief Joseph

Wallowa Nez Perce, 1832–1904

ALONG THE WALLOWA RIVER in northeastern Oregon was a clearing that for generations had served as a Nez Perce winter camp. In this late winter of 1877 the great longhouse, a good 100 feet long and covered in reed mats, dominated the snow-covered meadow. Nearby were a few tall tipis, their hide wrappings effective barriers against winter's wind. But it was a small four-foot high dwelling, made of mud, grass and thick hides, that was the camp's most important structure on this day. It was a sweathouse, and inside sat Chief Joseph. Although the sweathouse was used primarily for spiritual purposes, the chief sometimes retreated there to think. Perhaps he had acquired the habit from his father, Tuekakas, once also known as Chief Joseph. As Joseph poured water over the glowing rocks, he thought of his father's wise counsel and of what he might say had he been seated there. An important decision had to be made, one that would dramatically affect the future of his people.

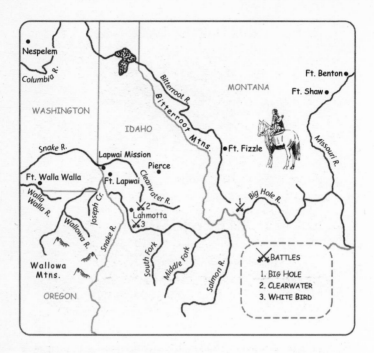

Joseph was chief of the Wallowa, a band of Nez Perce who refused to recognize the terms of the 1863 Lapwai Treaty, which demanded that they leave their ancestral lands and go to a small reserve in northern Idaho. The Wallowa refused to sign the treaty. The Wallowa valley region was the land of the people. Their fathers were buried there. They felt that to leave it was to abandon what made them Nez Perce. These strongly held beliefs made little difference to American officials who insisted that the Wallowa abide by the treaty's terms. That message had been conveyed through Joseph's own people. Rueben, his wife's brother and chief of the reservation Nez Perce, had led a delegation to his camp. He told Joseph that the commission (established to bring Joseph and his band under control) demanded that his band move by April 1, less than two moons away. In reply, Joseph said that he would not leave

A winter lodge built to hold four or five families at a Nez Perce camp in Idaho, likely around 1900.

until he was compelled. He hoped it would not come to that because he knew it meant war, an outcome he and his father before him had long sought to avoid. But the white men would not listen.

April 1 came and no one arrived in the Wallowa valley to force Joseph's people onto the reservation. It gave Joseph hope that the white men might yet be open to compromise. His hopes rose when word came that General Oliver Howard, military commander of the region and a member of the relocation commission, wanted to meet at Fort Walla

Walla in late April. Joseph had met Howard before, in 1875, and he was impressed by the soldier's apparent goodwill.

When Howard had first taken up his duties in the northwest, he had assigned his second in command, Major H. Clay Wood, to meet with Joseph and to investigate Wallowa claims in regards to the 1863 Lapwai treaty. Wood thought highly of the band, describing them as intelligent and self-supporting. He also concluded that the 1863 treaty had not extinguished Wallowa title to their land. On the basis of Wood's report, Howard recommended to Washington that a commission be established to work out the Wallowa land claim. Although Howard believed that it was best if the Wallowa were allowed to remain in their valley, he knew that the government did not want that. And there is no indication that Howard objected to the commission's final report to Washington: if the Nez Perce refused to move from the Wallowa valley, they "should then be placed by force upon the Nez Perce reservation." Only later would Howard's true opinion of the Nez Perce be revealed; he believed they were an inferior race. "Smart as [Joseph and Ollokot (Joseph's younger brother) were], their tendency to evil…was undoubtedly inherited."

Joseph knew neither of the recommendation nor of Howard's view of him, so he was enthusiastic about the forth-coming meeting. However, when the day came, Joseph was ill and could not attend. Ollokot went and spoke for the band. He returned with bad news. Howard had insisted that they move to the Lapwai reservation, despite Ollokot's objections that the geography there was not suited to the Wallowa lifestyle or economy. Yet, apparently, there was still reason to hope. Howard proposed another meeting for May, to which he invited all the chiefs who had not made treaty. But any hope the Nez Perce had was misplaced. Howard merely wanted to give the chiefs the government's ultimatum: get their bands to the assigned reservation. As the general put it, "the time for loving persuasion had now gone by. Positive instructions had come and obedience was required."

The Wallowa arrived at Fort Lapwai with faces painted and dressed in their finest clothes. They marched silently until they reached the fence surrounding the fort, at which point they began to sing a song that Howard later described as "shrill and searching; sad, like a wail and yet defiant." They marched around the compound three times, then finally laid down their weapons and entered through the gate. Only the reservation Nez Perce, whose presence was designed to encourage nontreaty capitulation, understood the meaning of the Wallowa actions—they believed they were to council with an enemy.

Once they were settled, Howard addressed Joseph. "I will listen to all you say, but you might as well know from the outset that in every extent the Indians must obey the orders of the government of the United States." Speaking for himself and the local Indian agent John Montieth, he added, "What [the government] commands us to do, that we must do.... If the Indians hesitate to come to the reservation, the government directs that soldiers be used to bring them hither."

So there it was. The council was a sham. There would be no negotiation; there would be war if the Nez Perce didn't obey. Frustrated and confused, Joseph demanded that the meeting be postponed until the other chiefs arrived. Howard agreed. They met again the next day.

"I am ready to talk today," began Joseph. "I have been in a great many councils, but I am no wiser. We are all sprung from a woman, although we are unlike in many things. We cannot be made over again. You are as you were made, as you were made you can remain. We are just as we were made by the Great Spirit and you cannot change us.... I do not believe that the Great Spirit Chief gave one kind of men the right to tell another kind of men what they should do."

Howard bristled at the impudence. A red man questioning his authority! Joseph turned to Toolhulhulzote, who the nontreaty chiefs had agreed would speak for them. He was an old man, but his voice had lost none of its power and his beliefs none of their conviction.

"I have heard about a bargain, a trade between some of these Indians," he said as he waved his hand towards the reservation Nez Perce, "and the white men concerning their land, but I belong to the land out of which I came. The earth is my mother."

"The Nez Perce did make such an agreement with Washington," declared Howard. "And all must honor that pledge."

"You are always talking about Washington. I would like to know who Washington is? Is he a chief or a common man, or a house or a place? Leave Mr. Washington, if he is a man, alone. He has no sense. He does not know anything about our country. He has no sense. Washington cannot think for us," replied Toolhulhulzote.

Howard did not like the direction the meeting was taking. He could see from the faces of the Nez Perce that they were taking strength from the words of the speakers. When Joseph asked to delay the meeting for another day, Howard readily agreed. He wanted to get more soldiers to the fort. It was two days before the council sat again. The Nez Perce were no more conciliatory, and Howard was emboldened by the knowledge that several army detachments were en route. Toolhulhulzote spoke again and he continued on the same theme.

"You white people get together, measure the earth and divide it.... We never made any trade. Part of the Indians gave up their land. I never did. The earth is part of my body and I never gave up the earth."

"You know very well that the government has set apart a reservation and that the Indians must go upon it...." replied Howard. "This large reservation is for you and your children, so that you may live in peace and prosper."

"The Great Spirit made the world as it is and as He wanted it, and He made a part of it for us to live upon. I do not see where you get authority to say that we shall not live where He placed us."

Toolhulhulzote's rebellious tone was too much for Howard, who barked, "Shut up! I don't want to hear anymore of such talk. The law says you shall go upon the reservation to live! You persist in disobeying the law. If you do not move, I will take the matter into my own hands and make you suffer for your disobedience."

Toolhulhulzote would not be intimidated.

"Who are you, that you ask us to talk and then tell me I can't? Are you the Great Spirit? Did you make the world? Did you make the sun? Did you make the rivers to flow for us to drink? Did you make the grass for us to grow? Did you make all these things that you talk to us as though we were boys? If you did, then you have the right to talk to us as you do!"

Toolhulhulzote turned to his fellow Nez Perce. "What person pretends to divide the land and put me on it?"

But it was Howard who answered.

"I am the man. I stand here for the president and there is no spirit good or bad that will hinder me!"

"So long as the earth keeps me, I want to be left alone. You are trifling with the law of the earth!" replied Toolhulhulzote.

Howard had had enough of talking. He gave orders to put Toolhulhulzote in the guardhouse. As soldiers guided him there, the old man shouted, "I have expressed my heart to you! I have nothing to take back!"

The Nez Perce murmured among themselves. They looked to Joseph for direction. All could see that the Natives outnumbered the soldiers. Should they let this happen? For a moment, Joseph was silent.

〜〜〜

The late spring night sky of 1844 was cloudy, shrouding the moon and stars, leaving the peaks of the Wallowa Mountains to the south as uncertain as the next bend in the Wallowa River. The low and sometimes piercing chant of the shaman carried along the water, calling to the salmon with which he had a special relationship. Tuekakas (Old Chief Joseph) listened and smiled. The conditions were perfect. Many salmon would be caught on this night. He called to his sons, who sat on the riverbank.

"Sousouquee, Hin-mah-too-yah-lat-kekht! Light the torches!" The third son, Ollokot, was still too young to help.

Tuekakas listened as they ran along the shore. Although the boys were young, 13 and 12, they had been responsible for lighting the pitch pine torches for some years already. Soon, a short stretch of the Wallowa River shone, as the rippling water threw back reflections of the torches that angled out from the river's bank. The light attracted the salmon, bringing them to the surface and making them easier to catch. Tuekakas took a moment to survey the scene. He felt a certain contentment, knowing that he was fishing on the same spot long used by his ancestors.

"Come! Into the canoe," directed Tuekakas. "It will be a busy night."

The quiet night was filled with shouts of triumph as the boys pulled bulging hand nets and dripping spears from the water. The catch was the most enjoyable part of fishing, much more exciting than the drudgery of mending nets or building small wharves. When the canoe was full, they went to the bank and tossed the fish ashore. Khapkhaponimi, Tuekakas' wife, and her daughters quickly gathered the salmon, deftly gutted and split them and placed them on wooden racks for drying. The activities went on for much of the night, little different than they had for countless other springs.

Tuekakas and his people were Nez Perce. For the better part of 2000 years the tribe had lived on the Columbia Plateau, west of the Rocky Mountains in what would become the southeast corner of Washington state, the northeast corner of Oregon and western Idaho. They were the most numerous and powerful of the Plateau tribes, with whom they were mostly friendly. The Nez Perce never knew themselves by that name. They called themselves Nimipu, meaning "the real people." It wasn't until French fur traders arrived, sometime in the late 1700s, that they became known as the Nez Perce, which meant "pierced nose" in French. The name was a poor choice, since few Nimipu actually pierced their noses with bones; nevertheless it stuck. The name was not the only change brought by white men. With them came useful trade goods, a strange new religion and diseases that even the most powerful medicine men could not cure. But most of all, the white men brought more white men. Their tribe seemed as countless as the stars.

On this night, the salmon were also countless. Eventually, Tuekakas called a stop to the fishing; there would be many opportunities to return to the river during the season. Later, when the fish had dried, the family returned to the winter camp farther down the Wallowa River, where there was much work to be done. Over the following days, the villagers prepared for the move to the plateau, where they would spend the summer hunting and harvesting the wild vegetation and berries. There was a sadness among the band members as the great longhouse, the winter dwelling, was dismantled for the summer. It housed as many as 30 families who lived in Tuekakas' village. Summer would see the Nez Perce separate into small groups of two or three families. They would not see each other again until the great camas bulb harvest later in summer when the band stocked up on that important food source. It would be a joyful reunion marked with ceremony and celebration—visiting, courting, storytelling—and thought of it dulled the sadness.

On the plateau, game was exceptionally abundant, and soon Tuekakas had killed enough to busy his wife and daughters with the preparation of meat for some time. His work done, Tuekakas turned his thoughts to the Lapwai mission. It had been his family's home away from the Wallowa valley for many years since his own conversion to Christianity in 1839. Tuekakas may have converted out of political necessity. He had become chief when his stepfather Takinploon died in 1836. Not all those who recognized Takinploon as chief looked to his stepson as successor. Choice was an important principal in the Nez Perce philosophy, and Tuekakas could not impose his authority on others. But by turning to the white man's religion he enhanced his position in the band because most believed that a Christian Native had greater standing among the white men.

Whatever his reason for converting, Tuekakas took the white man's teachings to heart. He became a good friend of the missionary Henry Spalding. Spalding, an evangelical Presbyterian minister, had preached at Lapwai since 1836. His fiery oratorical style served him well among the Nez Perce, who admired a talented speaker. Advocating acculturation, he challenged the Nez Perce to give up their nomadic ways and take up farming. That was difficult since Nez Perce women had always done the harvesting. Still, some Nez Perce saw Spalding's own determined efforts to farm to be respected. And, despite Spalding's scorn for traditional Nez Perce beliefs and practices, some responded to his religious message.

Tuekakas tried to be a model Christian, although in later years he abandoned the religion because of what he considered to be the white man's hypocrisy. While he had been at the mission, Tuekakas farmed a small plot of land, taught the children who attended the school in Spalding's home and participated in religious ceremonies by reading from the Bible. Tuekakas thought highly of Spalding, inviting him to visit his camp along the Wallowa. Spalding held a similar opinion of the Nez Perce chief, bestowing upon him the name of Joseph, his favorite Old Testament figure.

Tuekakas knew that Spalding depended on the chief's influence among his people, and that he was needed back at Lapwai. First, however, Tuekakas needed to have an important discussion with his son Hin-mah-too-yah-lat-kekht (Chief Joseph's name as a child). He went in search of the boy and found him nearby in a meadow bordered by an isolated stand of fir, where a few boys were gathered playing pinecone. He watched the boys throw the pinecones towards the small willow hoop that was their target. For a moment, his thoughts returned to his own childhood.

Finally, he called, "Hin-mah-too-yah-lat-kekht."

The boy, already well over five feet tall, ran to him.

"Come, we must talk."

Hin-mah-too-yah-lat-kekht waved to his friends, and father and son made their way to the horses. Tuekakas had told him a few days before that he had matters to discuss but he had revealed nothing else. Hin-mah-too-yah-lat-kekht

A Nez Perce group on horseback taken in 1906. Among the horses are some Appaloosa, a breed developed by the Nez Perce. The name of the spotted horse is a corruption of the Pelouse River (which flows through the Bitterroot River), where a Native once owned a large herd of the animals. People took to calling the horses Palousey, which later became Apalousey and eventually Appaloosa. A Nez Perce tradition tells that the Appaloosa were bred from the best mares of the Nez Perce stock and stallions acquired at a forgotten time from a Russian ship anchored off present-day Oregon. The first offspring were known as the Ghost Wind Stallions. Others suggest that the Nez Perce obtained horses at the turn of the 18th century through a trading network that linked Spanish settlers, Pueblo and Plains Natives. Selective breeding then produced the Appaloosa. Chief Joseph depended on the athleticism of the Appaloosa to help his people flee from the American army.

was most curious about what was so important. Arriving at the herd, Tuekakas mounted a fine Appaloosa, and his son mounted his own small cayuse. Together they set off at a leisurely pace towards the Wallowa River.

Tuekakas spoke. "Hin-mah-too-yah-lat-kekht, you have seen 11 winters. It is time to prepare for your spirit quest."

The Nez Perce believed in a *tiwatitmas*, a spirit guardian who gave assistance through spirit power in one's life journey. Tuekakas explained to his son what was expected of him.

"Alone, you will go to the mountains. There you will build a fire that must not die. You will sit and watch the sun as it travels across the sky. You will continue to watch the moon on its journey. When the sun wakes, you will turn around and greet it. Food or water must not pass your lips. All the time you will pray for a visit from a *tiwatitmas*."

"What will it look like father?"

"A *tiwatitmas* comes in many forms. Perhaps an animal."

"How did it appear to you?"

"A *tiwatitmas* is a personal matter. It is not to be spoken of. It is between a man and Ah-cum-kin-i-ma-me-hut (the Great Spirit)."

True to his father's words, when Hin-mah-too-yah-lat-kekht did embark on his spirit quest, whatever success he had he kept private. As they rode on, Tuekakas and Hin-mah-too-yah-lat-kekht continued to discuss spiritual matters.

"Father, do the white men go on spirit quests?"

"Every man must make his own journey and if it is traveled well, Ah-cum-kin-i-ma-me-hut provides protection."

"Are the journeys the same?"

Tuekakas was silent for some time before he replied.

"A man's path is his own, but there are laws that guide us all. Our fathers gave us those laws, just as they had learned them from their fathers. Treat all men as they treat us. Never be the first to break a bargain. It is a disgrace to lie. A man should speak only the truth. It is a shame for one man to take another's wife or property, unless he pays for it. Ah–cum–kin–i–ma–me–hut sees and hears everything and never forgets. He will give every man a spirit home according to his deserts. A good man will have a good home. A bad man will have a bad home. These are good laws."

"And they are the laws of the white men?"

"Good is good. It does not know tribe or color."

Hin–mah–too–yah–lat–kekht knew these matters to be important and he remained silent, reflecting on them as they returned to camp.

A few days later, Tuekakas' family made for the Lapwai mission, where they heard troubling news. In the summer of 1843, Marcus Whitman, a Presbyterian missionary among the Cayuse at the nearby Waiilatpu mission in the Walla Walla Valley, had led some 200 wagons with settlers into the region. Some Cayuse were upset. They wondered whether these white men wanted Native lands and feared that more might follow. Those concerns had been mostly forgotten throughout the winter and spring, when disease brought by the newcomers made many Natives ill. Whitman's limited medical skills proved inadequate and most died. While no one was yet ill at Lapwai, it was believed that the sickness would soon arrive and many were worried. Tuekakas thought too much of his duty to return to the safety of the Wallowa Valley.

No one in Tuekakas' family fell ill, but there was tragedy nevertheless. In late 1847, the Cayuse chief Tilokaikt, suspecting that his people's sickness was part of the white man's plan to take Cayuse territory, led an attack against the Waiilatpu mission. Whitman, his wife and 14 others died in what became known as the Whitman Massacre. Under pressure from his wife, who feared for her life and that of their daughter, Spalding closed the Lapwai mission in 1848 and moved to the Willamette Valley.

In the following months, Tuekakas thought often of the Lapwai mission. Occasionally he returned, but when he saw the empty log house on Lapwai Creek, his heart sank. On one occasion in 1850, however, when he traveled to the abandoned mission with his son, Tuekakas was happy.

"Spalding! My heart is glad to see you," he cried. "I did not expect to see you here."

"Joseph. It is good to see you too," smiled Spalding. "Had you arrived a day later, you would have missed me. My superiors have reassigned me and I will soon be ministering to Indians to the south. But I wanted one last look at the mission. I see that you have brought Ephraim." Spalding used Hin-mah-too-yah-lat-kekht's Christian name; he had been baptized days after his birth. Hin-mah-too-yah-lat-kekht's older brother was also baptized, but not his younger one. "He was one of Mrs. Spalding's favorites."

"How is Mrs. Spalding?" asked Tuekakas.

"She has gone to her eternal reward."

"Mrs. Spalding was a good woman. She will enjoy her rest."

Spalding nodded.

"How was your winter?"

"None were hungry."

"Not even for the Word of God?"

"Some do not understand those pangs."

"So right you are," chuckled Spalding. "Come, let us sit and talk."

They talked and laughed and even took some time to read from the Bible. Finally, Spalding went on his way. Tuekakas and Hin-mah-too-yah-lat-kekht headed back to their summer camp.

Once on the plateau, Hin-mah-too-yah-lat-kekht's eyes were drawn to the great rolling meadows that lay before him. He thought he saw movement in the distance to the south.

He squinted his eyes. Yes, a long, dark ridge moved on the horizon. He looked to his father, who had seen it also.

"White men. Traveling to the great waters," Tuekakas said.

"There are so many!" The line stretched on.

"There will be more. But they are not our concern. They do not wish to settle where the Nez Perce live," added Tuekakas, who was less suspicious of the white man's intentions than were the Cayuse.

Tuekakas could not be faulted for his belief that the white men would not cause the Nez Perce trouble. There had been nothing but good relations between the two groups since the arrival of the first Americans on a cold September day in 1805. The United States government had recently purchased the massive Louisiana Territory—all the land between the Mississippi River and the Rocky Mountains—from France. Officials were anxious to determine just exactly what they owned, so the Lewis and Clark expedition was dispatched west on a fact-finding mission. The explorers had only just managed to stumble into the Nez Perce camp on the Clearwater River. The horses they had not eaten were bony sacks, and the supplies of bear grease and candle wax that gave variety to their meals were almost gone. They were in such a poor state that it was doubtful they could continue their journey. The goodwill and assistance of the Nez Perce went far towards ensuring that they could. They remained with the Nez Perce for six weeks. In later life, Hin-mah-too-yah-lat-kekht remembered how important that first visit of white men had been to his people.

"They talked straight and our people gave them a great feast, as proof that their hearts were friendly. These men were kind. They made presents to our chiefs and our people made presents to them....All the Nez Perce made friends with Lewis and Clark and agreed to let them pass through their country and never to make war on white men."

But circumstances change. In 1853, a road was constructed linking the Oregon Trail with the West Coast via Fort Walla Walla. The route was less than 100 miles west of the Wallowa River and even closer to other Nez Perce bands. Just as threatening was the surveying party that was charged by the United States government with selecting the route for a rail line from Minnesota to Puget Sound in Washington Territory. Isaac Stevens, governor of the new territory, led the party. His proposed line ran right through the northern portion of Nez Perce territory.

As information about the region spread, settlers were increasingly drawn by reports of rich soil and thick grazing pastures. Natives held discussions about how to deal with the new presence. It wasn't the few newcomers that caused concern—land was plentiful and the Nez Perce were willing to share—but the belief that countless more would follow. Some argued for war before too many whites came to fight. Others counseled peace. The Nez Perce, both as bands and individual members, were free to make up their own minds. In April 1855, the time came when they were forced to make their choice.

To prepare the way for settlement, Governor Stevens sent a party of officials to Lapwai. Their task was to convince the Natives to meet for treaty discussions. Stevens wanted all the tribes of the Columbia Plateau to attend, but he especially wanted the powerful Nez Perce to be there. The officials were well received, and even those who had previously spoken of war agreed to parley. Stevens had to be surprised at the size of the Nez Perce contingent. Some 2000 people, including 57 chiefs and lesser chiefs, arrived at the Walla Walla Valley in May. In the end, likely more than 3000 Natives were at the council and a good half of them were warriors. The turnout was largely owing to good memories of their encounter with Lewis and Clark. Following the offer to meet Stevens, Tuekakas flew the American flag from the top of a pine tree that had been stripped of its branches—Lewis and Clark had left a Nez Perce chief with an American flag as a symbol of their friendship. When the Nez Perce arrived at Walla Walla, they gave their American flag to the white officials, who made a makeshift pole and raised it.

Stevens first outlined his position. Many more whites were coming and they would soon control the region. The most secure and certainly the most peaceful future for the Natives was for them to sign away land that would be inevitably taken and to set themselves up on reserves that would be theirs forever. While on the reserves, they would be provided with annuities, $200,000 over 20 years, to be distributed by the Indian agent. A good portion of the annuities would be in the form of tools and teachers' salaries, which could speed the acculturation process.

The Natives weren't enthusiastic about ceding the land they lived on and so the proposal was not well received. Stevens was cunning, however. He made it clear that the United States government wanted little of the Nez Perce territory. Rather, the proposed reservation would include their lands. By assuaging the fears of the most powerful tribe, he hoped that the Nez Perce would persuade others to sign what was for them a treaty that required minimal sacrifice.

Tuekakas was of two hearts when it came to the treaty. He was pleased that they were meeting to discuss an issue that was so important to their children, but he was not convinced that any man had the right to sell land because land was not owned by man. Perhaps he was influenced by Spalding, who was at the proceedings and who encouraged him to sign it. Ultimately, he and the other chiefs did sign. But Tuekakas did not sign away any of his band's territory along the Wallowa River, nor would he accept annuities or gifts, explaining to his people that "after awhile [the government] will claim that [we] accepted pay for [our] country." The reservation was just less than eight million acres in size, encompassing the southeastern corner of Washington Territory, the northeastern corner of Oregon Territory and a piece of Idaho stretching to the Bitterroot Mountains. Stevens assured everyone, "So long as the sun travels across the sky shall this reservation belong to the Indians and no white man shall be allowed on it."

The years following the making of the treaty put Stevens' pledge to the test and found it wanting. Stevens was for the most part responsible for many of the problems. In the mid-1850s, there was an economic depression in the Pacific Northwest. To reinvigorate the economy, Stevens declared that the treaty had opened the region for settlement. It had not. Some Native tribes (mostly southern Cayuse and Yakima), who were not at Walla Walla for the treaty negotiations but who nevertheless found their lands taken from them, were prickly even before the settlers arrived. Even those who had made treaty were none too pleased about the abrupt manner in which they were being forced from their lands. In response, they killed settlers. Throughout 1856, skirmishes occurred between Native warriors and American soldiers and territorial volunteers. There were also meetings to reconcile grievances. They resolved nothing, and the summer of acrimony came to a bloody end when a party of hostile Natives charged Stevens' camp on the Walla Walla River, only to be repulsed with howitzers. Thirteen Natives were killed or wounded, while the Stevens' party suffered only one death and one injury.

Tuekakas was opposed to the violence. Although he had concluded that the white man could not be trusted to live up to his promises, especially if breaking them meant material

gain, he continued to hold fast to the laws taught to him by
the missionary Spalding. What Hin-mah-too-yah-lat-kekht
thought about these struggles is known only through his own
subsequent relations with the white man. While this trouble
was ongoing, he was on the cusp of manhood, too young
to participate as an adult in council, but old enough to
think about the debates and to consider the effects of violence and peace. Undoubtedly, however, Hin-mah-too-yah-
lat-kekht was greatly influenced by his father's position.
Tuekakas' peaceful outlook, his concern for future generations, his suspicions about the intent of American officials
and his independent stand would influence Hin-mah-too-
yah-lat-kekht's own relations with the white man throughout his adult life.

Tuekakas' peaceful outlook was put to an even greater test
as the 1860s began. Many Natives were already angry
because the promised annuities had not yet arrived (the
United States Congress had not yet appropriated the necessary funds). Then, in 1860, gold was discovered on the
Orofino Creek, in the northern part of the Nez Perce reservation. Quickly, the town of Pierce appeared, bustling with
merchants and miners. The Nez Perce were accommodating
because they had no villages located in gold territory.
If compensated, they would allow the miners in, but they
would not give the newcomers title to the land. Predictably,
the miners couldn't be confined to Pierce. By the spring of
1862, more than 30,000 miners had moved into the region
and they spread across the northwestern part of the reservation like a prairie fire. When the Nez Perce asked officials
to enforce their treaty rights, they were presented with
a counter-offer—cede more territory. The army moved into
the region, and Fort Lapwai was built near the old Lapwai
mission to demonstrate that the government was serious
about its proposal.

Word that the American officials wanted to meet to discuss ceding territory came to the Wallowa band in late 1862. The council was set for the next spring. Tuekakas did not know what to do. It seemed as if the path he had chosen had not been best for his people. But what else was there? War? He thought of the recent news that Colonel Patrick Connor had attacked a Shoshone (Snake) village in southern Idaho as punishment for their attacks on miners and Mormon settlers. With 224 Natives killed and another 160 taken captive, Tuekakas knew that war was not the right path. He decided not to go to the council; the white officials knew his position well. He had a copy of the Walla Walla Treaty of 1855 and the deerskin map he had drawn of the land his band called home in a small trunk in his lodge. He had nothing new to negotiate and, hopeful (although uncertain) that he had the white man's word, he felt there was no need for more discussion. Then in late May, a messenger from the great treaty council arrived at his camp. Government officials wanted to reduce the Nez Perce reservation to just under 800,000 acres located wholly in northern Idaho. They wanted land that contained no gold. They wanted the land of the Wallowa band.

Tuekakas retreated to the band's sweathouse to more fully reflect on the situation. It was a good place to think. On this occasion Tuekakas was joined by Hin-mah-too-yah-lat-kekht.

Much had changed in Hin-mah-too-yah-lat-kekht's life over the previous few years. He had recently married Ta-ma-al-we-non-my, daughter of a chief in Lapwai. The marriage ceremony had been a great affair, with both families participating in the gift-giving feasts that served to join bands as well as relatives. Ta-ma-al-we-non-my was the first of three wives, although his subsequent marriages occurred after she had died. By all reports, Hin-mah-too-yah-lat-kekht was much sought after as a husband. His bearing alone—at least

six feet tall and handsome—had much to do with that. He
also came from a prominent and wealthy family; he was
quite skilled with horses; and already he showed an ability to
command attention and inspire enthusiasm with his well-
considered words. It was likely that Hin-mah-too-yah-lat-
kekht would be chief. Sousouquee (his older brother) had
died, a victim of the white man's firewater.

Inside the sweathouse, Hin-mah-too-yah-lat-kekht
poured water from a cedar root container onto the hot
rocks, causing steam to hiss into the air.

"Hin-mah-too-yah-lat-kekht, I will not be going to the
treaty council," said his father. "I am too old, too tired. All
know of my position, that it will not change."

"Then we will not participate?"

"Our voice may be of value. The messenger has told us
that Lawyer wishes all Nez Perce to be present to show the
white officials that we are united." Lawyer was a Nez Perce
who had emerged as the most prominent tribal chief,
largely because he was the government's choice during
the negotiations of 1855. Although many disagreed with
the appointment, the Nez Perce were comfortable knowing that the bands acted independently and that no one
man could speak for them all.

"If the messenger does not lie," added Tuekakas.

Hin-mah-too-yah-lat-kekht looked at his father.

"Lawyer is ambitious and I am not confident he will act in
the best interest of the Wallowa. He has shown that he is like
the willow and more than willing to bend to the will of the
white man. Someone must be there to speak for the Wallowa,"
continued Tuekakas. "Someone must remind the white men
of their promises. We have accepted white laws. We have lived
by them. Someone must tell them that the Nez Perce cannot
live on such a small piece of land. You must go."

Hin-mah-too-yah-lat-kekht nodded.

"When you go into council with the white man, always remember your country. Do not give it away. The white man will cheat you out of your home. I have taken no pay from the United States. I have never sold our land," Tuekakas declared.

With such advice from his father, Hin-mah-too-yah-lat-kekht traveled to Lapwai in early June. Accompanying him were his younger brother Ollokot (who served as a lesser chief) and those of the Wallowa band who wanted to go. They arrived at the treaty grounds to discover six companies of soldiers, considerably more than the regular contingent stationed at Fort Lapwai. Perhaps the government officials expected trouble. In total, some 2000 Natives were in attendance.

Hin-mah-too-yah-lat-kekht was greeted by many, especially the whites, as Young Joseph, a name that served to link him with his father. He had no objection. As he listened to Lawyer address the council, Young Joseph was undoubtedly pleased by Lawyer's words.

"In the same manner that my people receive the law of God as binding, so do we acknowledge and consider the law of your government as binding on us and on you, for the law is sacred," he reminded them. He went on to outline the past history between the white newcomers and the Nez Perce, careful to note that, while the Nez Perce had always welcomed them as friends, the white men could not say the same. They still hadn't met their obligations for the treaty of 1855. "We will sell you the sites where the whites have come in search of gold," offered Lawyer, "but we cannot give you all the country you ask for."

Young Joseph would not have disagreed with the offer, since it did not include any Wallowa land.

The government negotiators quickly dealt with any lingering grievances that the Natives had by arguing that it was

all water under the bridge. The prospectors were the new
reality that the Nez Perce must face and the government
could only protect them if their reserve was much smaller.
Seeing that the Natives were not inclined to listen to that
argument, the officials began to offer inducements to individual chiefs—houses, schools, mills. The chiefs met alone in
council to discuss the proposal. Some looked to the benefits
provided for their people and argued for treaty. Lawyer, who
had been secretly advised by the officials that his power
would be greatly augmented on the small reserve, was willing
to forget his previously stated powerful words. Ultimately, the
chiefs decided that Lawyer could no longer speak for the Nez
Perce as a group. Each band would make its own treaty with
the government negotiators if band members so decided. The
Nez Perce, who never really saw themselves as a single entity,
would no longer act as a unified body.

Young Joseph and other chiefs opposed to treaty said little during the council debates. Their minds were made up,
and they had no desire to force their will on others. Joseph
wasn't long back at Wallowa when word came that treaty
had indeed been made. It reduced the Nez Perce reservation to the size that the government officials desired and it
included *all* the Nez Perce! Apparently, once the opposing
chiefs had left, Lawyer had collected signatures from other
Nez Perce and substituted them for those who had rejected
treaty. The government representatives took the list as it was
and asked no questions. Whether they were suspicious or
not is unknown, but they were pleased enough to get what
they desired. A year later the treaty was ratified by the
United States Congress and all bands were directed onto
the new reservation.

Word came from Lawyer that he was not responsible for
the sale of their land. Government negotiators had tricked
them all. Tuekakas did not believe the feeble explanation,

This picture of Chief Joseph was likely taken after his epic flight from the American army in 1877. The hair flip (shown here) was a symbol adopted by followers of the Dreamer Religion. Smohalla, whose Wanapam tribe was located on the Columbia Plateau, preached the Dreamer Religion. In a dream Smohalla had in the 1850s, he visited the Spirit World and was given a message to take back to his people. Natives should reject white practices and return to their traditional ways. Smohalla also predicted that dead Natives would be resurrected, returning to overthrow the white man. The powerful message of renewal attracted many followers, all willing participants in the rituals Smohalla introduced to promote dreaming.

although he did not blame Lawyer alone for the unexpected turn of events. In 1855 the Americans had promised to leave his band in peace. They had returned to break their word. A despondent Tuekakas tore up his copy of the Walla Walla Treaty. Unsatisfied, he also destroyed a copy of St. Matthew's Gospel, written in his own Shahaptian language. It's likely that he abandoned Christianity at this point. If not, he did so within a few years when he (and Young Joseph) took to following the new faith of Smohalla, a Native from the Wanapum tribe located near the Columbia River. The rising wave of hair, seen in pictures of Young Joseph, was a symbol used by adherents of Smohalla's faith. It was probably easier for them to accept Smohalla's teachings about the sacredness of the earth and the unnaturalness of farming than it was to believe his words that dead Natives and buffaloes would return to overwhelm the white race.

Tuekakas had his own way of dealing with the increasing number of white men. He rode with Young Joseph and Ollokot to a trail that separated the Wallowa country from the Grand Ronde River to the north (the northwestern border of traditional Wallowa band territory), where many whites were beginning to settle.

He hammered poles into the ground and proclaimed to all, "Inside is the home of my people—the white man may take the land outside. Inside this boundary all our people were born. It circles around the graves of our fathers and we will never give up these graves to any man."

It would not be enough. Soon after the Lapwai treaty was ratified, surveyors came to Wallowa territory to begin dividing the land for homesteaders. In 1871 the first of the settlers arrived on the northern plateaus, the summer home of the Wallowa. Tuekakas saw them and, perhaps, it was a sight that finally broke the old man. Feeble and bed-ridden, he called for Young Joseph so that he might share one last piece of advice. The strong young man took his father's frail hand in his and listened to the whispery voice.

"My son, my body is returning to my mother earth and my spirit is going very soon to see the Great Spirit Chief. When I am gone, think of your country. You are the chief of these people. They look to you to guide them. Always remember that your father never sold his country. You must stop your ears whenever you are asked to sign a treaty selling your home. A few years more and white men will be all around you. They have their eyes on this land. My son, never forget my dying words. This country holds your father's body. Never sell the bones of your father and mother." The words came on his last breath.

The Wallowa shared the confidence that Tuekakas held in his son. Following the old chief's death feast, a council meeting was held and Young Joseph was elected chief. While they might have chosen his younger brother, a more skilled hunter and warrior, they instead selected the one known to be thoughtful, the one who had a gift for words. It was an important talent among the Nez Perce because the power of a leader came primarily from his ability to convince others about the appropriateness of a course of action. Even the white men recognized Young Joseph's ability as a speaker, although neither enthusiasm nor eloquence would give them cause to reconsider their positions.

Throughout 1872 more white men entered the Wallowa valley. Most were ranch hands, but a few were women, and with the start of the construction of a bridge across the Wallowa River, there was a suggestion of permanence about their presence. Joseph went to the town of La Grande, along the Grand Ronde River, to speak to the leaders of the immigrants. Joseph pointed out that they were on Wallowa territory, as settled by the 1855 treaty. The whites countered by noting that most tribal leaders had signed the 1863 treaty. Perhaps, they agreed, Joseph hadn't signed, but the American government had opened the land for settlement. In a rare example of level-headedness in Native-white relations, both sides recognized the legitimacy of the other's grievance, and they decided to call in the Lapwai Indian agent, John Montieth, for direction.

The parties met in August in the Wallowa valley. But it was Joseph, not Montieth, who did the talking. The Nez Perce chief spoke words that might have been voiced by his father.

"I did not want to come to this council, but I came hoping that we could save blood. The white man has no right to come here and take our country. We have never accepted presents from the government. Neither Lawyer nor any other chief had authority to sell this land. It has always belonged to my people. It came unclouded to them from their fathers and we will defend this land as long as a drop of Indian blood warms the hearts of our men."

Montieth remained for less than two days. Joseph's speech, however, had some impact on him. When there was word during the winter of 1872–73 that a band of Natives along the Oregon-California border had taken to the warpath rather than report to an assigned reserve, there was fear that Joseph might join them. To prevent an alliance, Montieth sent T.B. Odeneal, the superintendent of Indian Affairs for Oregon, to Joseph's winter camp. Joseph repeated his willingness to use violence to remove the newcomers, and he remained resolute when Odeneal pressed him to move to the reservation established by the 1863 treaty.

"I will not. I do not need your help. We have plenty and we are contented and happy if the white man will let us alone." Joseph gave his reasons for refusing. "The reservation is too small for so many people with all their stock...."

We can go to your towns and pay for all we need. We have plenty of horses and cattle to sell, and we won't have any help from you. We are free now; we can go where we please. Our fathers were born here. Here they lived; here they died; here are their graves. We will never leave them."

Recognizing that the Wallowa were not going to move, Odeneal took a new approach (perhaps under the direction of Montieth), again uncommon in Native-white relations: he sought a compromise. Would the Nez Perce be willing to share the Wallowa territory?

Despite his hard line, Joseph was a pragmatist and he agreed to Odeneal's proposal. But he had a condition: the reservation must be divided. As painful as it was to relinquish part of their Wallowa territory, Joseph concluded that a clearly identified piece of land free from white interference was the best option for his people. Odeneal agreed, and he drew up a proposal that split the traditional Wallowa reservation from north to south (from the Grande Ronde River to the Wallowa Mountains). Joseph's band would live on the eastern portion, bordered by the Snake River. Montieth sent the proposal to President Grant. On June 10, 1873, Grant signed an executive order authorizing it. The president's action was, as much as anything else, a recognition that the Wallowa had not signed the 1863 treaty.

On hearing the news, Oregonians were up in arms. Agreeing to such terms with the Nez Perce was bad enough, but the treaty had given the Wallowa control over the best farmland in the region. Even the Wallowa recognized this part of the treaty as unfortunate. They would have preferred the better grazing territory of the western section. The tense situation was made worse when a non-treaty Native was shot while he tried to stop a settler from plowing land that the Native considered unceded. The nontreaty chiefs met in the summer of 1874 to discuss going on the warpath. Joseph argued against it, suggesting that discussion with the white settlers would prove more fruitful. The council agreed. Throughout the remainder of 1874 and into 1875, Joseph was a common visitor at the farms and cabins of homesteaders. His efforts came to naught when, in 1875, President Grant bowed to pressure from the settlers and rescinded his executive order. White men could again settle where they wanted, and Montieth was charged with enforcing the terms of the 1863 treaty.

Montieth called Joseph to the Lapwai agency and informed him of the news. He insisted that Joseph move his people to the reservation in Idaho. It was, in his opinion, the only way to resolve the situation. Joseph was in a state of disbelief. How could the Wallowa be held to a treaty they did not sign? Years later, he tried to explain the absurdity of the demand.

"Suppose a white man should come to me and say, 'Joseph, I like your horses and I want to buy them.' I say to him, 'No, my horses suit me; I will not sell them.' Then he goes to my neighbor and says to him, 'Joseph has some good horses. I want to buy them, but he refuses to sell.' My neighbor answers, 'Pay me the money and I will sell you Joseph's horses.' The white man returns to me and says, 'Joseph, I have bought your horses and you must let me have them.'"

Despite Montieth's efforts, Joseph, enjoying the support of his band, would not move. It became increasingly difficult, however, to keep the band unified. Throughout 1876, more problems with settlers arose. The Wallowa cried theft and trespass. Matters came to a head when one of their own was killed, and government officials did little to bring the alleged murderer to justice. Then came news of the Sioux victory over Custer. There appeared to be another path that would ensure the Wallowa could keep their lands. The younger warriors were anxious to go on the warpath, perhaps even join with the nontreaty Sioux. What a force it would be! Although Joseph was unable to rein in fully the enthusiasm of the young men, he was able to keep them from doing what he called "rash things." Many settlers heard the Nez Perce war cry at night, but none suffered blows from their war clubs.

The Nez Perce were not the only ones to imagine that there could be an alliance among the nontreaty tribes of the northern plains and the plateaus. The settlers in Oregon were anxious and they made their concerns known to local politicians. It was not long before the government in Washington responded to their pleas by sending in the army under the direction of General Oliver Howard. Howard had been military commander of the Pacific Northwest since 1875, but he had few soldiers in the region. He seemed an ideal choice because he had valuable experience in dealing with reluctant Natives. In 1872, when it seemed that there might be war in the south between the army and the Apache, he had negotiated a treaty with Chief Cochise. What the government considered ideal, however, was somewhat different than what the Nez Perce did. Howard thought Natives were an inferior race, whose best course of action was to do as they were told. It was a common attitude among whites at the time.

Joseph's first official meeting with Howard was in 1876, when the Wallowa chief sat in council with the United States government commission (whose purpose it was to get the nontreaty Nez Perce onto the reservation set aside for them by the 1863 treaty). Howard was one of five commissioners. Joseph listened as the commissioners made their case. The Wallowa were bound by the treaty. If they remained where they were, they could not be protected from white men. And there would be more settlers coming.

"The Great Spirit, when He made the earth, made no marks, no lines of division or separation on it," replied

Joseph. "The earth is my mother. I was made of the earth and grew up on its bosom. The earth, as my mother and nurse, is sacred to me; too sacred to be valued or sold for gold or silver. I cannot give up my mother, the land that raised me....I ask for nothing of the president. I am able to take care of myself."

The commissioners explained to Joseph that the president did not want to take any rights from the Nez Perce. He merely wanted everyone to live under the same law. But it did not seem to Joseph that his people were being treated in the same way as whites were. It was only the Nez Perce who were being asked to give up their land. They pressed Joseph for an answer. Finally, he made a declaration.

"All I have to say is that I love my country."

It was not the decision the commissioners wanted him to make.

"Suppose several thousand men should come from Oregon with arms," posed Howard. "What would you do?"

Joseph looked at Howard's eyes, a rare act of defiance for a Native. "We will not sell the land. We will not give up the land. We love the land. It is our home."

Defiant Joseph might have been, but Howard was soon instructed to remove the Wallowa, by force if necessary. Howard was not anxious to use force, so in late April 1877, he met with the Wallowa again in an effort to persuade them to move peacefully. Joseph was sick, and discussions with Ollokot, his representative, proved only that the man was just as stubborn as his older brother. Howard would give them one last chance. In early May he called for a council of all the nontreaty Nez Perce. He would use the occasion to tell them in no uncertain terms that there would be no more delays, no more opposition. The Nez Perce would obey the terms of the 1863 treaty and move to their reservation.

As the council got underway, Howard discovered that the Nez Perce were under a misapprehension that he had organized it to continue negotiations. When he clarified his position, Toolhulhulzote (an insolent old Native in Howard's opinion), dared to challenge him and his authority. Frustrated, Howard had his soldiers arrest the man. As the soldiers led Toolhulhulzote away, Howard was not so sure that he had made the best decision. The Nez Perce were grumbling and their faces were angry. He could see them looking to Joseph. Howard prepared to give a signal to his men; he waited. He saw Joseph shake his head and breathed a sigh of relief.

Joseph realized that the situation was explosive. His word to rescue Toolhulhulzote would have resulted in the certain death of Howard and his men, and he knew that whatever the real cause, his people would be blamed. The army would not stop until they were hunted down and punished. Instead, he rose and addressed Howard.

"I am going to talk now. I don't care if you arrest me or not." Joseph turned to his people. "The arrest of Toolhulhulzote was wrong, but we will not resent the insult. We were invited to this council to express our hearts and we have done so." With that, he walked away.

But the council was not over, and they met again the next day. Surprisingly, Howard made a new offer. He would give the Wallowa the land around Fort Lapwai if they left the valley. Joseph did not want to dispossess those who lived in the proposed region so he declined the offer. Howard then drew his line in the sand.

"You have 30 days to go back to your home, collect your stock and move to the reservation. If you are not here in that time, I shall consider that you want to fight and I will send in my soldiers to drive you on."

"War can be avoided and it ought to be avoided," replied Joseph. "My people have always been the friend of the white man. Why are you in such a hurry? I cannot get ready to move in 30 days. Our stock is scattered and Snake River is very high [making a crossing dangerous]. Let us wait until fall and the river will be low. We want time to hunt our stock and gather our supplies for the winter."

"If you let the time run over one day, the soldiers will be there to drive you on to the reservation," declared Howard, "and all your cattle and horses outside the reservation at that time will fall into the hands of the white men."

Joseph fell silent. He did not want war. He did not want anyone killed, Nez Perce or white. He did not want to force others to move. He did not want to give up the land his people had known for so long as home, but his desire for peace was such that he had no choice.

"I listen to my heart. Rather than have war, I will give up my country. I would rather give up my father's grave. I will give up everything rather than have the blood of white men upon the hands of my people."

Once Toolhulhulzote was released, Joseph and his people returned to the Wallowa valley, but even this last journey was not to be a peaceful one. Rumors of approaching soldiers excited the Nez Perce warriors. There was talk of resistance. Toolhulhulzote was adamant that only blood could wash away the disgrace that Howard had brought upon him. His fiery rhetoric further inflamed the young Nez Perce warriors and many declared that they were ready to go on the warpath.

Joseph called for a council.

"It required a strong heart to stand up against such talk," he later admitted, "but I urged my people to be quiet and not to begin a war."

With the support of Ollokot and other prominent band members, the passions of the warriors were reined in and the Wallowa began to prepare for the move to their new home in Idaho. Somehow, they were able to round up their livestock and pack their belongings well within the prescribed 30 days. The greater challenge lay in crossing the Snake River that cut directly across their northeasterly path. As Joseph had said to Howard, spring run-off had swollen it, and the waters flowed with great speed. Scouts finally found a stretch that seemed less threatening. After two days of hard work, they could look back at the river and be thankful that no lives had been lost in fording it, although hundreds of animals had perished. They continued on past the Salmon River and when they arrived at the camas bulb harvesting grounds of Tepahlewam they made camp. There was no need to rush since Howard's deadline was two weeks away. Many of the other Nez Perce bands had already gathered at Tepahlewam to participate in the annual harvest and accompanying celebrations. In these last days of freedom, it seemed appropriate that the Wallowa join them.

Joseph and Ollokot traveled back across the Salmon River, where most of the livestock remained temporarily. They intended to slaughter some cattle for the feast. As they approached the camp after completing their task, they could see that something was wrong. The games and celebrations had stopped. People were packing their supplies and taking down their tipis; many had already left. A brave rode hard towards the brothers.

"Three white men killed yesterday!" he shouted. "War has broken out!"

Once in camp Joseph learned that Nez Perce warriors had killed a white man near the Salmon River. They had then come to Tepahlewam. Perhaps one act of violence might not have resulted in war, but as Joseph and Ollokot went from tipi to tipi encouraging people to reconsider fighting, they discovered it was much more than the one murder that inflamed the Natives. Toolhulhulzote had

continued to actively promote the warpath as an appropriate response to American treachery. His followers had
even been stockpiling ammunition in preparation.
Without the restraining voices of the brothers, it was not
difficult to persuade the Nez Perce that a bloody future
more honorably reflected their proud history than did
submission. Joseph and Ollokot listened to band members
tell them that their way was that of the coward.

Joseph later conceded, "I saw that war could not then be
prevented. The time had passed."

Joseph was first to admit, "…there were bad men among
[his] people who had quarreled with white men, [men
who] talked of their wrongs until they raised all the bad
hearts in the council."

But he did not hold them fully responsible for war.
"They had been insulted a thousand times; their fathers and
brothers had been killed; their mothers and wives had been
disgraced; they had been driven to madness by the whisky
sold to them by the white men; they had been told by
General Howard that all their horses and cattle which they
had been unable to drive out of Wallowa were to fall into
hands of white men; and, added to all this, they were
homeless and desperate."

Joseph contended that he would have given his own life
if it could have undone the killing of white men by his
people.

But once blood was spilled, the path seemed clear. He
and Ollokot decided to follow the bands. It made little
sense to continue to the reservation, for he knew that the
acts of Toolhulhulzote and his followers involved all
the Nez Perce in war. By the third week in June, they had
arrived at Lahmotta at the White Bird Canyon just across
the border in Idaho. They weren't there long when the soldiers arrived.

General Howard had been waiting at Fort Lapwai for the Nez Perce. By mid-June, he was aware of the events at Tepahlewam and was anxious to respond. He sent out two detachments, just over 100 soldiers, to investigate. They were green soldiers, only recently recruited and minimally trained. They rode hard, too hard in hindsight, and when they reached the White Bird Canyon, their horses were exhausted. The terrain, full of high buttes and sloping hill-sides, was ideally suited to defend. The Nez Perce were divided into small groups and well hidden—warriors followed their chiefs, who were likely positioned according to some predetermined plan. Even as the soldiers approached, the Nez Perce held out hope for talks that might prevent violence. They sent a delegation out to meet the soldiers, but a local volunteer who was assisting the force fired on it. The shots brought a response in kind from the Nez Perce. Killed first was the trumpeter, whom they knew relayed directions to the soldiers during battle. The soldiers retreated and attempted to reorganize, but it was too late. Although they outnumbered the Natives, 33 soldiers died. The Nez Perce suffered only 2 injuries.

As anxious as Howard was to rein in the hostile Natives, he had to wait for reinforcements. In addition to the 100 he had sent to White Bird Canyon, he had only another 20 under his command, a good indication that the army was unprepared for the course of action taken by the Nez Perce. By late June the reinforcements arrived and, with some 250 soldiers and volunteers, Howard made for White Bird Canyon. They arrived to find the Nez Perce gone, but they took time to bury the dead. Some soldiers marveled that the bodies were not brutalized, but none were surprised that all the weapons were gone. The gruesome work done, treaty Nez Perce scouts set out to find the trail of the fleeing Nez Perce. The scouts soon discovered that the Nez Perce had crossed the Salmon River and were headed west. Howard seethed as he thought of crossing the inhospitable river again.

Once on the other side of the river, trailing the Nez Perce proved even more difficult because they had slipped into the adjacent mountain range, where the going was treacherous. Even the Nez Perce had to abandon many of their supplies and stock. The chase proved all for naught. After a few days, the scouts discovered that the trail led back to the river, where the Nez Perce had crossed it. Howard could not ford the river at that point, and he was forced to retrace his steps to White Bird Canyon. Meanwhile, the Nez Perce were moving east and, although they didn't have Howard's men to worry about for the time being, numerous small detachments of soldiers were in the region. There were skirmishes and, for the most part, army deaths. By the second week of July, the Natives were camped near the south fork of the Clearwater River. It was necessary to rest because 500 of the 750 Nez Perce were women and children.

Taking care of the women and children while the men were engaged in battle emerged as an important task, and it fell to the camp chief. Traditionally a Nez Perce camp had two types of chief. The camp chief was responsible for the order of the village, both when it was stationary and during times of travel. The war chief became prominent when there was an enemy to fight. Joseph did not come from a line of warriors (although his brother was respected as such), he had no experience raiding or on the warpath and he had never desired to fight (although he did when it was necessary). He willingly took on the responsibility of camp chief for the five fleeing bands. Although reports, especially those written by Howard, described Joseph as a great war strategist, that was never his role during the Nez Perce War.

The Native's need to rest, however, gave Howard and his men a chance to catch up. Howard's appearance near the

Nez Perce camp caught the Natives by surprise, since they were not aware that he had forded the river. Fortunately for the Nez Perce, it took some time for Howard to arrange his soldiers properly and the warriors were able to take defensive positions in a broad arc around the enemy. It was surely a sight for the tenderfoot soldiers because the Nez Perce had stripped to their breechcloths and mounted the war cayuses they kept near their tipis. Quickly, the soldiers found themselves under attack. Although only about 100 Natives fought, the battle raged throughout the night. By morning, Howard had managed to bring his howitzer into range and the army was able to advance.

Throughout the mid-afternoon there was little significant change in the lines. Then a cavalry company out of Fort Klamath in southern Oregon appeared. They forced the Nez Perce down the hillside into their camp and quickly followed with cannonballs and rapid-fire bullets. Events had shifted so suddenly that the camp was caught by surprise. Joseph directed the bands to leave without packing. It was a chaotic flight across the Clearwater, but it proved effective. The soldiers weren't prepared to follow, so they turned to raiding what was left in the camp. Howard claimed victory, but he had lost 29 men and the Nez Perce only 4.

The Nez Perce headed east and made for the Bitterroot Mountains. At the encouragement of Looking Glass, chief of one of the more easterly bands, it was decided that the fleeing Nez Perce would continue into Montana. Looking Glass was one of the few Nez Perce who hunted buffalo on the plains. He felt that they might ally with the Crow or perhaps join Sitting Bull's Sioux in Canada. Joseph did not support the plan because it took his people farther from their homeland. It is possible that he thought about surrendering at this point, but perhaps he feared that the army would hang him. For the better part of two weeks, they followed the Loho Trail east. Howard was in pursuit, but he was hindered when several soldiers died in an ambush. When the Nez Perce reached the Bitterroot Valley, they discovered a detachment of soldiers had barricaded the eastern end of the pass.

The soldiers were out of Fort Shaw, Montana and not under Howard's control, although they had orders to detain the Nez Perce. Looking Glass had encountered them before, and they did not stir fear in him. Joined by Joseph and another chief, he rode to the barricades.

"These are meant to stop us," laughed Looking Glass, as he looked to the hastily made structures. "Even our children would be around them quickly!"

"If they don't stop you, we will," replied Captain Charles Rawn.

"Our dispute is with the soldiers in Idaho. If you let us pass, we will not fight you," answered Looking Glass.

"Our orders are to arrest you."

"We are going by you without fighting if you will let us, but we *are* going by you."

Rawn looked over the shoulders of the chiefs and took note of the many Nez Perce in the distance. They clearly outnumbered his men (he had only 44), even with the additional volunteers and Flathead braves.

"Leave us your weapons and we will let you pass," said Rawn.

The chiefs agreed to discuss it, but only out of respect. They were not going to give up their weapons because they were needed for protection and hunting. Later they parleyed again with Rawn and informed him of their decision. When Rawn suggested they reconsider, the chiefs returned to the Nez Perce and made plans to go around the barricades. Joseph organized the women, children and elderly and had them move out. Warriors rode between them and the soldiers to offer protection. By the time Rawn realized what was happening, most of the Nez Perce were beyond the barricades, thereafter called Fort Fizzle. Rawn barked orders to pursue, but the volunteers had heard that the Nez Perce would leave their property alone, and they were not anxious to fight. Before the few soldiers could organize, the Nez Perce were well into the Bitterroot Valley.

They continued unhampered, although there was concern when they again encountered some of Rawn's volunteers. Looking Glass assured them that the Nez Perce wanted no trouble. The white men were surely relieved because they had never before heard such reassuring words from Natives they considered to be hostile.

Joseph described what happened next: "We then made a treaty with these soldiers. We agreed not to molest anyone and they agreed that we might pass through the Bitterroot country in peace. We bought provisions and traded stock with the white men there."

Most behaved honorably. When a party of Nez Perce raided a homestead, Looking Glass made them return with three horses as compensation. They traveled on for four more days, finally making camp. At rest for the first time in many days, a council was called to discuss where the Nez Perce should go. Some called for flight into Canada. There was word that the Grandmother (Queen Victoria) might be willing to accept them because she had some other bands. Toolhulhulzote was one of those who approved of the plan. Looking Glass, however, was opposed. All looked to Joseph for his opinion.

"When we were fighting for our own country, there was little reason for flight...but since we have left our country, it matters little where we go. Perhaps Looking Glass is right and the Crow will assist us. But, as we cannot go back to the Wallowa, I have nothing to say...."

The council agreed to follow Looking Glass' plan. The decision wasn't long made before an unexpected attack nearly rendered it meaningless. Colonel John Gibbon, commander at Fort Shaw, had been on the trail of the Nez Perce since he'd been informed of Rawn's failure. He had about 160 men (the Nez Perce had about 250 warriors) and no Native scouts because local chiefs were unwilling to act against the friendly Nez Perce. Gibbon sent word to Howard, who was still on the Loho Trail, to hurry with reinforcements. Gibbon was certain he could catch the slow-moving Nez Perce, and he was confident that his howitzer and cannons would give the army the advantage. On August 9, Gibbon's men attacked under cover of night. They set the Nez Perce horses loose and then fired on the sleeping camp. Many were killed before they could get out of their tipis, and others didn't get far before bullets brought them down.

Joseph ran to round up the horses, while the warriors charged the soldiers. Hand-to-hand combat ensued and the army line broke under the skilled Nez Perce fighting. They retreated. Some warriors managed to get to the heavy weapons and damage them. But the Battle at Big Hole had been costly, perhaps the most difficult yet of all the fights that had involved the Nez Perce. They had lost 30 warriors and 50 women and children.

It was the death of the noncombatants that caused Joseph the most pain. "The Nez Perce never make war on women and children; we could have killed a great many women and children while the war lasted," he later said, "but we would feel ashamed to do so cowardly an act."

A final indignity occurred days later, when Howard's men finally reached Big Hole. His Native scouts dug up those who had been buried and scalped them.

Joseph had helped organize the burials, a difficult task given the number of children killed. Then, while the warriors kept the soldiers at bay, he led the families, the injured and the remaining stock towards the Plains, buffalo country. As they moved, more died and others, who knew they were burdens, asked to be left behind. Soon, the party slipped back into Idaho, near Yellowstone National Park. Their slow travel, however, allowed Howard to catch up with them. The Nez Perce decided to launch a surprise attack. They rode back to Howard's camp some 15 miles behind them and tried to drive off the soldiers' horses. It was risky because Howard had some 300 soldiers and volunteers. In the darkness, they mistakenly released the army's mules, and the warriors were discovered before they could retreat. The Nez Perce fought for a couple of hours before making their escape. Howard's men were exhausted from the stepped-up pace of their pursuit and did not follow.

By the third week of August, the Nez Perce were in Yellowstone. Along the way, they encountered settlers and tourists. Many Nez Perce were still enraged over the actions of the army at Big Hole and, despite pleas from the chiefs that they leave the whites be, they killed some. But it was not these deaths that spurred the United States government into more determined action. Howard's efforts were proving sadly inadequate. At almost every turn, the Nez Perce got the better of him. His superiors were questioning his ability. Rawn and Gibbon fared little better. Even worse, public opinion was beginning to unite behind the Nez Perce. Reports from Montana praised the peaceful ways of the Natives. Many were surprised—and pleased—that the Nez Perce did not scalp dead soldiers. Thanks to their restraint and to Howard, who was forced to justify his inability to catch the Nez Perce (by praising Joseph's abilities), many came to see Joseph as an intelligent and civilized leader. The government had to act before Joseph became an American hero.

William Sherman, general of the army, turned his efforts towards reining in the Nez Perce. He dispatched army units to Yellowstone and ordered them to take posts along routes that led from the park. He then ordered Howard to pursue the Natives into the park. Sherman figured it was an easy matter to force the Nez Perce into the waiting arms of one of the recently arrived companies. It might well have happened that way had the Nez Perce done as expected. Instead, they led Howard's scouts on a wild goose chase to the south, eventually leaving the park through a narrow, unprotected canyon to the north. By the time Howard and the reinforcements realized they had been misled, the Nez Perce were 50 miles into buffalo country.

The Nez Perce continued north to the Musselshell River, but it was not easy going. Although the army was well behind them, they discovered that the Crow (who they hoped would join them as allies) had thrown in their lot with the white men. They harassed the Nez Perce, raiding horses and even killing a few of the men. They reached Musselshell River by the middle of September, but it was without joy. The Nez Perce were tiring. They were traveling in unfamiliar territory at a rate of 25 miles a day, a fast pace for all but the warriors. Winter would soon arrive, and they had made no preparations. And the army was still chasing them. Some of the headmen renewed their calls to flee to Canada. Unlike the Crow, they argued, Sitting Bull was sure to welcome them. Finally, they agreed that Canada was the place to go. Looking Glass, however, was concerned with the pace of flight and determined that, since they had at least a two-day lead on the soldiers, they should take more frequent rests.

By late September they were across the Missouri River and at the Bear Paw Mountains. Canada was only 40 miles away, a two-day ride. But the weather turned cold, and the people were tired and hungry. Looking Glass ordered that they rest to recover their strength for the last leg of the journey.

"No!" cried Wottolen, a warrior. "It is not the time to stop and rest."

Looking Glass stared at him.

"I have dreamed that the soldiers will attack at dawn."

"Nonsense," laughed Looking Glass. "We have left them far behind."

Looking Glass *was* correct. The men who rode with Howard were days behind. However, a new force led by Colonel Nelson Miles was very close, and his Cheyenne scouts were watching the Nez Perce. Miles had experience fighting Natives. He had fought the Sioux and forced Crazy Horse to surrender and Sitting Bull to flee into Canada. He was preparing an escort to lead commissioners to Canada (they were to negotiate Sitting Bull's return) when an appeal came from Howard to assist in cutting off the Nez Perce escape route. He rode towards the Bear Paw Mountains with the better part of eight companies (400 soldiers) under his command. They attacked on the morning of September 30, just as Wottolen had dreamed.

When the Nez Perce saw the Cheyenne painted and dressed for war, the call went out that attack was imminent. Joseph ran to the horses at the first crack of gunfire. Quickly Miles' men swept into the valley that the Nez Perce were using for their camp. Joseph later described what happened to him.

"I thought of my wife and children, who were now surrounded by soldiers and I resolved to go to them or die. With a prayer in my mouth to the Great Spirit Chief who rules above, I dashed unarmed through the line of soldiers. It seemed to me that there were guns on every side, before

and behind me. My clothes were cut to pieces and my
horse was wounded, but I was not hurt. As I reached the
door of my lodge, my wife handed me my rifle, saying,
'Here's your gun. Fight!'

"The soldiers kept us under continuous fire. Six of my
men were killed in one spot near me. Ten or twelve soldiers
charged into our camp and got possession of two
lodges....I called my men to drive them back. We fought at
close range not more than twenty feet apart and drove the
soldiers back upon their main line...."

The battle raged throughout the daylight hours, stop-
ping with nightfall. It grew colder and snowed; the Nez
Perce were forced to dig trenches for shelter as well as
graves for the dead. It was a costly fight. Although only
18 Nez Perce were killed (26 soldiers died), among the
dead were Ollokot and Toolhulhulzote. The soldiers had
them surrounded, but six warriors slipped through. They
were sent to find Sitting Bull and to ask for his help. Events
would play out before they could fulfill their mission.

The next morning, Miles sent word to Joseph that he
wanted to meet. The Americans continued to believe that
Joseph was the leader of the renegade Natives. Joseph was
the man to talk to, but not for that reason. The Nez Perce
knew that negotiation was rapidly becoming their only
option if they did not want more bloodshed, and Joseph was
best at that. Although he was suspicious, Joseph agreed. The
meeting was not amicable. Miles demanded that the Nez
Perce surrender. Joseph declined. He remained hopeful that
the messengers might return with assistance from Sitting
Bull. Joseph stayed in Miles' tent for the night. The next
morning when he still hadn't returned, Yellow Bull, a Nez
Perce headman, went to see if he was still alive. Yellow Bull
learned that Joseph was not allowed to leave, but they were
permitted to meet as long as soldiers were present.

"They have got you in their power and I am afraid they will never let you go again!" lamented Yellow Bull. "I have an officer in our camp and I will hold him until they let you go free."

"I do not know what they mean to do with me, but if they kill me you must not kill the officer," replied Joseph, ever aware of the need for peace. "It will do no good to avenge my death by killing him."

Throughout the night there was renewed fighting. Joseph was permitted to return to the Nez Perce the next day, perhaps in an effort by Miles to calm the Natives. They held a council but were divided on whether to surrender. Some suggested they continue to run for the Grandmother's country.

Joseph agreed, "We could have escaped from Bears Paw Mountain if we had left our wounded, old women and children behind." None, however, was willing to do this and Joseph revealed why. "We had never heard of a wounded Indian recovering while in the hands of white men."

Instead, Joseph met with Miles again.

"If you will come out and give up your arms, I will spare your lives and send you back to the reservation," offered the general.

"I could not bear to see my wounded men and women suffer any longer; we had lost enough already," Joseph later remembered. "General Miles had promised that we might return to our country with what stock we had left. I thought we could start again. I believed General Miles or I never would have surrendered. I have heard that he has been censured for making the promise to return us to Lapwai. He could not have made any other terms with me at that time. I would have held him in check until my friends came to my assistance, and then neither of the generals nor their soldiers would have ever left Bears Paw Mountain alive."

At council, Joseph listened as Nez Perce leaders spoke of their fears. Some told stories of Natives who had been hanged once they surrendered. They believed that Howard would ensure the same fate awaited Joseph.

The old warrior Looking Glass would not surrender. "I have my experiences with a man of two faces and two tongues. If you surrender, you will be sorry and in your sorrow you will feel rather to be dead, than suffer that deception."

"One should look twice at a two-faced man," agreed Joseph. "But I do not believe that Miles is such a man."

Looking Glass shook his head. "I will never surrender to a deceitful white chief," he declared. He never did. A few moments later he was shot dead by a Cheyenne. He was the 120th and last Native to die in the Nez Perce War.

Joseph made his decision. Likely it was prompted by Miles' decision to turn his cannons on the muddy shelter pits used by the women, children and elderly. His people needed rest and wanted peace. On the fifth day of the fight, October 5, he went to Miles.

"Our chiefs are killed....It is cold and we have no blankets. The little children are freezing to death. My people, some of them, have run away to the hills and have no blankets, no food—perhaps freezing to death. I want to have time to look for my children and see how many of them I can find. Maybe I shall find them among the dead. Hear me, my chiefs! I am tired. My heart is sick and sad...." He gave Miles his rifle. "From where the sun now stands I will fight no more."

Although over 200 Nez Perce escaped from the Bears Paw Mountains and continued for Canada, the Nez Perce War was over.

General Sherman grudgingly summed up the remarkable exploit: "Thus has terminated one of the most extraordinary

Indian wars of which there is any record. The Indians throughout displayed a courage and skill that elicited universal praise; they abstained from scalping, let captive women go free, did not commit indiscriminate murder of peaceful families, which is usual, and fought with almost scientific skill, using advance and rear guards, skirmish lines and field fortifications."

Apparently, he didn't believe that Natives were capable of such things. Likely his real feelings regarding Natives were less than flattering, which he revealed in different communication. "The more we kill this year, the less will have to be killed in the next war, for the more I see of these Indians, the more convinced I am that they all have to be killed or maintained as a species of paupers."

To their surprise, the Nez Perce were not led to their homeland but taken east. Joseph complained to Miles, who declared his opposition to the order.

"You must not blame me. I have endeavored to keep my word, but the chief who is over me has given the order...." He explained that the relocation was being done for economic reasons. It would be cheaper to provide for the Nez Perce where they were going.

For a time, there was concern among the Nez Perce that Yellow Bull's fears might be realized. But a noose did not await Joseph when the Nez Perce arrived at Bismarck, North Dakota. Well-wishers, cheering crowds and a marching band greeted them!

The local paper even printed an invitation to Chief Joseph: "Sir: Desiring to show you our kind feelings and the admiration we have for your bravery and humanity, as exhibited in your recent conflict with the forces of the United States, we must cordially invite you to dine with us at the Sheridan House in this city. The dinner is to be given at 1 PM today." Whether Joseph attended is uncertain, but the next day his people were on a train bound for Fort Leavenworth, Kansas, and they arrived in late November.

"At Leavenworth we were placed in a low river bottom, with no water except river water to drink and cook with," explained Joseph. "We had always lived in a healthy country....Many of our people sickened and died [most from malaria] and we buried them in this strange land. I cannot tell you how much my heart suffered for my people while at Leavenworth. The Great Spirit who rules above seemed to be looking some other way and did not see what was being done to my people."

The Nez Perce petitioned Sherman to allow them to return to Oregon, but he denied it and directed fort authorities not to bother him again with such requests. Seven months later, however, they were moved to the Quawpaw Indian Reserve at Baxter Springs, Kansas. Baxter Springs proved no better a location than Fort Leavenworth. Over the next year some 70 more Nez Perce died from disease. Authorities gave them little medicine.

While at Baxter Springs, numerous sympathetic politicians, journalists, army officers and civil servants visited the Nez Perce. Most promised help, but rarely was any forthcoming. The most prominent visitor was Commissioner of Indian Affairs E.A. Hayt. On meeting him, Joseph reminded Hayt that he expected Miles' word to be honored.

"It cannot be done," replied Hayt. "White men now live in that territory and there is no land left. If you return to Wallowa there will be no peace, for there are warrants out for the Nez Perce warriors who caused trouble there. The government cannot protect you there."

Hayt was willing to let the Nez Perce move to a more desirable site nearby, and the pair spent time searching for one. They found a place that was better than Baxter Springs, but it paled in comparison to the mountains and rivers of

Chief Joseph, taken at age 69 while at Nespelem where he spent his final years.

home. Joseph was not sure that his people could live well there. Perhaps they wouldn't have to. When Joseph met with Indian Inspector General John O'Neill, the official was so taken by the plight of the Nez Perce that he agreed they should be permitted to live in the northern mountain country. He felt the Nez Perce case could best be made if the chief appealed in person to the president, so O'Neill arranged a meeting between Joseph and Rutherford B. Hayes.

Joseph arrived in Washington in early January 1879. He met many prominent people, including Hayes, his secretary of the Interior and numerous congressmen. The most memorable meeting was on January 14 in Lincoln Hall before an audience of prominent Washingtonians. There, Joseph spoke of his people's history from the arrival of the white man to the Nez Perce relocation at Baxter Springs (many of Joseph's words included in this biography are taken from a version of that speech). The history complete, Joseph turned his powerful oratorical skills to the problems of the present.

> I have heard talk and talk, but nothing is done. Good words do not last long until they amount to something.... I am tired of talk that comes to nothing. It makes my heart sick when I remember all the good words and all the broken promises. There has been too much talking by men who had no right to talk....
>
> If the white man wants to live in peace with the Indian, he can live in peace. There need be no trouble. Treat all men alike. Give them all the same law. Give them all an even chance to live and grow. All men were made by the same Great Spirit Chief. They are all brothers. The earth is the mother of all people and all people should have equal rights upon it. You might as well expect the rivers to run backwards as that any man who was born a free man should be contented penned up and denied liberty where he goes.... If you pen an Indian up on a small spot of earth, he will not grow contented nor will he grow and prosper. I have asked some of the great white chiefs where they get their authority to say to the Indian that he shall stay in one place, while he sees white men going where they please. They cannot tell me.

I know that my race must change. We cannot hold our own with the white men as we are. We only ask an even chance to live as other men live.....Let me be a free man— free to travel, free to stop, free to trade where I choose, free to chose my own teachers, free to follow the religion of my fathers, free to think and talk and act for myself—and I will obey every law or submit to the penalty.

Whenever the white man treats the Indian as they treat each other, then we shall have no more wars. We shall all be alike—brothers of one father and one mother, with one sky above us and one country around us and one government for all. Then the Great Spirit who rules above will smile upon this land and send rain to wash out the bloody spots made by my brothers' hands upon the face of the earth. For this time the Indian race are waiting and praying.

Perhaps everything Joseph said in his speech did not stand up to careful historical scrutiny, but his impassioned vision was beyond criticism. He struck a chord when he addressed concepts the white men understood: justice, dignity, fortitude, resilience. Joseph was given a great ovation from the audience, but it did not change his people's lot. He returned to Baxter Springs with empty hands.

In July his people were moved, not nearer to home but to a 90,000-acre reserve near the Chikaskia River, Indian Territory in Oklahoma. The terrain was a little better there, but his people were still sick. Nearly every child died in infancy. As the years passed, Joseph grew despondent.

"The white men forget us," he told one visitor, "and death comes almost every day for some of my people. He will come for all of us. A few months more and we will be in the ground. We are a doomed people."

Joseph's cause, however, continued to gain supporters. Two of them were old war enemies, General Miles and Major

Wood (who had served under General Howard). Miles appealed to President Hayes, asking that the Nez Perce be allowed to return to the Northwest. Wood started a letter-writing campaign in Joseph's support. On July 4, 1884, the United States Congress passed an act that allowed the Nez Perce to return to Idaho. Many in the state, however, continued to blame Joseph for the Nez Perce War. They spoke of violence should Joseph return. The government succumbed to this new pressure: half the Nez Perce would be returned to the Lapwai reservation, while the rest would go to the Colville reservation in Washington state. Joseph was among the latter group and he settled his people in a place called Nespelem, which was similar in appearance, at least, to the Wallowa valley.

The Nez Perce prospered at Nespelem because few white people interfered with them (although the Indian agent controlled most aspects of reserve life), and the hunting was good. Still, Joseph longed to return to the Wallowa. In 1887 he was given an opportunity to move closer to it. The government passed a Severalty Act that divided up the reservations into individual plots of land. It was an effort to further acculturate the Natives by breaking communal ties and making each responsible for his own success. Joseph was offered title to a piece of land in the Lapwai reservation, but he declined. He had accepted teachers and religious men, but he would not live as a white man and he still held out hope for a home in the Wallowa valley.

A report from the office of the Indian agent says much about Joseph's unfaltering determination. "He will remain landless and homeless if he cannot have his own again. It was good to see an unsubjugated Indian. One could not help respecting the man who stood firmly for his rights, after having fought and suffered and been defeated in the struggle for their maintenance."

Joseph returned to Washington, D.C., in 1897 to complain about white squatters on the Colville reservation and to again request that the Wallowa valley be restored to them. President William McKinley said he would look into the matter of the squatters, but that Joseph's people would never again live around the Wallowa River. He also met General Miles there. Miles invited Joseph to participate in the dedication of President Grant's tomb in New York. He agreed and found himself riding at the front of the parade between General Miles and General Howard, among the thousands who jammed onto Madison Avenue.

Joseph was able to visit the Wallowa valley twice in the summers of 1899 and 1900. It was not the land he remembered, cut up and packaged as it was by the fences of settlers. He was moved to tears, however, when he found his father's grave. Although it was within a farmer's field, the man had carefully fenced it off. Joseph met with some of the settlers, who declared as had McKinley that he would never return. Joseph made one last attempt to do so, meeting with President Theodore Roosevelt in 1903. The results were no different than any of his previous meetings with the president.

Joseph died on September 21, 1904 in Nespelem, collapsing while sitting near the fire outside his tipi. The doctor on the reservation declared that he had died of a broken heart. It was a heart attack. Dressed in his finest clothes with his face painted, Joseph was placed on a litter and carried to his burial site. Once there, a shaman spoke over the wails of his wives and the sobbing of his people. He was interred on a gently sloping hill in the Nespelem Valley.

CHAPTER THREE

Quanah Parker

Quahadi Comanche, 1845–1911

IN THE EARLY SUMMER OF 1874, the southern Plains, likely somewhere in southern Kansas, provided the setting for an unusual event. The Comanche *puhakut* (medicine man) and prophet Ishatai had called for a Sun Dance, and the Cheyenne, Kiowa and Arapaho joined his people in celebration. None would have come if an ordinary man had called for it. But Ishatai possessed great *puha* (power). It was said that he had visited heaven and had returned bullet-proof, with the ability to bring back the dead. Recently he had predicted a comet that had blazed across the sky. When Ishatai visited the bands of the southern Plains in the spring and promised them victory against the white men if they purified themselves, the Natives listened. For the first time, the Comanche performed the Sun Dance.

It was not the Sun Dance known by the Sioux and Crow of the northern Plains. There was no self-mutilation or sacrifice. There was no appeal to the Great Spirit for a vision that

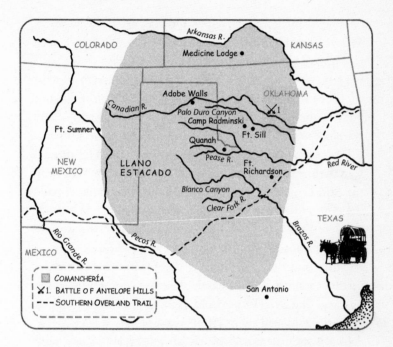

might help the people in the task that lay ahead. But the celebration was lively nevertheless. For days they danced and sang. In quiet times, men gathered around fires, smoked their pipes, told stories of bravery and made pledges of friendship. Women and their daughters prepared the feasts and boys joined in the mock battles. Like the Sun Dances of the north, the Comanche ceremony served to unite the tribes so that they might meet their enemies with greater confidence.

"We will enjoy success," Ishatai assured them. "Everything will again be like it once was. Buffalo will darken the plains. The people will be strong. The enemy will be crushed underfoot."

The ceremony continued for seven nights. A declaration by Ishatai brought it to a close.

"It is enough. We are one. We are ready."

The Comanche war chief Quanah Parker was ready.
When Ishatai had first proposed the idea of a Sun Dance
to him, he was skeptical. The ceremony was not his people's way and he did not believe that it would benefit
them. But the more he considered the idea, the greater
was its appeal. A gathering of tribes would bring many
warriors together. United, the warriors could be a powerful force against the *tejanos* (the white men). The shrewd
leader threw his support behind Ishatai's idea. Watching
the Sun Dance had convinced Quanah that he had made
the correct decision. As the *puhakut* predicted, many bands
answered the call, and the ceremony united the diverse
peoples as nothing had before.

Discussions among the war chiefs after the ceremony
further solidified the bands because consensus came
quickly. The warriors would fight as one and Quanah
Parker would lead them. At 30 years old, he was relatively
young, but Quanah had already proven his ability as a warrior. He and his Quahadi band were well known by all
who called the southern Plains home. Natives respected his
cunning and courage, while settlers feared his blazing six-
shooter and his war whoop. Most had lost count of the
number of successful raids he had led, but few had forgotten that he had forced pursuing cavalry into retreat more
than once. Quanah suggested that the warriors should first
strike at the buffalo hunters, the hated white men who had
done so much to destroy the Native way of life. They chose
Adobe Walls, an abandoned trading post fashioned into
a small village and used as a headquarters by a party of buffalo hunters, as the site of their first strike.

In June, 700 Natives rode south to the Canadian River in
the Texas Panhandle. Twenty-eight men and one woman were
at Adobe Walls and, as fate would have it, two of them were
working on repairs throughout the night of June 26, 1874,

when the Natives arrived. They gave the alarm before
Quanah Parker could give the signal to attack. The element
of surprise, always crucial in the war chief's battle strategy,
was lost. Nevertheless, he had his warriors attack the walls
of the post. It was an unusual move, since the more traditional method of Native warfare had them surround a target, shoot at enemies as they became visible and retreat
quickly. Original though it was, charging Adobe Walls
proved to be a poor strategy. The buffalo hunters stayed
holed up in the handful of buildings inside the post. The
warriors had no targets. But the buffalo hunters did. They
were expert marksmen and disinclined to waste ammunition. Many warriors fell.

Quanah Parker pulled the warriors back, but he was not
done. He led a second attack. The warriors killed the buffalo hunters' horses, thereby preventing any escape.
Quanah's own horse was shot from under him. He scram-
bled for cover, but was unlucky to catch a ricocheting bullet in the back. Another warrior pulled Quannah onto
a horse and carried him to safety. For a time, the opposing
sides exchanged shots from a distance, but the Natives'
weapons were no match for the buffalo hunters' powerful
Sharps rifles, which were designed to pack a punch at more
than 1000 yards. As more warriors fell, the Natives turned
on Ishatai. He was reminded of his bulletproof powers and
was challenged to approach the post and retrieve the body
of a fallen comrade. When he wouldn't, many of the warriors left in anger, leaving only the Comanche at Adobe
Walls. Eventually, Quanah called a retreat.

It was the Comanche war chief's worst defeat yet.
It wasn't merely the retreat and the loss of warriors (13 died
during the fight and more died later from their injuries),
although those were bad enough. He realized that any hope
of a Native alliance to resist the encroaching *tejanos* was lost

Quanah Parker, taken after his surrender in 1875. The feathers he holds may be symbolic of his vision quest.

forever. Within months, many of the chiefs that had ridden with him to Adobe Walls had surrendered at the Fort Sill reservation. They were tired of a life one step ahead of the pursuing cavalry. Some were placed in jail, but Quanah Parker would have none of that. He held the code of the Comanche warrior close to his heart and was prepared to die before he handed over his war bonnet. He took his own people back to the Llano Estacado, the Staked Plains they called home.

While Quanah Parker was determined to avoid defeat, the U.S. government was set on insuring just that. In the summer of 1874, the government declared that Natives who failed to report to the reservation by August 3 would be attacked as hostile. In early fall, Colonel Ranald Mackenzie and his Fourth Cavalry were directed to carry out the government order. Mackenzie was anxious to return to the Llano Estacado, where Quanah Parker had eluded him on two different campaigns a few years previously. He was confident that he would not be humiliated a third time. His men knew the territory and they were better prepared for what waited. In late November, the cavalry found the Quahadi, without Quanah, at Palo Duro. The soldiers attacked, but most of the Natives escaped, although they were forced to abandon their horses and supplies. Mackenzie had 1000 of the recovered horses killed. Experience had taught him that the Comanche were expert raiders, likely to be successful in any attempt to retrieve the animals.

Without supplies, it was a difficult winter for the Quahadi. Plants, grubs and rodents did little more than dull sharp hunger pains. Even if they had horses to use in the hunt, they would have been of little value since no one saw any buffalo, and everyone knew that to go in search of them was to risk an encounter with the cavalry. The women and children were exhausted. The youngest knew only of a life in flight. Some Quahadi wanted to continue to run and they suggested Mexico or New Mexico Territory as likely destinations. Quanah Parker was no longer sure. No one doubted his commitment to the traditional way of Comanche life. He had fought for it with such determination that he had become recognized as the greatest of Comanche warriors.

But, he wondered during that cold winter of 1874–75, *even if we win, is there such a life to which we might return?* As chief, he had to make the decision that was in the best interest of his people. That such a decision might turn the stomach of a warrior was a matter of secondary importance. He would make his decision known in the spring.

~~~~

Naduah pulled the scraper down along the buffalo hide. How many times had she made the same motion that morning? Hundreds? A thousand? She had no idea; it was not a thing to be measured but one to be done. Once the hide had been thoroughly scraped, it would be tanned and sewn together with 15 or 20 more to form the cover for a tipi. Naduah took a moment to wipe the sweat from her face. She glanced at a nearby rack from which strips of buffalo meat hung. They were nearly dried and she would soon have to pound them to make pemmican. Like any Comanche, she was pleased that the recent buffalo hunt had been successful. But the work it involved! The lot of a Comanche woman was not an easy one, but Naduah accepted it as necessary and went about it without complaint.

An attentive observer would have noticed that Naduah had blue eyes and not the dark eyes of a Comanche. She was born Cynthia Ann Parker. In 1836, when she was nine years old, a raiding party of Comanche, Caddo and Kiowa warriors had attacked her family's stockade, Parker's Fort, in east-central Texas. As with most Comanche raids, it had been bloody and frightening. She had heard the screams of those tortured, her grandfather who was scalped and castrated and her grandmother who was violated. The Comanche raiders killed most of the men, but they took several women and children captive, a common practice. The Comanche and Kiowa headed back to their band's village with two boys, a girl and a woman. The children were adopted by band members and were treated no differently than Comanche children. Cynthia Ann was given the name Naduah and accepted her fate. She grew to love her new family. When American traders discovered the white children in the early 1840s, negotiations resulted in the return of the two boys to their white families. Naduah, however, refused to go. She wouldn't even speak English to the traders.

Now 18, Naduah had never regretted her decision. Raised as a Comanche, she knew the skills, stories and expectations of her people as well as any in her band. She could cook a tasty stew, repair damaged tools or set up a tipi. She knew where to find fruit, vegetables and plants with medicinal properties. She could ride a horse and bring down an antelope as well as most men. Her abilities were such that young Peta Nokona, skilled as a hunter and warrior and already respected by fellow band members, sought her as a wife. They had courted for some time. Peta Nokona had composed a love song and it whistled on his flute for Naduah's ears alone. Their hands had rested on each other's shoulders as they shuffled to the beating drums of the Love Dance. Save for the rare opportunity that Naduah was able to slip unseen from her family's tipi, the Love Dance was the only occasion when the pair was allowed to touch. Young women were well protected in Comanche society.

Eventually Peta Nokona visited Naduah's family with horses as a marriage gift. He tied his riding horse outside their tipi and hobbled another eight animals nearby. He slipped away and watched from a distance. If Naduah turned the horse loose, it would mean that she rejected his offer. If she drove the animal to the herd, then she was ready to take care of his horse and other property. Soon Naduah emerged from the lodge. She was dressed in a fine, fringed buckskin dress. She took the horse and led it back to the herd. They would marry! While the custom suggests that Naduah could choose whom she wanted as a partner, the reality was that Comanche women had little influence in the family's decision. Naduah's wishes would have been a minor consideration in her family's discussions. All that remained for the consummation of the marriage was the ceremony. It would wait until the buffalo killed during the recent hunt had been prepared.

When the work was done, Peta Nokona and Naduah settled on an appropriate night. She told her parents and her siblings. On this night they were all required to sleep in same tipi, even if they had moved out on their own. It was dark when they heard the first rustle outside the tipi. Then a hand slipped under the pegged hide! As those inside the tipi moved towards the intruder, the hand was pulled out. A peg was tugged from the ground. Peta Nokona stuck his head inside, laughed and was gone again. This went on for some time, until he was confident that those inside the tipi were sufficiently confused to allow an attempt to breech their defense. Peta Nokona plunged in through the entrance and dived for Naduah's bed. Success! The pair lay together under the buffalo robe and, by morning, they were considered married.

In 1845, while the band was camped at Cedar Lake in west-central Texas (about 50 miles east of New Mexico), the couple had their first of three children. He was named Quanah, meaning "fragrant." A second son and daughter soon followed.

Quanah was born into the Nokoni (Those Who Move Often) band, one of the largest of the 13 autonomous Comanche bands. Their tribal name is either a corruption of the Ute word *kohmaths* (one who wants to fight me) or the Spanish phrase *camino ancho* (main road). The Comanche called themselves *Nermurnuh* (true human being). In the 1600s, the Comanche had been part of the Shoshone and lived in present-day Wyoming. During that century, they acquired the horse, split from the Shoshone and began a migration that saw them settle on the southern Plains of present-day south-central United States (in parts of Texas, New Mexico, Oklahoma and Kansas) by the mid-1700s. It was not an easy transition. The territory included the traditional homelands of Pawnee, Navajo, Ute and Apache, and the Comanche had to take it by force. They were skilled warriors whose mastery of the horse made it possible. Not all Comanche, however, had the stomach for migration and battle. Some returned to Wyoming. Quanah later suggested that this was the reason other Natives often referred to his people as the Snake Indians because those who retreated resembled a snake moving backwards.

The Comanche called their new homeland Comanchería. The Nokoni tended to live in the eastern regions of Comanchería, but they were a nomadic people whose travels took them throughout the southern Plains. As with the other bands, the Nokoni consisted mostly of extended families. The bands operated independently; there was no tribal leadership among the Comanche. Even leadership within bands was shared. While there was usually a permanent leader, a council that comprised all adult males made decisions by consensus. Bands also had war chiefs, who were selected because of their skill as warriors, and peace chiefs, usually respected elders who offered advice and settled disputes as it was necessary. Peta Nokona was emerging as a war chief at the time of Quanah's birth.

Little is known of Quanah's boyhood, but it would likely not have differed significantly from that of any Comanche boy. A mother was important in the raising of infants, but as a boy's education became more specific in the responsibilities of a Comanche man and the ways of a warrior, his education became the task of his mother's father. Since Naduah's father was dead and not Comanche in any case, Pohebits Quasho, Peta Nokona's father, shouldered the duty of educating Quanah. Pohebits Quasho was a great Comanche war leader, who wore a Spanish coat of mail in battle because he believed that it protected him from bullets. At the knees of his grandfather, Quanah became well versed in the ways of a warrior.

Quanah was on a horse from infancy and, by the age of five, rode bareback alone. A year later Pohebits Quasho gave him his first bow and small quiver of blunt arrows and taught him to shoot. It was then Quanah's responsibility to practice until he mastered the weapon. Comanche boys had great freedom and much of it was used in hunting birds and small animals, ensuring that practicing skills was enjoyable. Quanah also listened intently to the stories told by Pohebits Quasho. He learned of his grandfather's own youth, of the secrets of the hunt and of the legends and history of the Comanche. The stories were not always happy ones, but they always carried a lesson.

Quanah and his grandfather rode their cayuses on an old trail that snaked along the shore of a nearby river. Quanah's eyes sought out tracks and he identified them on sight. He was good at it. But he was stumped when his eyes fell upon long, straight lines that cut across their path. They were too far apart to have been made by a travois. The lines were accompanied by what looked to Quanah like hoofprints, but they were deeper and cut more cleanly than those that were familiar to the boy. Pohebits Quasho noted his grandson's puzzlement, pulled his cayuse to a stop and spoke.

"It is important to know the tracks of the animals," said Pohebits Quasho, "but a Comanche warrior needs to know all markings. There are the tracks of your people, remembered in story. Where we have come from reveals much about where we are."

He fell silent for a moment.

"When I was your age, I listened to the stories that told of our warriors' bravery against the Apache, Navajo and Spanish. They took the fight to our enemies, raiding into Mexico, taking horses to increase our wealth and captives to make us stronger. No one dared to raid on the Comanchería, for they knew they would leave their dead there.

"The Comanchería is no longer as it was. The lines that stretch out before us were made by a *tejano* wagon. It rides on round wheels and is pulled by horses with iron shoes. In my youth, we saw few *tejanos* on the Comanchería. Their villages were far to the south and east. But with each passing winter, they come closer to our territory. Today they are as drops of rain in a storm. And like the thunder and lightning, they are not to be trusted."

Quanah shuddered as he thought of the booming spirits that set the sky on fire. They were to be feared.

"We tried to make peace with the newcomers," explained Pohebits Quasho. "Many winters ago Comanche chiefs visited the *tejano* village of San Antonio. They spoke of their desire to parley. The white war chief said that the Comanche must bring in those they held captive. It was so agreed.

"Twelve Comanche chiefs went to the *tejano* Council House to parley. With them were their wives and families and two captives. They wanted to know how much the *tejano* would pay for the captives before they brought them all in. Mookwarruh spoke for the Comanche. He asked what the *tejano* would give for peace. The room then filled with soldiers. The *tejano* attacked! In council, they attacked!"

Pohebits Quasho shook his head as he recalled the treachery. "The chiefs tried to escape, but all were killed. So were
others. Those who lived were put in jails.

"The *tejano* showed themselves to be without honor.
There has been no talk of peace since the Council House
Fight."

Pohebits Quasho looked to the horizon.

"The sun goes to its tipi. Let us return to ours," he
concluded.

As Quanah reached his teenage years, the playful times
of his youth became memories. Life became much more
serious as he prepared to go through the rituals to become
a man. The first step was to move out of the family tipi, so
that he would not be close to his sister Topsannah. Tradition
dictated that brothers and sisters be separated from one
another, so Quanah erected small tipi behind the family's.
He had little time to think about the sudden separation
from his family, however, because his first buffalo hunt
accompanied the move. The hunt was an important step
along the path to manhood. If he failed, he could not
become a warrior. Quanah was successful. His father
marked the occasion with a Give Away Dance. Band members, who had been informed of the ceremony days in
advance, gathered in a great circle at the appointed time.
Drummers occupied the center of the circle and beat out
a rhythm. Quanah was the first to dance, but others soon
joined him. When the dancing was complete, Quanah's relatives placed gifts at his feet. Anyone who wanted could
approach the youth and take one of the items. The sun ran
across the sky before the ground before Quanah was
empty. His family had given much, which increased their
prestige within the community.

All that remained for Quanah to become a man was to
undergo his vision quest. As with all youth, Quanah needed

no prompting to seek out his vision. He shared the dream of other Comanche boys: he wanted nothing more than to become a warrior of repute. Achieving his goal required a vision quest because success on the warpath depended on *puha* (power) provided by a strong guardian spirit, whose presence could be revealed during the ceremony. Quanah was about 15 when he visited the village *puhakut*, a medicine man blessed with special power from the spirit world. The *puhakut* explained what he must do. Quanah listened carefully. Days later he was still thinking about the words of the *puhakut*, anxious to be certain that he understood what was expected of him. As he reflected, he prepared the buffalo hide robe, bone pipe, tobacco and flint that he would need. He could take nothing else. Confident that he was ready, and hopeful that the Great Spirit would agree, he set out on his journey.

Where Quanah went is not known, although it was a solitary place where he could see both east and west. Traveling, dressed only in a breechcloth and moccasins, he stopped along the way at a spring to cleanse himself. Finally arriving at his chosen location, he waited for darkness to descend. He lit his pipe and smoked, praying silently for *puha* that he might use for the good of his people, watching the rising smoke lift his prayer to the Great Spirit. He lay down facing east so that he might greet the rising sun and covered himself in his blanket. Throughout the night he watched the stars and listened to the cries of the nocturnal animals. The next day he waited as the sun crossed the sky and watched as it slipped below the western plateau. For three days he waited. He was tired and hungry, but he did not grow discouraged. The *puhakut* had told him that the sun might make its journey four or five times before he was granted a vision, if he was granted a vision. He was granted a vision on the fourth day.

As Quanah shivered under his blanket, he caught sight of a great eagle that circled above him. It floated lazily, as if a cloud. Without warning, the eagle descended abruptly to the ground. It struck hard between two small rocks near Quanah. Quickly it rose again with a snake dangling from its talons. A feather broke loose and slipped through the air. As it fell, Quanah heard a voice.

"Your vision is complete."

The feather landed at his feet. Weak though he was, Quanah rose and retrieved the feather and two small stones. He put them into the rawhide pouch that was his medicine bag. When he returned to his village, he sought out the *puhakut* to explain his vision.

"You have strong power, very good medicine. The eagle is a skillful hunter with no equal in the skies. The rocks do not wear out and they promise long life. The snake has long been a symbol of the Comanche," explained the *puhakut*. As he said this he moved one hand in a backward, waving motion in the manner of a snake.

"The Great Spirit knows you as Serpent Eagle," he concluded.

Quanah would seek out and have other visions in his life, but none were as important as his first one. He was finally a man and allowed to accompany the warriors on their raids. It was a difficult time to become a warrior. Raiding and warfare in the late 1850s challenged even the best of the Comanche braves. As Pohebits Quasho explained to Quanah, the face of the Comanchería had changed dramatically within a generation. Until the 1820s, the present-day state of Texas was under Spanish rule. In 1821, following Mexico's successful battle for independence against Spain, Texas became part of Mexico. Over the next decade, many white homesteaders began to settle in the region. In 1835, the Texas Revolution began and, in a year, Texas was a republic. Nearly 10 years later the United States annexed Texas. Of all the changes, the one that had the most impact on the Comanche was the formation of the militia known as the Texas Rangers. Their mandate was to protect settlers from the Natives, bringing the Rangers into direct conflict with the Comanche, the most powerful of the Native tribes in the region.

The Comanche learned something of the Texas Rangers' determination during the Council House Fight in 1840. At the urging of the Texas government, Chief Mookwarruh led members of his Comanche band to San Antonio. Both government and Comanche motives for the council remain uncertain. Perhaps they sought peace or maybe the government simply wanted the Comanche captives returned. Either way, Mookwarruh arrived, believing that there would be negotiations. The Rangers were at the Council House to lend support to the government. When the Texans saw the horribly mutilated condition of a female captive brought by the Comanche, they decided that there would be no negotiations. They wanted the rest of the captives freed, and the Rangers were directed by government officials to hold the Native delegation hostage until their demand was met. The Comanche chose to fight the Rangers because their warrior code demanded death before capture. News of the attack sent Comanche across Texas on the warpath. Their raids caused much damage, but the Texas Rangers won a major victory at the Battle of Plum Creek in August 1840. Eighty Comanche were killed, and as a result, the warriors scaled back the size of their raids.

When Texas became a state, the United States Army joined the Texas Rangers in its efforts to subdue the Comanche. Seven forts were built in a line, spanning the breadth of Texas, between the Red River and the Rio Grande. The soldiers stationed at the forts were mostly

infantry and largely ineffective in pursuing the mobile
Comanche. Nevertheless, the presence of the army had the
desired effect. In 1855, the Penateka band of Comanche
made treaty with the United States. The Penateka had been
ravaged by a cholera epidemic in the early 1850s that killed
half of its members. In its weakened state the band had no
desire to continue fighting. The Penateka people were
placed on a reservation in western Texas, and they permitted the government to build a fort at Clear Fork on the
Brazos River, just west of the border of the Comanchería.
The Penateka had not consulted other bands before making treaty, which was customary since the Comanche didn't
operate in a unified manner. Still, other bands were
incensed when they learned of the Penateka's action. To
demonstrate to the *tejanos* that all Comanche did not share
the Penateka's view, warriors from other bands intensified
their raids on settlers. Texans, however, were not shrinking
violets so they determinedly set about driving the
Comanche out of their state and killing those who would
not go.

In May 1858, Native scouts (who had signed the 1855
treaty) led Texas Rangers in search of the Nokoni. Riding
north into Indian Territory, the Rangers chased Peta
Nokona's Comanche raiders along the Canadian River.
The Comanche were unaware that they were being pursued, and the Rangers, after dispensing with a small look-
out camp, caught those in the main village by surprise. The
Nokoni thought they were well protected by a canyon in
the Antelope Hills, but the attack came suddenly and their
defenses deteriorated quickly. It didn't help that most of the
warriors were absent. Pohebits Quasho took the lead in
protecting the women, the children and the elderly.
Quanah watched as his grandfather was struck down by
a shot from an enemy warrior's rifle. His bulletproof coat of

mail had failed to protect him. The few warriors were dis-
heartened when their great war leader fell and perhaps
they did not fight with their usual intensity. Many
Comanche died. A rout seemed inevitable but was
avoided when Peta Nokona arrived later in the afternoon
with some 500 warriors. The fighting continued until the
Comanche retreated through a side canyon. The Battle of
Antelope Hills was costly; 75 Comanche died and the
band lost most of its supplies and food.

Throughout the summer Peta Nokona led the Nokoni
on raids in Texas and into New Mexico. They attacked and
burned wagon trains, farms and ranches. So fierce was the
intensity of their raiding that the United States government lifted the ban that prevented troops from riding into
Indian Territory (present-day Oklahoma) in an effort to
stop the Comanche offensive. It proved to be a sound
decision. In the fall, Peta Nokona's band clashed again
with the soldiers. Few Comanche were killed, but they
were forced to flee, leaving behind their depleted supplies.
With winter coming on, the loss of their supplies was
a major blow. Peta Nokona decided to go southwest onto
the Llano Estacado, the great plateau that straddled the
border of New Mexico and Texas. There he made camp in
the Palo Duro Canyon. It was hidden and difficult to
access, and the Nokoni were able to endure the winter
without encountering cavalry or the Texas Rangers.

In the summer of 1859, word arrived at the Nokoni camp
of a government directive that forced the Penateka to relocate
to Indian Territory because settlers wanted their reservation
land. The Penateka were not even given sufficient time to
round up their livestock or to harvest their crops. Angry, Peta
Nokona and his warriors again began raiding, and for months
they lay siege to central Texas. By the fall, warriors had to
abandon their raiding to hunt buffalo for their winter needs.

Cynthia Ann Parker (Naduah), taken at age 33 probably while in Texas where she was forcibly reunited with white relatives.

Quanah joined his father on the hunt. When they returned to their new village on the Pease River, they found it burned. The few warriors left to defend it lay dead, along with some women and children. Many others were captured and taken to Fort Radziminski.

Among the prisoners were Naduah and her daughter, Topsannah. Naduah was recognized as a white woman,

and when questioned, she revealed that she was Cynthia
Ann Parker. Against her wishes, she was returned to her
white relatives in Texas. Despite her continued pleas,
her family would not allow her to return to Peta Nokona,
her husband. Topsannah died within a year. Two years
later, depressed and likely ill, Naduah also died. Quanah
never saw his mother again after she was captured, and he
did not know until years later of her struggle to return to
the Comanche.

The death of his grandfather and the capture of his
mother were not the end of Quanah's personal tragedies. In
the spring of 1861, Peta Nokona led a raid against Apache
warriors who were raiding in the Comanchería. He was
injured in the encounter and died soon after returning to
his Comanche village. The death of a warrior caused considerable mourning, but the death of a great war chief
launched an even more intense response. Female relatives
tore their clothing and cut themselves. The village echoed
with their wails and moans. Men cut their hair and, some,
their flesh. Mourning continued for almost two weeks.
During this time, Quanah prayed, smoked and offered the
first piece of every meal to the spirits for the benefit of his
father. As tradition dictated, he also burned or gave away all
of his father's possessions and killed his horses. The ceremony complete, the village moved to escape the place of
death. Peta Nokona's name was never again mentioned.

Only Quanah and his younger brother Pecos remained
of his family. Pecos, still a boy, was sent to live with and be
reared by the Yamparikas, a Comanche band. He died soon
after. But Quanah was a man, and there was no one to take
care of him. Eventually, he chose to make a name for himself away from his family's band of Nokoni. He joined with
the Kotsoteka (the Buffalo Eaters), who lived in the territory around the Wichita Mountains in southern Indian

Territory. He was determined to make his reputation with them, but he had far to go. He owned nothing and could claim only a little raiding experience. While he was a warrior for the Nokoni, he had participated in a mere handful of raids. He had much to prove to his new band, and to himself.

Quanah gave the Kotsoteka little cause for concern. At first, they asked questions about Quanah's ability, questions that were rightfully raised about any young, unknown warrior. The Kotsoteka wanted them answered before they would let him join them on raids. Within months they were satisfied, and Quanah was invited to do more than menial camp chores. On one memorable occasion he saved the band chief from certain death. A Mexican soldier was training his rifle on the chief when Quanah, who had identified the soldier's target, broke for the enemy and drove his spear into him. Such quick, courageous action elevated Quanah's prestige within the band.

But it was not with the Kotsoteka that Quanah was to gain his reputation. In the fall of 1862, Yellow Bear's band of Quahadi (Antelope) arrived from the Llano Estacado to visit their Kotsoteka relatives. Yellow Bear learned of young Quanah's skill and bravery and invited him to join his Quahadi. Quanah had spent some of his childhood in the Llano Estacado and the thought of returning to the region that he likely considered his home territory was appealing. He accepted Yellow Bear's offer. The Quahadi were not disappointed. It was a good time to raid because many of the soldiers had been sent east to fight in the Civil War. Within a few years Quanah was leading hunts and raids. By 1866, he was also running for his life.

Quanah had fallen in love with Weckeah, Yellow Bear's daughter. While the Quahadi chief was not opposed to their marriage, there was the matter of gift giving. Custom required Quanah to give horses to Yellow Bear for the right to marry his daughter. As yet, Quanah had no herd from which to draw such animals. Yellow Bear declared that Weckeah would marry Tennap, the son of an important and wealthy war chief. On hearing of Yellow Bear's decision, Quanah and Weckeah eloped. Elopements were unusual among the Comanche, but when they did occur, it was almost always a result of the suitor's inability to pay the bride's family. In such cases, the band members ostracized the couple until relatives of the man could come up with the required number of horses. Eloping with the daughter of the band's chief, however, was a different matter. With no hope of acquiring the horses in the near future, Quanah and Weckeah fled.

It is likely that the escape had been long planned because some 20 young warriors joined them. The warriors were impressed by Quanah's leadership and abilities, and it seems that they were determined from the start to form their own band, hunting and raiding as they saw fit. Aware that Yellow Bear would be in pursuit, the group traveled at night and hid during the day. They didn't stop until they neared the Mexican border.

In the months that followed, Quanah's band swelled to over 200. Warriors were attracted to Quanah's new band by the success they enjoyed on their raids into western Texas. White settlers came to fear the quick and determined strikes of his Comanche braves. By winter's end, they had amassed a herd of more than 300 horses and acquired a solid reputation as skilled warriors.

Yellow Bear and Tennap searched for them during these months, and it may have been the renegade group's prosperity and fame that resulted in their discovery in the spring of 1867. Yellow Bear and Tennap were intent on striking a blow for their honor; they were determined to

fight Quanah. The bands were preparing to do battle, when
a Quahadi elder counseled them to reconsider. He suggested that the Comanche could ill afford to lose warriors
with the white men pressing into the Comanchería.
Perhaps tempers would be soothed if Quanah gave both
men a gift of horses? It was so agreed, and once the grievances were appeased, Quanah and his band reunited with
the Quahadi.

The reunion did not bode well for the settlers of western Texas because, with their greater numbers, the
Quahadi intensified their raiding. Army detachments and
government workers also became targets. The Quahadi
became known as the much-feared Red Riders. The
United States government was anxious to put an end to
the violence. While many wanted the cavalry to be dispatched in force to deal with the Comanche, the government saw the proposition as too costly and perhaps
without a conclusive outcome, especially given the country's financial state following the Civil War. In the summer
of 1867, the United States Congress appointed an Indian
Peace Commission, whose task it was to ensure a lasting
peace with the Natives of the southern Plains. The assignment was challenging. Previous agreements with some of
the tribes had seen neither Natives nor government officials live up to their promises. Trust was at low ebb.

Nevertheless, the participants met at Medicine Lodge
Creek in south-central Kansas in October 1867. It was the
largest gathering yet of southern Plains peoples to bargain
with the government. Five tribes, including some
Comanche bands (but not officially, the Quahadi), were
present. Quanah attended because he wanted to hear for
himself the intentions and proposals of the white men. The
government commissioners arrived accompanied by a large
escort of cavalry in full dress uniform. The Natives, not to

be outdone in matters of appearance, presented themselves in full war dress, with faces painted and bonnets secured. Following an introductory ceremony of giving gifts and smoking pipes, the negotiations, such as they were, began.

The well-respected Yamparikas chief Ten Bears, an elder whose life had been characterized by peacemaking rather than fighting, opened the council on behalf of the Comanche.

"My heart is filled with joy, when I see you here, as the brooks fill with water, when the snow melts in the spring, and I feel glad, as the ponies do when the fresh grass starts in the spring of the year....My people have never first drawn a bow or fired a gun against the whites. There has been trouble on the line between us, and my young men have danced the war dance," he conceded. "But it was not begun by us. It was you who sent out the first soldier, and it was we who sent out the second....

"The Comanche are not weak and blind, like the pups of a dog when seven sleeps old! They are strong and far-sighted, like grown horses....I was born upon the prairie, where the wind blew free, and there was nothing to break the light of the sun. I was born where there were no enclo-sures, and where everything drew a free breath. I want to die there, and not within walls!" he declared with a meas-ure of defiance in his voice. "I know every stream and every wood between the Rio Grande and the Arkansas River. I have hunted and lived over the country. I lived like my fathers before me and, like them, I lived happily...."

With the past adequately addressed, he turned to present considerations.

"The white man has the country which we loved and we only wish to wander on the prairie until we die. Any good thing you say to me shall not be forgotten! I shall carry it as near to my heart as my children and it shall be as

often on my tongue as the name of the Great Spirit. I want
no blood upon the land to stain the grass! I want it all clear
and pure, and I wish it so, that all who go through among
my people may find peace when they come in, and leave it
when they go out," concluded Ten Bears.

Words and sentiment were fine, but the government had
a concrete offer and the commissioners outlined it. The
Natives would be placed on a reservation in Indian Territory,
far from the settlements of white men. They would be given
food, seed and clothing amounting to a total of $25,000
a year for 30 years. Instruction in farming and carpentry
would be provided, as would teachers and a doctor. All that
was required of them was to stop fighting and allow the
white settlers to move onto their traditional Native lands.
The commissioners concluded by noting that the Natives
had behaved badly, but that the Great Father was willing to
forget their bloody misdeeds.

The Natives wanted peace, but they did not want to
farm. They did not want to be cared for by the government.
They did not want to give up any of the Comanchería. But,
what the Natives wanted mattered little to the commissioners. If they weren't willing to make treaty, the government
would send in the cavalry to force them into submission.

General William Tecumseh Sherman was present at the
council as the army's representative and he emphasized
this point. "Your desires are no longer relevant. You have
to give up your old ways and follow the ways of the
white men. Roads and rail will be laid in your old hunting territories. There will be no more buffalo and you
will have to live like the white settlers, either farming or
ranching. In the past, the Great Father had agreed to let
you keep your lands," he conceded, "but those former
agreements had not made allowances for the rapid
growth of the white race. You can no more stop this than

you can stop the sun or moon; you must submit and do the best you can!"

In the end, some Natives did just that. Ten chiefs touched the pen. Even though only a few of the Comanche chiefs agreed, the United States government considered the Treaty of Medicine Lodge Creek binding on all Comanche. The Comanche, however, did not see it the same way. Unlike the United States government, which allowed for a group to negotiate on its behalf, no such arrangement existed among the Comanche. A chief could not sign away Comanche rights, especially for bands over which he had no authority. As a result, most Comanche did not recognize the treaty.

Quanah was upset at what he heard and left the council, determined never to surrender. "My band is not going to live on a reservation!" he declared to other Comanche. "Tell the white chiefs that the Quahadi are warriors!"

Perhaps a chance meeting with Phillip McCusker influenced Quanah's attitude. McCusker was a white man who lived with the Comanche and who knew of Quanah's mother. He related the story of Naduah's unhappy few years with her white relatives and of her tragic death. From McCusker, Quanah learned of his mother's surname, and from that point onwards, the Quahadi warrior called himself Quanah Parker.

The Medicine Lodge Treaty created the Comanche-Kiowa reservation of just under three million acres in southern Indian Territory. The reservation was significantly smaller than the region the Comanche considered their ancestral land, which stretched from the Arkansas River to the Rio Grande. And, while it was good land and part of the Comanchería, it did not include the best hunting territory on the Texas plains. To ease Native fears, government officials promised that settlers would not be permitted to hunt buffalo south of the Arkansas River. Some Comanche

bands did settle on the Comanche-Kiowa reservation, but
even the little enthusiasm that existed for such a move dissipated quickly.

The government didn't ratify the treaty until the following August, and it wasn't until December that the first
annuities arrived. The inappropriate supplies—clothing,
food and assorted sundries—did nothing to improve the
situation. The clothing was unsuitable, the meat was
unknown salt pork, the cornmeal was fed to the horses and
the soap was discarded once tasted. Money that was to be
set aside for capital improvements was spent on more palat-
able beef rations. The government assumed that crops
grown by the Comanche would supplement these food-
stuffs, but the Comanche would not farm. Perhaps the
greatest indignity was that the reservation Natives found
themselves raided by non-reservation warriors for the few
meager supplies they were given. By the summer of 1869,
two-thirds of the reservation Natives had left the reservation and returned to the plains. And it was not uncommon
for those who remained to use the reserve as a base from
which to send out raiding parties.

The Quahadi were one of the few bands that lost no
members to the reservation. Indian agents (local government officials) looked on the resisting band with suspicion
and blamed them for the misdeeds of their own reservation
Natives. Such finger pointing was an effective way to avoid
any responsibility for the actions of their charges. While the
Indian agents overstated their case, their stories had some
truth to them. The Quahadi's successful raids throughout
central and western Texas seduced reservation Natives.
Quanah Parker often directed their efforts since he had
continued his ascent to the position of band war chief. An
encounter with soldiers near Gainesville, Texas enhanced
his reputation considerably. Quanah assumed control of the

warriors when the raid leader was killed, and all later agreed that he exercised good judgment in leading the warriors out of the near disaster.

However, misfortune awaited the Quahadi on the Sanchez Creek in the spring of 1869. Settlers were surprised to see a Comanche dressed in a blue Yankee jacket with shiny brass buttons slip into their herd and make off with some horses. It was Quanah Parker and with him rode 16 Quahadi. Although they knew the Comanche were fearsome warriors, Texans were not averse to taking matters into their own hands. Seven of the settlers gave chase, catching up with the raiders and forcing the warriors to abandon the stolen horses. Watching the Natives scamper behind shelter, the Texans assumed they were victorious. What they didn't count on was that the Comanche were seasoned fighters who would not surrender. When one of the settlers was shot and killed, the others retreated. Perhaps they might have persisted had they known that nine of Quanah's men were either killed or wounded.

The Quahadi didn't usually suffer such losses. More commonly the warriors returned to their village with their booty of supplies and horses and everyone accounted for. They were so successful that the size and number of their raids increased throughout 1869 and the opening years of the 1870s. The number of dead settlers mounted and their herds of cattle and horses diminished, and the situation became urgent. The cavalry was called on to address the matter of the defiant Quahadi. Aware that the soldiers were looking for them, the Comanche took the offensive and attacked detachments where they found them. There were major skirmishes that pitted the Quahadi against the Fourth and Ninth cavalries and the Twenty-fourth Infantry. But it wasn't until the late spring of 1871, when Comanche warriors (not the Quahadi) captured Henry Warren's wagon train on the Southern Overland Trail in north-central Texas, torturing and murdering its teamsters, that the army put a determined shoulder into its effort to rein in the Comanche.

One of the wagon party escaped and staggered into nearby Fort Richardson. William Tecumseh Sherman, General-in-Chief of the United States Army, was at the fort on an inspection tour, and he ordered the capture of the attackers. The Comanche were tracked to the Fort Sill reservation. The Indian agent admitted knowing that reservation Natives were responsible for the raid. Frustrated, he also argued that there would be no peace on the reservation as long as the Quahadi were allowed to pursue a traditional Comanche way of life. Young warriors found it appealing and too readily rode in imitation of the Quahadi. Sherman agreed with the assessment and he authorized the resources necessary to bring the Quahadi to their knees.

Colonel Ranald Mackenzie had command of the operation. Even though he was just 30 years old, Mackenzie had a great deal of commended service during the Civil War. He spent the summer of 1871 training his men, and in August, the Fourth Cavalry left Fort Richardson heading west for the Llano Estacado. Six weeks later, they were on the way back to Fort Richardson. All they had found of Quanah Parker and the Quahadi were their cold fire pits. Frustrated, but a little smarter, Mackenzie set out again in mid-September, this time with 20 Tonkawa scouts and nearly 600 soldiers. But even the Native scouts had little knowledge of the interior of the Llano Estacado. The great plateau covers 50,000 square miles and is mostly inhospitable territory. Any who ventured up the steep eastern escarpment encountered large, sweeping dune fields; deeply cut, usually dry riverbeds; wind-eroded basins filled mostly with water too salty to drink; and thousands of playas (small depressions). Ignorance of the terrain was not the army's only weakness. No one had any idea how to fight the Quahadi.

Quanah Parker had the advantage of knowing the soldiers' every move. He employed creative tactics that demoralized Mackenzie's men and kept them off-stride for the duration of the Blanco Canyon campaign. He held his braves back until the cavalry camped near Blanco Canyon, just west of where the Clear Fork joins with the Brazos River. The moon was high in the sky on the early morning of October 10, 1871 when Quanah signaled the attack. Ringing cowbells, war whoops and gunfire roused the startled soldiers. Before they could defend themselves, the Quahadi were gone, taking with them some 60 horses. Shrewdly, Quanah did not allow his men to engage in any lengthy pitched battles. Instead, he employed lightning strikes followed by equally abrupt retreats, before the soldiers could respond adequately. If Mackenzie harbored any doubts about the ability of the young Comanche war chief, they disappeared rapidly.

The day after the Quahadi stole the army's horses, Mackenzie dispatched an advance party of 21 men under the command of Captain R.G. Carter to track them. As the soldiers neared Blanco Canyon, they spotted a small party of Quahadi in the distance. Seeing that his men outnumbered them, Carter probably smiled with satisfaction as he pursued the Quahadi around a bend. But when the soldiers rounded it, they discovered the main body of the Quahadi warriors. Leading them was a young warrior on a coal-black mustang. The beaded fringes of his buckskin pants danced as he as drove his horse towards the soldiers. He was naked from the waist up, but down his back hung a long, flowing bonnet of eagle feathers that glittered as they caught the sun's rays. His facial features were all but hidden beneath the layer of mostly black paint. Rings pierced his nose and hoops dangled from his ears. It was Quanah Parker, and he rode without fear. As he approached the soldiers, he slipped to the side of his horse, thus removing himself as a target for the soldiers—an old Comanche trick mastered in boyhood. His own six-shooter smoked, one shot taking an officer's life. Carter called to his men over the noise of shouting Quahadi and cracks of gunfire, ordering them to hold fast. Then, as quickly as it had begun, the Quahadi vanished into the canyon and the clash ended.

Mackenzie's men eventually caught up with Quanah Parker's Quahadi, presenting the Natives with a real challenge. Quanah had to devise a strategy that would not only engage the soldiers, but also protect the women and children who accompanied the warriors. Instead of meeting the cavalry head on, he divided the braves into smaller groups and had them attack the soldiers from various positions. It was an unorthodox strategy that Mackenzie did not anticipate. His surprised men had their hands full fighting a multi-fronted battle. Meanwhile, the rest of the Quahadi escaped from the Blanco Canyon and fled across the Llano Estacado. The warriors followed them soon after. Yet again, Mackenzie was left empty-handed.

But the Quahadi were suffering. Despite their successes against the cavalry, weeks on the run were taking their toll. The women and children were tired and hungry. The horses were exhausted and the band was forced to abandon equipment that the animals could no longer pull. To make matters worse, the weather turned. Cold rain and sleet fell from dark skies. A less imaginative leader might have dwelt on the apparent inevitability of the situation. It was impossible for the Quahadi to outrun the soldiers. Perhaps it was best to give up and avoid the suffering and death that waited. Quanah Parker was shrewd enough to realize, however, that if his people were hurting, the soldiers, who had no experience on the Llano Estacado, were desperate as well. His scouts told him that the blue coats rode without enthusiasm; they rarely took time to cook their meals; their horses lumbered along without energy; and they each had no more than a single blanket to keep warm at night. Surely they must be discouraged.

Quanah Parker leaped at what he saw as an opportunity. He and his warriors doubled back on Mackenzie's men. Waiting until the early morning hours when sleep was deepest, they attacked. The camp was thrown into chaos as horses were cut free and stampeded in fear. Still groggy, the soldiers were slow to react to the shouting and gunfire. Once up and ready, they found it difficult to respond on the cloudy, moonless night. When they finally got their bearings, it was too late. The Quahadi, as usual, were gone. The next day, a demoralized Mackenzie, who had taken an arrow in the side, ordered his men to head across the Llano Estacado for Fort Sumner. The men didn't want to make the arduous journey and the horses were too exhausted, so they straggled back to Blanco Canyon to wait for supplies. The campaign was over, and the Quahadi still called the Staked Plains home.

Throughout late 1872 and for most of 1873, the cavalry directed no major offensive specifically at the Quahadi. But Mackenzie was determined to complete his assignment. After all, he didn't become known as the best Indian fighter in the southwest for his failures. Operating out of the forts along the Southern Overland Trail in west-central Texas, he kept his soldiers busy patrolling to the west, and occasionally, he led larger detachments into the Comanchería. When the soldiers found Comanche, they attacked. In one major encounter in September 1872, Mackenzie found a village of

some 200 Kotsoteka Comanche. The soldiers killed 50
Natives and captured another 130. But the massacre of the
Kotsoteka on McClellan Creek was unusual because few
major encounters occurred during these months. Perhaps it
suited Mackenzie, who wasn't really interested in racking up
a tally of Comanche deaths. He simply wanted to drive
home the point that they had no alternative to peace and no
choice about the terms dictated.

By the early 1870s, government and army officials agreed
that the most effective way to achieve their surrender was to
cut off the Comanche's access to buffalo. Roaming cavalry
patrols effectively disrupted Comanche hunting, although
the activity was hardly time-consuming. The great herds of
buffalo that had roamed the plains a decade earlier were no
more. Despite the United States government's pledge in the
Medicine Lodge Treaty that forbade the hunting of buffalo
south of the Arkansas River, white hunters increasingly pursued the animal for easy money. In 1872, a hide was worth
$3.75 in the East, where buffalo leather was particularly val-
ued. The average hunter could kill over 30 a day and an
expert 200. There's no record of the total number of animals
killed but Dodge City, Kansas alone shipped 1.5 million
hides between 1872 and 1874.

The Comanche were all too aware of the decimation of
the herds and harbored their deepest hatred for the buffalo
hunters who they blamed for destroying their way of life.
Then came word that, indeed, they need not lose their way of
life, that the old ways might continue indefinitely. In 1874,
Ishatai, a Comanche *puhakut,* informed Quanah Parker that
he had envisioned an alliance among the southern Plains
tribes so powerful that it could defeat the *tejanos* and bring
back the buffalo. Ishatai proposed that the tribes gather for
a Sun Dance. Although the Sun Dance was not a Comanche
ritual, that didn't bother Quanah because he wasn't interested

in its spiritual or mystical properties. He recognized the military potential of the ceremony and threw his support behind it.

In the early summer of 1874, bands of Kiowa, Cheyenne, Arapaho and Comanche performed the Sun Dance. Later, their war chiefs decided to unite and strike as a single arrow against the newcomers. Quanah Parker was chosen to be the arrow's sharp point. The first target was chosen easily. They attacked the buffalo hunters at Adobe Walls. The operation was a disaster. The buffalo hunters repelled the Natives and their fragile alliance splintered. Quanah took the Quahadi back to the Llano Estacado where he found Mackenzie's men scouting the plains and scouring the canyons. The soldiers made it difficult to hunt what little game there was, and within weeks, they made it impossible. In one devastating blow, the soldiers captured most of the Quahadi's horses, and the band lost most of its meager supplies.

Quanah Parker had a decision to make. The Llano Estacado were as familiar to him as the feel of his horse. The plains ran deep and he could hide there for a long time. Perhaps if his companions were only warriors, they could continue to flee. But he had women and children to think about. His greatest obligation was to provide for the members of his band and he was no longer certain of his ability to do so. Word arrived from Mackenzie promising the Quahadi safety if they surrendered, extermination if they would not. On June 2, 1875, Quanah surrendered. Surrounded by his band headmen, he walked into Fort Sill, with his open hands empty. The women and children would follow later. Mackenzie greeted him, all too aware that what appeared as an easy victory on the surface was in reality the culmination of hard years of action. Perhaps he might have agreed with the Quahadi war chief's assessment of the situation, spoken sometime after the event.

"I came into Fort Sill, no ride me in like horse or lead me by halter like cow....I fought....[Mackenzie] brave man, good soldier, but uses 2000 men; many wagons, horses and mules. Me, I had only 450 braves, no supply train, ammunition and guns like him....Mackenzie no catch me."

Quanah Parker was the final Comanche chief to come onto the reservation and the last to accept the terms of the Medicine Lodge Treaty. Never again did he lead his people against the *tejanos*. As he settled into life at the Comanche-Kiowa reservation, he made a determined effort to adapt to *tejano* ways. While he enjoyed great success, the *tejano* road was not always an easy one to travel, and Quanah did not follow it slavishly. In all decisions, he exercised careful consideration about its impact on Comanche well-being. In doing so, he helped both himself and his people, and he demonstrated the leadership qualities demanded of a chief.

Life was difficult for the Quahadi when they first settled on the Fort Sill reservation. The immediate problem was one every reservation Native in the land knew—rations. The government simply did not provide enough food because officials anticipated that Natives would augment government supplies with game. Therefore, the Comanche were allowed to hunt, occasionally even off-reservation, but they could find few animals and no buffalo. Understandably, Natives greeted ration days with excitement. Occasionally the beef was issued on the hoof, bringing at least some joy to their desperate situation. Braves would choose their animal while it was in the corral. Then they would line up, wait until their cow was set free, ride after it and take it down as if it were a buffalo. Women ran to the kill site to butcher it as in days gone by. Exciting though it might have been, it was also a sad reminder of a past never to return.

To remedy the situation, Quanah Parker sought a source of income to supplement government rations. He turned

Quanah Parker, taken at age 60 with three of his five wives and two of his 25 children. Dressed in his citizens suit, Quanah's appearance often surprised tejanos (white men). They expected to see him dressed as a Quahadi war chief who had terrorized the settlers of western Texas and surrounding area. But Quanah was much more than a war chief. While he desired to fight until victory or death, Quanah came to realize that continued resistance would result in the decimation of his band. Because nothing was more important than the well-being of his people, Quanah ignored his personal inclinations and surrendered at Fort Sill. He remained a leader on the reservation where his actions demonstrated an ongoing commitment to improve the lives of his people. While he refused to reject traditional Comanche ways, he also adapted to tejano ways, both in appearance and practice. Quanah was always a role model for the Comanche, a responsibility he never took lightly.

to the *tejano* cattlemen. Texas ranchers had to drive their
steers north to Kansas, and once there transport them to
marketplaces. It was imperative that cattle drives be kept
short because the steers lost weight—and the ranchers lost
money—with every mile traveled. The shortest route to
Kansas cut through the Comanche-Kiowa reservation and
the ranchers had been using the route freely, and illegally,
for some time. Quanah negotiated a deal whereby the
ranchers paid $1 a head for the right of way. The money
went towards building up the Comanche's own herds.
Within a few years, he had arranged leases with the cattle
barons for the use of reservation land as pasture. The money
thus acquired was divided up among the Comanche.
Quanah had struck profitable deals. Every man, woman and
child received as much as $50 a year in lease payments.

However, it took time to reach these agreements and for
the Comanche to realize the benefits. To fill their bellies in
the meantime, Natives slipped off the reservation to raid
nearby farms and ranches. Sometimes violence occurred
when they returned, and the Indian agent ordered their
arrest. Quanah Parker shared the Indian agent's belief that
theft was no longer appropriate and violence was unac-
ceptable. Like it or not, his people would have to abide by
tejano rules if they were to live and prosper in the *tejano*
world. The Comanche chief worked tirelessly to control
the Quahadi. But he would not do it by blindly accepting
the Indian agent's dictates, unless he believed that they
made sense for his people. Usually his decision was shaped
by what was appropriate within Comanche tradition.

When the Indian agent proposed the creation of
a Comanche police to ease the problems associated with
white men arresting Natives, Quanah Parker opposed the
idea and advised his people not to join the force. He
thought it would be wrong for a younger Native to arrest

an older one. But he relented when the Indian agent threatened to eliminate off-reservation hunting. Once the force was operating, Quanah quickly saw its value. There was less anger among his people when Comanche arrested alleged lawbreakers. Realizing he'd made a mistake, he came to support the Indian Agency police and even served as a member. Flexibility and pragmatism were to define Quanah's outlook in this new world.

He also took an unofficial role in enforcing the law on the reservation. In 1878, he sent warriors into the nearby mountains to arrest a Comanche who had tried to kill a reservation guard. Two warriors were killed during the arrest, and Quanah feared the killings might spark revenge raids, so common in the pre-reservation days. Quanah interceded and the matter was closed without incident. The Indian agent took note of Quanah's ability to maintain peace on the reservation, and when a judicial Court of Indian Offenses was established in 1888, the agent recommended that Quanah be made a judge. Quanah's sound reasoning on the bench impressed many, including *tejanos*. His decisions were informed by tradition, as is evident in one case remembered by Eagle Tail Feather who, at the time, was the chief of the Indian Police.

"One Comanche beat another to a claim for a half-section of land. The one who had lost out was making a big complaint about it, and the man who received the land said that if he lost the land because of this fellow's objection, he would kill him.

"Quanah Parker decided the case on old lines. He called in two well-known warriors to decide on the war records of the two men. One of these warriors was late coming in so he sent me out in his place to get the record of the man who felt he was being beat out of his claim. I was chief of the Indian Police. The man who had the claim asked if he could go along too.

"When we found the warrior, this man who had the land said, 'Who is the better man, I or this other fellow?' He thought the warrior would give him the credit.

"'All right,' the warrior answered him, 'you asked me. I'll speak right out. This other fellow is the better man. I was in a battle where I saw him get off a horse and help a dismounted comrade out of the midst of the enemy. He is a brave man and he did a great deed. You had better look out or he will whip you or kill you!'

"I took this report back to Quanah. It was then up to this fellow to come out with a true account of a braver deed or else give up the land and abide by this decision. He could not do this, so Quanah and the two warriors decided for the complainer. That man had to give up the land and keep quiet."

While the judicial appointment was an important position, Quanah Parker began to serve his people in other official capacities as well. As chief, he considered it his duty to lead where possible. In 1901, Quanah was elected a school trustee and was subsequently chosen to be president of the Parker School District. He was a strong advocate of education, believing it to hold the secret of success in the *tejano* world. He sent his own children to the Carlisle Indian School in Pennsylvania, and eventually he had several schools built on the reservation so that the Comanche parents would no longer have to send their children away for an education (although many refused even local schooling). In 1902, Quanah was elected deputy sheriff of Lawton, Oklahoma. He accepted the position because he believed that he could help keep Comanche youth out of trouble, and he was successful in this. He was even appointed assistant farmer for the reservation, thereby demonstrating to his people the importance of accepting the *tejano* way of making a living.

In the early 1900s, Quanah Parker was also appointed to the Comanche, Kiowa and Kiowa-Apache Business Council. It was the governing body of the reservation, and the Indian agent made such appointments. As a chief, Quanah might have expected to be appointed, but the agent had confidence in him because of Quanah's business savvy.

And he *was* a shrewd businessman. By this time, he was said to be the richest Native in the United States. Much of his money came from his relationship with the cattle barons. They were pleased to be working with a man who was open to dealing. Burk Burnett, one of the wealthiest ranchers, advised Quanah on personal investments and built him a large house in Cache, Oklahoma. So impressive was its two stories, with 12 rooms and 22 stars on the roof (reflecting the star insignias of cavalry generals), that locals came to call it the Comanche White House. Quanah had enough money to invest $40,000 in the Quanah, Acme and Pacific Railroad. He was present in 1910, when it made its inaugural run from the town of Quanah, Texas. Because of his reputation, both the railroad and the town were named after him.

Onlookers watched him slide his fingers along the train and heard him whisper, "My engine, my railroad." To those gathered, he spoke more loudly. "May the Great Spirit always smile on your new town."

Quanah Parker often traveled in these years. In 1889, a newspaper in San Antonio reported on Quanah Parker's arrival in that city. His notoriety as a Comanche war chief and his reputation as a leader among reservation Natives ensured that he was a newsworthy subject wherever he went. The reporter's description is interesting because it illustrates Quanah's successful adaptation into the *tejano* world. It also hints that he did not sacrifice everything to do so.

"Quanah Parker is chief and speaks fair English....He bears papers from Agent C.M. Hunt that he has permission to

Quanah Parker with braided hair and citizens suit, symbols of
the two traditions he embraced.

leave the reservation and travel to Old Mexico....Mr. Parker
is the prominent half-breed Comanche Chief. He is also
a successful rancher and farmer near Cache, Oklahoma.

"The chief wears a citizens suit of black broad-cloth,
neatly fitting his straight body. His shoes are the regular dude
style, with toothpick toes. A gold watch, with chain and
charm dangles from his close fitting vest. He wears a beautiful
black beaver hat that is pulled down in front. The only pecu-
liar item of his appearance is his long black hair, which he
wears in two plaits down his back."

Quanah's double braid was the most visible of his decisions to maintain links with Comanche tradition. That he also kept five wives vexed local government officials. They expected him to take a lead in the assimilation of his people and he did so in many things. But he needed to see value in any proposed change, and he could see no reason for a man to have just one wife if he could support more. On one occasion, the Indian agent's wife interested Quanah in Christianity by explaining to him that it was the religion of his mother. He asked what he would have to do to become Christian. She told him that he would first have to give up four of his wives.

"In that case," Quanah Parker replied, "I keep my religion."

He kept it at some sacrifice. In the 1890s, he was removed from the Court of Indian Offenses because he would not abandon polygamy.

Quanah Parker's greatest challenge in maintaining the traditional ways of his people involved land ownership. The Quahadi weren't long settled on the reservation when homesteaders pressured the federal government to reduce the size of the Comanche-Kiowa holdings. Little came of it until 1887 when the United States Congress implemented the Dawes Act (General Allotment Act). Its purpose was to destroy the communal structure of reservation life, which many government officials saw as a barrier to Native assimilation. It did so at the expense of Native territorial rights. The Dawes Act proposed to divide reservations into 160-acre parcels (the size of a standard homestead) and to allot these quarter sections to individual Natives. The anticipated effect was to encourage a work ethic among Natives by making each responsible for his own success as a farmer or rancher. Land not allotted would be sold off, thereby assuaging the homesteaders' demands, and the proceeds would be held in trust for the local Natives.

Quanah Parker traveled to Washington to protest the changes. The destination was not new to him. He had been in that city before, when he lobbied for the leasing arrangements with the ranchers. With the support of the cattle barons (who didn't want to lose access to the pasture), the changes proposed by the Dawes Act were put on hold until 1892. In that year, the United States government sent the Cherokee Commission to the Comanche-Kiowa reservation to negotiate the implementation of the Dawes Act. The commissioners were able to get three-quarters of the reservation Natives to agree to its terms: 160 acres per individual and the sale of the remainder of the land for $1.25 per acre.

Many later argued that the Jerome Agreement (named after the lead commissioner) was obtained with threats and translations designed to deliberately mislead the Natives. Again Quanah traveled to Washington to protest the agreement. Assisted by other chiefs, he was successful in further delaying its implementation. And when the Jerome Agreement finally became law in 1902, Quanah had finessed from the government an additional 480,000 acres of communal land that the Natives continued to lease to the ranchers.

While much of the success that Quanah Parker achieved with land matters was due to the influence of the cattle barons, his personal relationship with President Theodore Roosevelt was also important. Quanah was one of six chiefs invited to Roosevelt's inauguration in 1905. Later, Roosevelt accepted Quanah's invitation to join him on a five-day wolf hunt. Quanah was impressed with the man.

He explained, "When he with cowboy, he cowboy; when he with rough riders, he roughest rider of all; when he with statesman, he statesman; when he with Indian, he just like Indian...."

Many chiefs asked Roosevelt to intercede on their peoples' behalf, but like most presidents, he rarely did. He made an exception in Quanah's case. In 1906, lobbyists succeeded in convincing Congress to sell the communally held land on the Comanche-Kiowa reservation for a paltry $1.50 an acre. Even the local Indian agent saw the sale as unfair. He suggested that the land be given to Natives born since 1887 and that the remainder be leased. Congress ignored the proposal. Quanah knew some sort of sale was inevitable, and he supported the Indian agent's proposal. He traveled to Washington, where he expressed his view to Roosevelt. The president agreed to veto the bill unless it was modified to reflect the Indian agent's plan. It was so changed.

In one significant matter, Quanah Parker diverged from both Comanche and *tejano* ways. In 1884, he became an advocate of the peyote ritual that came to his people from the Apache. Chewing the peyote button (the aboveground part of the peyote cactus) produced visions and feelings of tranquility. Visions were an integral part of Native life, and these serene effects were much appreciated during the years of intense change. And, as a communal ceremony, it reinforced tribal bonds. The peyote ritual was held in a special tipi and usually only attended by men. Prayers, songs and rhythmic drum beating and rattle shaking accompanied the ingestion of the peyote buttons. The ceremony lasted throughout the night. Quanah became an adherent after attending a peyote ritual during which he was cured of a stomach ailment.

Despite his spiritual beliefs, Quanah Parker was not against Christianity. He thought that the "Jesus road" was a good one. Willie Parker, one of his 25 children, even became a Methodist minister. Quanah was, however, suspicious of *tejano* religion. There seemed to be a great gulf between what the religious men preached and what the *tejanos* did. It was not an issue that he often discussed, but his view was expressed clearly in the early 1890s, when the government created Indian cavalry battalions to post in forts across the West. Quanah used his influence to keep the Comanche from enlisting.

"Me and my people have quit fighting long ago," he noted, "and we have no desire to join anyone in war again."

He pointed out that the missionaries were teaching his braves that violence was wrong so it would be wrong for them to fight. Quanah was not the first Native to point out the inconsistencies found in *tejano* words and practices.

He defended his own religious choice. "The white man goes into his church house and talks about Jesus; the Indian goes into his tipi and talks *to* Jesus."

Quanah Parker achieved much as a leader after his people settled at the Fort Sill reservation. But not all his efforts were for his peoples' benefit. He was curious about his white family, and he obtained permission from the Indian agent to travel to Texas and Mexico to meet with them. In Texas, he found his mother's grave, and he set his mind to moving her body to the reservation. There was great opposition among the local settlers to the idea of a white woman being buried among Natives, and they threatened to protect her remains armed with rifles. Hoping to change their minds, Quanah wrote a letter that was read in several churches in the vicinity of his mother's cemetery.

My mother. She fed me. She held me. She carried me in her arms. Her boy. See me, she happy. I play, she happy, I cry, she sad. I laugh, her eyes shine. I sleepy, she roll my blanket, she pat me. I sick, she awake. I thirsty, she get water, she not tired, not deep sleeping, not cross, her boy. He want, she get. Laugh with boy, cry with boy. Love boy, my mother. Don't say Indian, say boy. They took my mother away. They kept her. They would not let me see her. Now she dead. Her boy want to bury her. Sit by her mound. My people, her people. Our people. We now one, all our people. Comanche had

much land. Sunrise, sunset, broad grasslands, buffalo, deer,
wild horses, now little land. No more Texas. Few Indians
little land. Lonesome. White boy, boy bury mother, my
mother. She mine. Me bury her, you keep her, she mine.
Her dust, my dust. White brothers, your mother, you bury.
My mother, I boy. Her dust I bury. I sit on her mound.
Love mother. Boy plead. My mother.

Opposition dissipated before the heartfelt appeal. The United States Congress gave him $1000 to remove and re-inter the body. Cynthia Ann Parker was buried at the Post Oak Mission, near Cache, Oklahoma in 1910. Quanah Parker spoke during the ceremony at her gravesite. What he said revealed much about his attitude towards the *tejanos*.

"Forty years ago my mother died. She captured by Comanche nine years old. Love Indian and wild life so well no want to go back to white folks. All people same anyway, God say. I love my mother. I like white people. Got great heart. I want my people follow after white way, get educated, know work, make living when payments stop. I tell um they got to know pick cotton, plow corn. I want um know white man's God. Comanche may die tomorrow or 10 years. When end come they all be together again."

Quanah Parker fell ill early in 1911, and despite a heal-ing ceremony and the efforts of a *puhakut*, he died on February 23. Over 1000 people, including white dignitaries and Natives from across the country, attended the funeral of the last principal chief of the Comanche. He was buried next to his mother, under a gravestone provided by the United States government that read, "Resting here until day breaks and shadows fall and darkness disappears."

CHAPTER FOUR

Red Cloud

Oglala Sioux, 1821–1909

IN THE EARLY 1860s MINERS with gold fever turned from the played-out diggings of British Columbia and Nevada, and made their way to the southwest corner of present-day Montana. By 1863, some 14,000 prospectors had rushed into the territory, giving rowdy life to places like Bannack City and Varina (Virginia City). Perhaps even more would have come if the place hadn't been so inaccessible. The popular Oregon-California, Mormon and Overland trails ran too far south to be convenient. John Bozeman and his partner John Jacobs decided to address the problem. Between 1863 and 1865 they carved out the Bozeman Trail, linking Julesburg, Colorado on the South Platte River and Varina, Montana, to the northwest. While the trail provided western-bound prospectors with easier access to the Montana gold fields, it did so by cutting through the best of what remained of Sioux buffalo-hunting territory in the Powder River country, roughly bound by the North Platte River, the Bighorn

Mountains and the Powder River in Wyoming.* Prospectors only wanted an efficient route, but what they brought down on the United States was Red Cloud's War.

For the Teton (western) Sioux it was a war of self-preservation. They rarely objected to white men crossing their lands, but they wanted them to do it where it would not disrupt their way of life. For Americans, it was a war of territorial expansion. They were not interested in protecting what many of them considered an inferior and dying culture, as was evident when the United States government protected the Bozeman Trail by constructing several forts along the route. The Sioux resisted American intrusions and, in one shocking battle masterminded and led by Red Cloud and fellow Sioux Crazy Horse, wiped out Captain William Fetterman's 80-man army detachment out of Fort Phil Kearny, one of the posts along the trail.

The army wanted to mount an all-out offensive for retribution, but the American government, tired of bloodshed after the Civil War and with a nearly empty treasury, decided that an investigation of the "Fetterman Massacre" was more appropriate. The Phil Kearny Commission visited various forts in Nebraska and Wyoming, and even sent a special invitation to Red Cloud, asking him why he was at war. The question was an insult; they knew well why he fought so he ignored the message. The commission ultimately reported that much of the Sioux problem could be traced to an aggressive army. It concluded that warfare could only be avoided if Americans stayed out of Sioux territory, which would require a reconsideration of American western policies and a new relationship with the Natives.

---

*Refer to the map on page 8 in the chapter on Sitting Bull for locations and events related to Red Cloud.

American officials thought hard about the recommendation. Red Cloud's War had proven the Sioux to be a for-
midable enemy and, with ongoing raids along the North
and South Platte rivers, it didn't appear as if they were tiring of the fight. News reports from the West made it clear
that settlers were tired of warfare and the army's ineptitude,
so many decided to take matters into their own hands. In
Colorado, the governor called for volunteers to defend the
territory. He also gave his approval to a citizen-initiated
scheme, where those concerned about frontier peace collected $5000 to be used for buying Native scalps. Men
would be paid $25 for each scalp with the ears on. And
there were new financial considerations. The American
government guaranteed the bonds of the Northern Pacific
Railroad, which intended to lay track through Sioux territory. It would be a disaster if the Sioux harassed the construction crews and delayed the laying of steel.

In mid-summer 1867, the federal government finally
authorized an Indian Peace Commission. It was charged with
discovering why the Natives were hostile and with making
a treaty that would remove the causes of war, allow for the
safety of settlers and railroad construnction and begin the civilization of the Natives. Although there was continuing violence throughout the late summer (much of it led by Red
Cloud), the commission made its way west in September.
General Christopher Augur, commander of the Department
of the Platte, met the commissioners in Omaha and exhibited
to them the army's intransigence. He informed them that it
would be necessary to send 100,000 soldiers to the West if the
Natives were to be brought under control. As for Red Cloud,
Augur declared that he was on the warpath to the death.

Throughout November, the commissioners met with
Native chiefs and leaders. To the dismay of the commissioners, neither Red Cloud nor his warriors attended.

However, Red Cloud did send word. He informed the commission that he had gone to war against the whites to save the hunting grounds of the Powder River country. When the troops were removed from forts Phil Kearny and C.F. Smith, he would stop making war. The commissioners returned to Washington for the winter disappointed that they had never met with Red Cloud, but buoyed by his assertion that he was willing to cease hostilities.

In the spring, the Peace Commission was back at Fort Laramie where they learned that Red Cloud's demands for peace had grown to include the right to hunt north of the North Platte River and annuities for 30 years. It was a good time to seek such concessions because the government simply could not afford the troops necessary to keep the Bozeman Trail open. Throughout April and into May, the commissioners waited with wagonloads of presents and a treaty guaranteeing all Red Cloud's demands. Finally, word arrived; Red Cloud would be in the fort by the middle of May.

Red Cloud did start for Fort Laramie in early May. But rather than ride directly south to the fort, he headed west to the Bozeman Trail. There he saw that the forts were still manned. A wily war chief, he trusted his eyes more than the too often misleading words of the white man.

He sent a message to the commissioners: "We are on the mountains looking down on the soldiers and the forts. When we see the soldiers moving away and the forts abandoned, then I will come down and talk."

The commissioners were enraged, so most of them left. But by the middle of July, Red Cloud's demands were finally met. Forts C.F. Smith, Phil Kearny and Reno were abandoned. Within days, Red Cloud's men burned Smith and Kearny to the ground. All expected his immediate arrival at Fort Laramie, and when word came that he was going to hunt buffalo after which he might come in and listen to the

Red Cloud, taken in the 1880s, wearing a single feather perhaps earned after taking his first coup.

white men, a wave of concern swept over American officials. Was it possible that Red Cloud would not make treaty? Suddenly there was renewed trouble because the southern Plains Natives were raiding with increased enthusiasm. Was it mere coincidence? General Augur didn't think so, and he issued a circular to his troops advising that Natives be treated with suspicion. Others suggested that Red Cloud had manipulated the negotiations and that he had never intended to make peace, but wanted to demonstrate that he could force the United States to its knees. Surely other Natives would follow suit, pulling the army into a protracted and bloody Plains war. Everything depended on Red Cloud. What would he do?

≈≈≈

Camped comfortably along the Platte River east of its forks was a band of Oglala (Dwellers of the Plains) Sioux, known as the Bad Face. It was a summer day in 1837 and while women cooked outside, cradleboards harboring infants hung from trees and toddlers played nearby. Older children ran through the camp between lodges and into the stands of sheltering trees. Elders gathered in small groups, smoke from their pipes drifting skyward. Only a careful observer would notice that few men were present. Most had joined a war party that rode against the Pawnee and, although the routine actions of the band suggested few were concerned about it, all were preoccupied with thoughts about its success or failure.

Walks as She Thinks had a special reason to be concerned. Her son had joined the war party. It was the first time he had been invited to participate as anything more than an errand boy. At 16, he was of an age to count his first coup. Nevertheless, Walks as She Thinks was worried, and her fear was founded on more than a mother's natural anxiety for her son's safety. His father, Lone Man (also known as Red Cloud), had died when the boy was an infant. Roaring Cloud, the boy's twin brother, had also died when he was young. Although he had sisters, there were no other boys in the family. She was troubled because she felt that bad omens had foretold disaster. The raid was sent in retaliation for the Pawnee's killing of her nephew, whose name was also Red Cloud. Before her son left, she had pleaded with him to wait for another day. He laughed at her superstitions, a response she knew was meant to ease her fears.

When news of the approach of the returning war party reached camp, band members spilled onto the trail. The runner had reported that the warriors had successfully met the Pawnee and had counted many coups. The gathering erupted into shouts and songs; all, that is, save Walks as She Thinks. Search as she might, she could not see her son. She called to the other warriors.

"Where is my son!"

"He is coming," someone called.

"Why does he trail behind? Is he hurt?"

"No Pawnee could touch him. His heart failed him and he did not fight!" came the reply amidst much laughter.

Walks as She Thinks' face darkened and she lowered her eyes to the ground. She was glad to hear that he had not been injured, but there was no pride in having a son whose courage failed him in battle.

Then came a cry. "Red Cloud's son comes."

Then another. "Red Cloud comes."

As easily as that, the youth left behind the name of his childhood, which remains unknown, and took on that of his father. Walks as She Thinks was about to scurry back to her lodge. Surely, she believed, the name by which the community was calling her son was given derisively. His father had died of alcoholism, unable to resist the white man's firewater. She had left her husband's Brulé Sioux band and with neck bent had returned to her people. Although many seasons had passed and her son had excelled in the activities of Oglala childhood and early youth, the shame of the manner of his father's death tainted them still. The unkind words about her son's courage were too much for her to take and she knew they would only get worse as he rode into camp.

Then another cry. "Look, he is painted black as the warrior! He is leading a bay!"

The braves had played a cruel joke on Walks as She Thinks. The Sioux, like most Natives, thought little of such joking and she had made too much of it. Red Cloud had done the war party proud. He had counted first coup, one of some 80 that he would take during his life. Throughout the following days he was invited into many lodges to share the story of his victory. Ceremonies followed, and during one Red Cloud received an eagle feather in recognition of his first coup. Everyone recognized the young man as a warrior, and his father's failure receded into distant memory.

Little is known about Red Cloud before the time he counted his first coup but many tales have been told about him. Some myths allege that he was given his name because a meteor flew across the sky on the day of his birth. However, Red Cloud's own words suggest he was born in 1821 and not a year later when the fiery ball flew through the sky. Other stories suggest that the name reflected the power he commanded among the Sioux. A single command could bring enough scarlet-blanketed warriors to cover the hillsides like a red cloud. However, he had the name Red Cloud long before he gained such prominence. While their accuracy is open to question, both stories capture something of the special character of the man.

Red Cloud was born in the buffalo-rich Platte River country, near where the Blue Water Creek flows into the larger river. His people hadn't had been there for long, no more than a generation or two. Their presence marked the end of a century-long migration from the Great Lakes region. Mastering horsemanship in the early 1700s allowed

them to refine their nomadic lifestyle, which was so necessary to the hunting of buffalo. Their entire way of life—
cultural, spiritual and physical—depended on the buffalo.
When their skills with horses were combined with the
introduction of the gun around the turn of the 19th century, the Teton Sioux (of which the Oglala were one tribe)
came to dominate the western plains. They pushed back
their enemies—Crow (in the Powder River country) and
Kiowa (around the Black Hills)—and became allies with
the Cheyenne. When Americans first arrived in the early
1800s, they recognized that the Teton Sioux were supreme
on the plains west of the Missouri River.

While Red Cloud was born into a powerful people,
there was little reason to think that he would eventually
lead them. He was a nephew of Old Smoke, the leader of
his mother's Bad Face band. But his father's weaknesses and
Brulé heritage worked against him, since the Sioux gave
great consideration to heredity when choosing leaders.
Positions of leadership generally went to the sons of prominent band members, but the rule was not fixed. A man
could elevate himself if he was an exceptional hunter or if
Wakan Tanka (the Great Mystery) revealed visions to him.
He could also prove himself as a warrior. When fighting an
enemy, bloodlines paled before courage, daring and cunning. Red Cloud was always ambitious and, given his
exceptional ability as a warrior, it's clear that he decided
from an early age to earn respect and attain position on the
battlefield.

Everyone agreed that Red Cloud's strength and intelligence were his defining characteristics. Elders in his camp
were not surprised; they recalled that even as a child he was
strong and smart. He learned the lessons of childhood mostly
in games and activities, but they were far from childish competitions to Red Cloud, who regularly demonstrated a fierce

determination to best others. His uncle White Hawk, who took on the primary responsibility of educating the boy, consistently found himself lecturing or scolding the boy on the necessity of restraining his reckless impulses. It could not have been a comfortable task for White Hawk, since the Sioux preferred to lead by example rather than by word. However, sometimes Red Cloud's rash and occasionally ill-considered behaviors became bullying. While there was little doubt as to Red Cloud's bravery and fortitude, White Hawk was forced to abandon traditional notions of non-interference and to rely on direct instruction in other matters. He told his nephew what was proper and what was not so that Red Cloud might more fully appreciate the remaining two of the Sioux's four cardinal virtues, generosity and wisdom.

For the most part, however, Red Cloud's education was like that of other Sioux youth. He learned about the land his people called home, the resources that Wakan Tanka provided and how to use them respectfully. Sioux boys weren't much more than toddlers when they were first placed on a horse and not long after they were given their first set of bows and arrows. By the time they reached manhood, the skills needed for hunting were deeply engrained. They learned about plants that were edible or provided medicinal aid, and they were taught to know the power of and to respect all things that came from nature. Learning about their environment also meant that Sioux youth were steeped in the ways of their people. Through stories of legend and coup and through observation, they learned about Sioux culture and its rituals.

Red Cloud's character made him most fond of competitive activities and warriors' stories. Some competitions were especially popular among the Sioux. Boys spent many afternoons playing the top game, the object of which was to keep one's top spinning longest. They were always racing and swimming, and they hunted long before bringing down their first animal. Speedy boys were sent onto the plains with a supply of meat and the other boys were challenged to chase them and take their food. All these activities served to strengthen and coordinate the body. The stories men told around fires at night or on forest walks whetted appetites and ensured that boys were anxious to put their learned skills to use. By the time Red Cloud was ready to embark on the rituals of manhood, few in his tribe doubted that he was one of the most capable of his generation. He was soon to show that their observations were accurate.

When Red Cloud was a young man, there were plenty of raids against neighboring tribes during which a brave could show both his courage and ability. Only a couple of months after he counted his first coup against the Pawnee, Red Cloud counted three more during an attack on the Crow. He had taken the much-respected first coup, striking the three men with his bow without killing them (left alive, there was always the possibility that they might strike back). On a subsequent expedition against the Crow, he again demonstrated his bravery. The Oglala were out to steal horses, a popular activity. Red Cloud seethed as the leaders of the expedition took their time approaching the Crow camp. He was less concerned about avoiding detection than he was anxious for engagement. Against orders, he joined with a fellow Sioux and left the party, intent on a quick strike. Before they encountered the main body of the Crow, they came upon a lone Crow sentry tending a herd of about 50 horses. Red Cloud had his scalp before the brave knew he was under attack. He had already developed a taste for hand-to-hand combat and he was merciless. When they met up with the others, they fully expected to be whipped for disobeying orders. Seeing the horses and recognizing that the main body of the Crow camp still had not been alerted, Red Cloud was praised for his daring instead.

While Red Cloud's success in fighting the enemy was impressive, it was an attack on a fellow Sioux that got everyone talking around their fire pits. As a nation, the Sioux were a confederation of autonomous tribes. In times of dire circumstances, the tribes banded together as a more cohesive unit, but to do so wasn't the norm. At most, they gathered once a year, usually to celebrate the Sun Dance. While they pledged not to go to war against each other, raiding horses and women and the subsequent reprisals were not unknown. Red Cloud was involved in such a situation.

In the 1830s the Bad Face had fallen out with another Oglala band, the Cut-Off. Bull Bear, chief of the Cut-Off, was the most powerful Oglala chief. Old Smoke, chief of the Bad Face, was jealous but he was also worried. Bull Bear and his band wielded such influence among the Oglala that Old Smoke was concerned his band might simply be assimilated into the Cut-Off. Matters deteriorated when the two bands found themselves drawn to the territory around Fort Laramie where fur traders were operating. The traders had learned that the Oglala wanted whisky in trade for their furs, but the alcohol also increased the tension between the Bad Face and the Cut-Off. Bloodshed seemed inevitable, and it happened following the abduction of a Cut-Off woman by a Bad Face warrior. The Cut-Off rode into the Bad Face camp, their determination for revenge fueled by booze. They killed the father of the man who stole the girl, and onlookers feared that Bull Bear wanted to destroy the entire village. A group of Bad Face warriors, Red Cloud among them, quickly organized to defend the camp. Bull Bear took a bullet in the leg, and Red Cloud ran to the injured chief, finishing him off with a shot to the head. The episode demonstrated Red Cloud's courage as well as his impetuosity. When there was an opportunity, he took it. Consequences seemed, at best, fleeting considerations. In this case, his action opened a chasm between the two bands that took decades to close. But the immediate effect of Red Cloud's action was that it enhanced his reputation among the Bad Face.

It was a reputation that almost became a memory soon after. Red Cloud led a party that set out to raid horses from the Pawnee. The expedition was poorly planned because they had underestimated the numbers of their enemy. The Sioux were routed. Red Cloud was separated from his warriors, and they watched from a distance as he was felled by an arrow. They feared that he had died and he very nearly did. The Oglala braves pushed towards their leader and found that the arrow had pierced just below his ribs. They removed it and treated the wound, but there was great blood loss. Weak and slipping in and out of consciousness, Red Cloud was transported back to camp on a pony drag. It was a difficult two-week journey. For two months he was cared for and given medicines. Prayers were offered for the brave whose survival seemed precarious. He pulled through eventually, although the wound bothered him for the rest of his life. Red Cloud was subsequently permitted to wear a red eagle feather on his headband, a mark that he had been injured in battle.

On his recovery, Red Cloud took a final step towards Sioux manhood. He offered twelve horses to the father of his intended bride and, when accepted, he married Pretty Owl. Although it is not known when she died, it is believed that Pretty Owl outlived Red Cloud, which means they were married for some 60 years. Depending on whether one believes Red Cloud or his wife, they had either three or five children. What was most marked about their relationship, however, was its monogamy. Red Cloud took no other wife, which was uncommon for a Sioux of his stature. The reason, however, appears tragic. When he was first married, Red Cloud had intended to take Pine Leaf as his second wife. But he wanted to allow a respectable amount of time to pass before he made an offer to her family. Pine Leaf did not know of his intent. In despair, on the night of his marriage, she hanged herself from a tree whose branches sheltered the newlyweds' lodge. The episode so affected Red Cloud that he never sought a second wife.

Throughout the 1850s, Red Cloud's reputation as a warrior and a strategist grew. He modified traditional raiding practices by dividing the Bad Face warriors into small groups of 8 to 12, effective for quick strikes and rapid retreats. All the Oglala soon adopted the method. Smaller raiding parties did call for more vigilant reconnaissance and care in target selection. Enemy camps could be large, and if they were too large, a small Oglala raiding force was likely to suffer defeat. And Red Cloud's impatience, ambition and courage occasionally saw him attack without the necessary due diligence, as was evident in a series of raids in Ree territory along the Missouri River in 1857.

Red Cloud's band was in that unfamiliar region in search of food. They sent out some raiding parties to ease the monotony of hunting. Unsure of the enemy's number and location, Red Cloud led an unusually large party of 24. They could not find the Ree, but all was not lost because they discovered a Gros Ventre camp. The Oglala attacked and, although they managed to steal 100 horses, they did little damage to the camp. One Oglala was killed and three more were injured, increasing the remaining warriors' desire for blood. While some returned to the Oglala camp with the horses, 13 warriors, including Red Cloud, continued to search for an enemy.

They eventually found a Ree camp, but the Gros Ventre
had warned them of the Sioux presence so the raid was
a disaster. Four Oglala were killed and Red Cloud escaped
with his life by ingloriously paddling down the river in
a stolen canoe, but the story doesn't end there. The following year, Red Cloud's warriors encountered a band of
50 Native families near the Black Hills. The Oglala weren't
sure whether they were Cheyenne or Arapaho. It was
decided that if they were Cheyenne (Sioux allies) they
could go in peace, but if they were Arapaho (relatives of the
Gros Ventre), the Oglala would attack. When a scouting
party discovered that the band was Arapaho on its way to
visit the Gros Ventre, the Sioux raised their war clubs and
shouted their war whoops. Only the women and children
were left alive. When it came to warfare and honor, Natives
could hold strong grudges.

Red Cloud served his people well as a warrior; a good
blotahunka (war leader) brought wealth to the tribe and
expanded its hunting territory. His reputation also helped
him fulfill his own aspirations. In the 1840s he was likely
a member of an Oglala warrior society. By the end of the
1850s (the mid-1860s at the latest), Red Cloud was a shirt
wearer, one of those who wore a colorful shirt and was
responsible for carrying out the decisions of the tribal council. Being a shirt wearer was an honor because there were
only four shirt wearers in the tribe. But it wasn't enough for
Red Cloud, whose ambitions would be satisfied only when
he was named a band *itancan* (chief). His Brulé heritage
continued to be an impediment; many believed that a leader
of the Oglala needed to be a full-blooded member of the
tribe. Red Cloud worked hard to change such opinions.
And, although it went against his nature as a man of action,
changing opinions meant being political and forming
alliances, sometimes with amusing results.

In the mid-1850s Red Cloud lived near Fort Laramie. On one occasion, some prominent chiefs visited the fort. Red Cloud wanted to make a good impression on the leaders and decided he would do that with his hospitality. He prepared a great feast and went in search of a bottle of whisky for the pleasure of his guests. The fort's surgeon willingly obliged him and took two quill-ornamented buffalo robes as payment. As the feast began, Red Cloud took the bottle and passed it around the circle of chiefs. When the first chief tilted it to his lips, his brows furrowed and his eyes fixed on Red Cloud. He quickly lowered the bottle and passed it on. All the guests drank from the bottle, but none seemed pleased. When it finally returned to Red Cloud, he took a swallow and discovered that it was water. Incensed, he left the feast in search of the surgeon. The officers of the fort knew something of Red Cloud's temper and the surgeon, who was undoubtedly playing a trick on a man who was at least a good acquaintance, was well hidden by the time Red Cloud arrived. A few days later, he was able to make reparations to a cooled Red Cloud. But from then on, folks at Fort Laramie called Red Cloud Two Robes, but probably not to his face.

Eventually, a sufficient number of Oglala believed that Red Cloud would make an able leader. Although it is not certain, he probably became a chief before the signing of the Fort Laramie Treaty of 1868. In the late 1800s, Red Cloud himself asserted that he held such a position. Skeptics suggest that any such claim was self-serving and point out that, at the time Red Cloud made the assertion, the United States government had made legal changes that enhanced the status of Native chiefs. In claiming he had long been a chief, the ever-ambitious Red Cloud was merely giving credence to his alleged right to continue to hold the position. According to Red Cloud, he was invested as chief during a pipe-dance ceremony in 1855. If his story is true, Old Smoke, the previous chief, chose him above his son. Chief or not, in the late 1860s Red Cloud was the unquestioned *blotahunka* of the Oglala, and it was to him they turned when the white man came.

By the 1820s only a few white men were in Oglala territory, and these were mostly employed by the American Fur Company. A decade later more independent traders came to settle in the region. The Oglala didn't object to their presence. The fact was that trade goods (knives, guns, pots) made their lives easier, although the liquor often made it more tragic. Throughout the 1840s, thousands of immigrants bound for Oregon made their way through the territory. Although Sioux eyes widened at the great numbers, they weren't overly concerned because few from this western rolling wave remained in their territory. But problems surfaced. The Natives accused the immigrants of driving off the buffalo. The immigrants replied that the Natives were attacking them and stealing from their wagons. The allegations of the white immigrants were sufficient for the government to act. Colonel Stephen W. Kearney led five companies of dragoons into the Platte country and informed the Sioux that he wanted to parley. Mostly he wanted to impress them with his well-disciplined men and to warn them not to harass those using the Oregon Trail (from Independence, Missouri to Astoria in the Oregon Territory). Red Cloud attended the meeting, but he was not yet prominent enough to speak.

As Red Cloud watched the wagons roll west, he must have believed that the final stragglers of the white tribe would soon pass through Sioux hunting territory, bringing the matter to a close. That never happened. A two-year span in the late 1840s saw some 50,000 Mormons headed for Utah and forty-niners bound for California gold.

While they were only passers-by, they came in sufficient enough numbers to seriously disrupt the seasonal buffalo hunts. Whether they killed the animals or interfered with their migratory patterns, the end result was the same—the Sioux faced a greater challenge when it came to finding buffalo. Even worse than the waning buffalo numbers was the disease the immigrants brought. Entire Native bands were wiped out by cholera. Red Cloud's band fled, but they were not unaffected. To combat the deadly effects of the disease, Red Cloud successfully concocted a medicine derived from cedar leaves. He never claimed to be a medicine man, but certainly his efforts improved his standing in the band.

Unlike the Sioux, the United States government was well aware that there would be no end to the people making their way west and that more would choose to remain in the Platte River country. To protect the newcomers, the government purchased Fort Laramie from the American Fur Company in 1849 and turned it into an army post. However, the government was not inclined to spend much money on manning the post, so instead decided that the best way to ensure no harm came to its citizens was to try to make peace with the Sioux and the other Native tribes of the northern Plains.

The Natives were receptive to the idea, and in the early 1850s they arrived by the thousands at Fort Laramie to negotiate peace. Their enthusiasm dimmed when Colonel David Mitchell, who led the American negotiations, announced that the United States would not negotiate with the bands independently. He demanded that each group select one person to speak as a chief for his entire tribe. Once selected, the government would support and sustain that chief in his position. This method flew in the face of Native political structure. The Sioux had no concept of a supreme ruler; even the head chief had limited decision-making powers. While they objected, Mitchell pressed, eventually choosing his own chief, a Brulé called Conquering Bear. The Sioux accepted the appointment as some strange white custom. Certainly they did not recognize the authority Mitchell had given Conquering Bear. When the Fort Laramie Treaty of 1851 was finally signed, five Oglala marked their X on it, including Old Smoke for the Bad Face band. The Natives agreed to cease intertribal warfare, to live in specified territories (within which the government reserved the right to establish roads and military posts) and to make restitution for wrongdoings done to settlers. In return, the government promised that the Natives would be protected against white depredations and that they would receive $50,000 worth of goods for 50 years.

The treaty was broken almost immediately. The United States Senate reduced 50 years to 10 without telling the Natives. The Sioux and the Crow renewed their hostilities and the Sioux again harassed the Americans. These confrontations took an unfortunate turn in 1854, when a Sioux killed and ate a stray cow. Its Mormon owner went to Fort Laramie and demanded compensation. The fort's commander sent Lieutenant John Grattan to Conquering Bear's camp to seek payment for the dead animal. Unfortunately Grattan was a poor choice; only 21, inexperienced and a vocal critic of the Sioux, he believed he could best them easily and was determined to prove it. Conquering Bear's offer of money was met with army gunfire. Soon, the entire contingent of 31 men was dead. The army responded with force. Within a few weeks, Brigadier General William S. Harney and his 1200 men attacked the Brulé, killing almost 100. Harney then led his troops north through Sioux country, a visible warning to keep the peace. It proved persuasive and many Sioux, including Red Cloud's Oglala, left the

Fort Laramie area and the many white immigrants on the California/Oregon Trail traveled with less fear.

Red Cloud did not want to leave Fort Laramie because he had good relations with several officers there, but the northern move served him well. The Oglala ended up in Powder River country. There, they joined other Sioux tribes. At a council during the annual Sun Dance in 1857, the tribes pledged to act in a more unified manner. They agreed that any whites who entered their lands would be turned back. There were fewer to be seen, though, since most Americans were soon preoccupied with their own Civil War. Nevertheless, the Sioux did not want for an enemy because the Powder River was traditionally Crow territory, and that tribe continued to fight for it. Thus began the Crow Wars, a concerted effort by the Sioux to drive the Crow from the region and gain control of the hunting territory. In the winter of 1861–62, Red Cloud led a war party against the Crow, killing Little Rabbit, their chief, thereby adding to his reputation as a *blothunka*. It wasn't long before his considerable military skills were turned against the white man.

In spring 1865, Teton Sioux and Cheyenne war leaders met along the Tongue River west of the Powder River to discuss the increased violence to the north and south. Many prominent warriors attended the council, including Red Cloud and Crazy Horse. They all agreed that the past few years had not been good ones for the Plains Natives.

The problems started in 1862, with the Minnesota (Santee) Sioux uprising. Frustrated by the government's failure to meet treaty obligations (delays in supplies and annuities), agency mismanagement and continued settler intrusions into Sioux territory, the Santee went on the warpath. In the late summer of 1862, they killed some

800 whites. The uprising set a gruesome stage for the Plains Native wars of the mid-1860s. In 1863, the Cheyenne and Arapaho in Platte country set about raiding anything that smacked of a white presence—stage stations, wagon trains, telegraph offices. The government responded by strengthening its military presence.

In July 1864, General Alfred Sully and a 2220-strong army contingent attacked some 1600 Santee Sioux led by Inkpaduta, a prominent figure in the Minnesota uprisings. His followers fled west and Sully finally caught up with them in North Dakota. At the Battle of Kildeer Mountain, 100 Santee were killed or wounded before the warriors retreated. In November, Colonel J.M. Chivington directed his 700 men to attack Black Kettle's band of Cheyenne at Sand Creek in Colorado. Chivington's men knew that Black Kettle was a friendly (the term referred to those Natives who desired peace), who believed his band was under the protection of the army. Ignoring all protests and declaring that he had "come to kill Indians, and believe it is right and honorable to use any means under God's heaven to kill Indians," Chivington ordered the attack. His men killed 163 Cheyenne, many of them women and children.

When the survivors of Black Kettle's band limped into another Cheyenne camp, a war council was held. It was decided to send the war pipe to neighboring tribes. All were incensed at the news, as had been the American public. Faced with a court-martial, Chivington resigned. By December, 800 lodges, representing some 1000 warriors, gathered for revenge. Red Cloud was not among their numbers, but Crazy Horse was. They raided ruthlessly along the South Platte into Colorado. By summer, the bands dispersed, providing immediate, but temporary, relief to the settlers. When the warriors returned to their villages, they brought home news of the struggle against the whites and incited a determination to continue it. The war council of 1865 was a result of these events.

As they prepared for the council on the Tongue River, three Oglala sat together in a forest glade—Red Cloud, Young Man Afraid of His Horse and Crazy Horse. The smoke from their pipes drifted skyward and the sound of the creaking trees mingled with that of the rushing river. Their discussion belied the peaceful setting.

"Tell us of the raids along the Platte," said Young Man Afraid of His Horse as he looked to Crazy Horse.

"Our hearts were strong. Where there were white men, we attacked. We took supplies and burned mail. We destroyed Camp Rankin, burning it to the ground," smiled Crazy Horse. "Black Kettle had no stomach for it," he chuckled. "He took his Cheyenne and left. But we were effective. Neither wagon nor Long Knife could make its way west." For a time, the Natives blockaded much of Colorado from the eastern United States.

"We have heard stories that, since we left the Platte country, there are many more whites," said Red Cloud.

"More than there were," agreed Crazy Horse. "But not so many. And few Long Knives." Army resources were still tied up with the Civil War. The Natives weren't aware that the Civil War was the reason for the limited number of soldiers, and they didn't anticipate that many more would inevitably arrive. "Their numbers are no match for us. We must continue to attack if we are to keep our lands," suggested Crazy Horse.

The trio fell silent. Although Young Man Afraid of His Horse was the hereditary chief of the southern Oglala, in recognition of Red Cloud's military abilities, he deferred to Red Cloud in matters of war. He wanted to know Red Cloud's opinion before he spoke. He was no way certain of it. To this point, Red Cloud had remained mostly passive when it came to the white presence. He had been on good terms with the Long Knives at Fort Laramie. He had shown no indication that he wished to fight them. Finally, he spoke.

"It is the trail that bothers me, the one they call the Bozeman Trail. It cuts through our hunting territory, like a wound in one's chest," said Red Cloud, dragging his hand down along his own chest. "It is not land given to the white man. The Great Father promised we would be free to hunt there. We have seen few white men yet, but I fear their tribe is large."

"It is time to resist," persisted Crazy Horse. "The white men cannot be trusted. They have broken treaty with us. They have done the same with the Santee."

"They smoke the peace pipe while they hold a knife. Their actions are greedy and treacherous," agreed Young Man Afraid of His Horse. "They have no honor."

"Honor!" laughed Crazy Horse. "They understand nothing of the word," he spat. "We should do as Sitting Bull and the Hunkpapa have and declare that no white men will pass through our territory."

"We have said as much," noted Young Man Afraid of His Horse.

"Perhaps it is necessary to show that we mean it," decided Red Cloud. "If we are not to suffer the fate of the Santee. Yes. We must go on the warpath to preserve our way of life."

The war council agreed so through the spring and early summer of 1865 strategies were outlined and preparations were made. They decided that the Sioux would arrange themselves into a single large fighting unit. At 1500 (some accounts suggest as many as 3000), they were confident that they could intimidate any Long Knives and settlers in the region. Before the war party set out there was a Sun Dance held to unify the tribes and seek Wakan Tanka's support. In July, they moved into Platte country. They had one encounter at the Platte River Bridge, where a handful of soldiers were killed. After the events of the previous years and the great war council, it seemed anti-climactic, but it was victory enough for the Natives. After a suitable cele-bration, they disbanded to hunt buffalo, which was, after all, the main reason for their actions.

But even the hunt provided opportunities to raid. When Red Cloud and the Oglala returned to their hunt-ing grounds along the Powder River, they encountered a large wagon train, equipped for road building. Red Cloud himself addressed the leader of the party, Colonel Sawyer, who was a retired army officer.

"You are in our hunting territory," stated Red Cloud.

"Just passing through," replied Sawyer. "We're on the way to the Montana gold fields."

Red Cloud trotted his horse to the wagons and lifted some of the covering tarps. He looked up at Sawyer.

"You must not go near the Powder River. Your wagons will scare the buffalo."

Sawyer nodded.

"You may continue west if you give us a wagonload of supplies."

At this, the commander of the military escort with the train rode to Sawyer and voiced his objection. Sawyer ignored him. Red Cloud got his provisions and the wagon train continued on unmolested.

To the army, raiding was theft and they were determined to put an end to both it and Native attacks. The late sum-mer and fall of 1865 witnessed the army searching for those they called the hostiles. They did so without success, but at great expense, which was a significant problem because there was little money that was not tied up in southern reconstruction after the Civil War. The government wanted to make treaty with the Plains Natives. Many Sioux, including Red Cloud, were receptive to the idea. The winter of 1865 had been harsh and many were destitute. Some of the younger warriors, like Crazy Horse, were unwilling to negotiate; however, they did not have the weighty responsibility of the tribe's well-being on their shoulders.

Red Cloud went to Fort Laramie in June 1866. E.B. Taylor, head of the peace commission, greeted him. Oglala leaders demanded that the treaty be explained in great detail so Taylor enthusiastically obliged. When he reached the clause concerning the construction of roads through Powder River country, Red Cloud raised his hand.

"We will never sign such a treaty," he declared.

"The government doesn't want to build new roads through Powder River country," noted Taylor. "It wants only to maintain the Bozeman Trail."

"It is bad enough," answered Red Cloud and he ended the discussion so the Oglala could confer.

The Oglala left the fort and returned to their camp. While they smoked and discussed the treaty, Standing Elk brought news that many Long Knives were marching up the North Platte River, headed for the Powder River to build forts and to guard the Bozeman Trail.

In April Colonel Henry B. Carrington, in charge of the Department of the Platte, had taken some 700 soldiers to the Bozeman Trail to oversee the trail's development, to protect those who traveled on it and to construct forts.

The Oglala were incensed. When the peace council reconvened, Taylor knew he was in for trouble.

"Standing Elk has told us that the Long Knives march along the Bozeman Trail," said Young Man Afraid. "I hope he is mistaken."

"They are there to protect the settlers." replied Taylor.

Red Cloud leapt from the stage on hearing Taylor's response.

"In this and Wakan Tanka I trust for the right," he shouted. He then walked from the council arena, a symbolic act indicating he no longer wanted any relationship with the commissioners. He sat on the floor wrapped in his blanket, refusing to talk to Taylor, who tried to explain his government's position. Finally Red Cloud shouted over him.

"The Great Father sends us presents and wants us to sell him the road, but the Long Knives steal the road before the Indians say yes or no. I will take no gifts. You treat us as children, pretending to negotiate for a country you have already taken by force. My people called the plains home. You have forced us north. We are crowded around the Powder River. There is not enough buffalo. Our women and children starve."

Red Cloud spoke to the Sioux. "It is better to fight. What else is there? To starve? To die in a land no longer ours? We should fight and we will win."

Red Cloud, Crazy Horse and their supporters quickly left Fort Laramie.

While some friendlies, including the Brulé chief Spotted Tail made treaty, the peace commission was in a shambles. Ironically, the United States Senate subsequently rejected the treaty, but they did not inform the Natives.

If there had been questions about Red Cloud's leadership, they disappeared. Many looked to him as the leader of the nontreaty Oglala. He led some 500 lodges to the Tongue River and set about organizing the Native resistance. In addition to most of the Teton Sioux tribes, the Yanktonai, Santee, Northern Cheyenne and Northern Arapaho were also willing allies. Red Cloud sent tobacco to his traditional enemies, the Crow, as a sign that he wanted to discuss an alliance with them. He offered the

Crow much of the hunting territory that the Sioux had taken from them over the past decade if they would fight the Long Knives. While some of the younger warriors wanted to join the resistance, the Crow leadership felt that their most secure future lay with the Americans. With or without the Crow, most Plains Natives were determined to drive the Americans out of the Powder River country. Thus began what was known as Red Cloud's War.

In the summer of 1866, Red Cloud and the other Native leaders watched with anger as the army built Fort Phil Kearny in the eastern foothills of the Bighorn Mountains in Wyoming. Since it was designed to protect the Bozeman Trail, the Sioux considered that it was a slap in the face. Clearly, the Americans did not intend to close the route. Within weeks of its opening, Colonel Carrington was forced to send for reinforcements to relieve him of Red Cloud's constant siege of the fort. His command strengthened, Carrington ordered the construction of Fort C.F. Smith, 90 miles to the north. Along with Fort Reno, it was expected that the three forts would provide adequate protection to travelers. While the soldiers were poorly trained in Native warfare, they were a confident bunch, and getting Red Cloud's scalp dominated barracks talk.

Red Cloud, Crazy Horse and the other Native leaders made their plan of attack in the summer of 1866, but they waited until after the fall buffalo hunt before putting it into action. When they did, Red Cloud and his allies inflicted the greatest single defeat suffered by the American army on the plains up to that point. On December 21, Carrington dispatched Lieutenant Colonel William J. Fetterman to assist a wood train (civilians out gathering wood for the fort) that was pinned down by the Sioux. Carrington was careful to give Fetterman specific orders not to travel out of sight of Fort Phil Kearny. He was concerned that the Sioux planned an ambush, as they had unsuccessfully attempted a few weeks before. But Fetterman was an egotistical hothead when it came to the Natives; he had often been heard to claim that with 80 men he could wipe out the Sioux nation. Fetterman set out for Lodge Trail Ridge, only to see the Sioux fall back at his approach. Emboldened by their withdrawal, Fetterman directed his men to pursue them. Perhaps his blood quickened when he realized that Crazy Horse led the retreat. Undoubtedly, it turned cold when Sioux, Cheyenne and Arapaho warriors suddenly appeared from behind rocks and brush. Within half an hour, Fetterman and his company were wiped out. Ironically, Carrington had given him command of 80 men.

After the Fight of 100, as the Sioux called the battle (they believed that 100 soldiers fought under Fetterman's command), the Native bands dispersed for the winter. While they told stories of their victory, American officials searched for a cause for the Fetterman Massacre. The army sent additional reinforcements to Fort Phil Kearny, even while government representatives back east were pointing fingers at the army's intolerant attitude towards the Natives as the root of the problem. Ultimately, a commission was called to investigate the Fetterman affair. Red Cloud would not participate in its hearings and, as a result, the effort was a failure.

The summer of 1867 saw the Natives continue their offensive, but they were no longer unified. The Cheyenne wanted to mount an assault on Fort C.F. Smith, which they believed to be more vulnerable than Fort Phil Kearny. The Sioux held the opposite position and the result was two major battles. The Hayfield Fight saw some 500 Cheyenne attack Fort C.F. Smith. Less than 30 soldiers and civilians managed to hold their position, and the Cheyenne retreated after suffering losses. A day later Red Cloud and Crazy

Horse led the Sioux against a detachment of 26 soldiers guarding a wood train near Fort Phil Kearny. The number of Red Cloud's force in the Wagon Box Fight is unknown, but it was certainly in the many hundreds. The Sioux also suffered losses and were forced to retreat, but in both encounters the Natives took enough horses to allow them to proclaim victory. Americans also considered both battles victories, although any success was due less to forethought or strategy than to the new rapid fire Springfield-Allen breechloader, a weapon unfamiliar to the Natives, who still depended mostly on muzzle-loaders and arrows.

Red Cloud did not fight the American army again, largely because government officials were no longer willing to spend the money necessary to wage war against such demanding adversaries. By fall of 1867, the Indian Peace Commission arrived at Fort Laramie; however, it returned to Washington without meeting Red Cloud. The commissioners were in Fort Laramie again in the spring of 1868. Their superiors had made it clear that the government was willing to close the Bozeman Trail and abandon the forts along it if that was the price of peace. Red Cloud was pleased to hear it, but he was not ready to deal with the commission until he saw with his own eyes that the Americans would be true to their word. When the forts were abandoned in the summer, Red Cloud was still unprepared to go to Fort Laramie because he had more important matters to consider. A supply of buffalo had to be put aside for the winter. In November, with that done, he led a contingent of 125 chiefs and leaders to the fort. Red Cloud was ready to make treaty, but to the end, he would leave the Americans uncertain.

It was a sullen Red Cloud who sat in the conference room. He was not pleased with the government delegation and remained seated when they came to shake hands with him.

"I came to Fort Laramie to speak with the peace commissioners. They are not here," observed Red Cloud. "I see only the shirt wearers of the Long Knives. I think this council will not serve anyone well."

"I have been given the authority to allow Red Cloud and others to sign the treaty," replied Brigadier General William Dye, the fort's commander. He might have added that the commissioners had tired of waiting for him and had left, but he could not risk offending the Sioux chief. Dye had no authority to change the terms of the treaty; he could only explain it. The next three days were spent doing just that. Dye clarified each of the treaty's terms point by point. When he began to explain the sections about reservations, farming and agencies (locations where supplies would be issued and education provided), Red Cloud interrupted him.

"I need to know nothing about those things," he declared. "My people do not wish to leave their home for a new one. We will not give up the hunt to dig in the earth. These matters are not important to me. I have come to talk and get powder and lead to fight the Crow."

"The government will not issue ammunition to Indians at war. Your people must go to a reservation. Once there, the government will supply all your needs," promised Dye. "Tonight there is a feast. I advise you to think over these matters and we will discuss them again tomorrow."

When the talks resumed, Dye emphasized that the government especially wanted peace with Red Cloud, whom it considered to be "a big chief." Despite the flattery, Red Cloud remained noncommittal. On the third day, Red Cloud satisfied himself as to the territory set apart for the Sioux and the regulations that forbid white intrusion on the reservation. The Fort Laramie Treaty of 1868 established the Great Sioux Reservation (which

William T. Sherman and commissioners in council with Native chiefs at Fort Laramie, 1868.

became the state of South Dakota west of the Missouri River) and prohibited Americans from entering there unless on official business. Then he stood and began to walk to the document. He hesitated. He washed his hands with dust from the floor and finally put his mark on the document. He looked back to his fellow Natives, who rose to make their marks. At his urging, the Long Knives also touched the pen. Red Cloud ended the conference with a speech.

"I am tired of fighting and want peace. Many of my people feel the same. But I cannot speak for the young braves. I do not know whether they will lay down their weapons," he conceded. "I will ask them to, but their hearts are strong and their blood is hot. They are not ready to go to the reserve. Neither am I. We will continue to go where the buffalo is. We will trade with who we like."

Red Cloud was true to his word. He led his people to the territory as outlined in the treaty and they hunted. He was next seen the following spring, when he arrived at Fort Laramie in search of provisions. He was told he would only receive them if he went to the appropriate agency, Fort Randall on the Missouri River. Red Cloud went north instead. When he showed up again the next year at Fort Laramie, he had a new request. He wanted to meet the Great Father in Washington to discuss the treaty. His timing proved fortuitous. While leading army officials recommended against any such meeting, President Grant had embarked on new peace policy with regards to the Natives and he was willing to meet with Red Cloud and his people.

Red Cloud and the Oglala delegation finally arrived in Washington on June 1, 1870, where they were well feted. Newspapers welcomed the great Sioux chief and proclaimed him that nation's most powerful leader. Americans still did not understand Sioux political structures and continued to assume that they mirrored their own. Government officials wanted to show Red Cloud something of the might of the United States and so they took him to the Navy Yard where weapons were being assembled. The sight had no more of an impact on Red Cloud than did a subsequent full-dress parade of marines.

Red Cloud had several meetings with prominent officials. He outlined his demands to the secretary of the Interior and the commissioner of Indian Affairs. He wanted more rations for the women and children, additional ammunition for hunting buffalo and, always suspicious of American intent, a telegram sent to his people informing them that he had arrived. Only the latter was granted.

Throughout the meetings, Red Cloud continued to push for increased aid. "We only want to raise our children in peace. Many whites have come. They continue to come from where the sun rises. They have taken our land. We are surrounded by a great lake of whites! We are nothing but an island," sighed Red Cloud. "We were strong but they had many guns. Now we are melting like snow on the hillside, while you are growing like spring grass!

"The buffalo are few and those that remain are scared away by the settlers. The army must abandon Fort Fetterman," he then demanded. Fetterman was north of Fort Laramie, along the old Bozeman Trail in the southern range of Oglala hunting territory.

The government was unwilling to bend on any of these key demands until Red Cloud proclaimed that he had no knowledge of the Laramie Treaty of 1868 and certainly did not sign it. He further declared that he would not follow it. When presented with the document, he barked that it was all lies. At that point, the government agreed that Red Cloud and his Oglala could remain in Wyoming. No longer would they have to travel to Fort Randall for supplies. Before they returned home, Red Cloud and his delegation were taken to New York City. They were paraded down Fifth Avenue before curious onlookers anxious to see the man who had forced the government to close the Bozeman Trail. Red Cloud was also given the opportunity to speak before a forum put together by Peter Cooper, a Native sympathizer who had been a member of the Indian Peace Commission. The chief's comments were both reflective and pragmatic.

"I was brought up among the traders; those who came out there in the early times treated me well and I had a good time with them," he said. "They taught us to wear clothes and to use tobacco and ammunition. Since then the Great Father has sent whites that cheated and drank whisky.

This drawing of Red Cloud appeared in the July 1870 edition of *Frank Leslie's Illustrated Newspaper*. The accompanying caption describes the scene: "The Sioux chief, Red Cloud, in the Great Hall of the Cooper Institute, surrounded by the Indian delegation of braves and squaws, addressing a New York audience on the wrongs done to his people." After Natives had been placed onto reservations, their chiefs often traveled to major eastern cities, where their presence served to confirm America's military might in the mind of citizens. Red Cloud, like most Native leaders, seized such opportunities to publicize the terrible conditions endured by his people. While there were Americans, like those at the Cooper Institute, who sympathized with the Natives' plight, the chiefs' stories of poverty, hunger and administrative corruption usually fell on deaf ears and rarely produced change.

Commissioners are sent out to us who do nothing but rob us. The good times are like the snow of past winters. Still, I have made treaty. I will keep my word!" he declared.

Red Cloud followed his words with an act of good will. In the early 1870s, with access to food supplies more of a necessity, Red Cloud finally agreed to move from the Platte River valley and settle his people close to a more northern agency near the White River. As with most decisions he made, Red Cloud hesitated at the last minute. For a time, it appeared as if the relocation was in doubt. Red Cloud realized that many in his band opposed such a move. To solidify his position as chief, Red Cloud demanded more supplies in return for the move, some of which were granted. He also warned that no white men should travel north of the White River. When they did, only the influence of Red Cloud and their speedy withdrawal stopped incensed warriors from attacking.

In the mid-1870s, when prospectors illegally invaded the Black Hills, the Sioux's sacred *Paha Sapa*, Crazy Horse and Sitting Bull exerted considerable pressure on Red Cloud to join them on the warpath, but the Oglala chief remained true to his treaty obligations. Red Cloud and Crazy Horse were no longer the close allies they had once been. Crazy Horse had never been an advocate of Red Cloud's peace, but the dispute became irreparable when Red Cloud refused to allow Crazy Horse to marry his daughter.

Sitting Bull, at least, could not have been surprised at Red Cloud's position. The Oglala chief had sent him a message in the early 1870s, one that Sitting Bull was surely not pleased to hear.

"I shall not go to war anymore with the whites. I shall do as my Great Father says and make my people listen." He went on to give Sitting Bull and his allies some advice. "Make no trouble for our Great Father. His heart is good. Be friend to him and he will provide for you."

Red Cloud's decision to keep the peace did not mean he would simply accept from the government what it was willing to offer. In 1875, on what would prove to be the eve of the Sioux War, Washington dispatched the Allison Commission to the western plains in the hope of negotiating the sale of the Black Hills. The Sioux were not of one mind on the issue, but Red Cloud was willing to listen when the commission arrived at his agency.

After the large collection of Natives met to consider the commission's request, Red Cloud addressed the council.

"I want seven generations ahead to be fed....These hills out here to the northwest we look upon as the head chief of the land. My intention was that my children should depend on these hills for the future. I hoped that we should live that way always hereafter. That was my intention. I sit here under the treaty, which was to extend for 30 years. I want to put the money that we get for the Black Hills at interest among the whites, to buy with the interest wagons and cattle. We have much small game that we can depend on yet for the future, only I want the Great Father to buy guns and ammunition with the interest so we can shoot the game."

Red Cloud obviously had a good grasp of the economics of the situation. He went on to identify a list of supplies, including Texan steers and other food, tobacco, wagons, farm animals and tools, a saw mill and frame houses like those of the white people. He considered it the least the commissioners could do if they wanted to make white men of his people. He concluded by justifying his demands.

"Maybe you white people think I ask too much from the Government, but I think those hills extend clear to the sky—maybe they go above the sky and that is the reason I ask for so much...."

Other chiefs echoed his demands, but they proved far too excessive for the commission to meet and so there was

no sale of the Black Hills. Events would force the matter.
After the Sioux defeated Custer at the Battle of the Little
Bighorn in 1876, the government created a new commission, with the purpose of issuing an ultimatum—no more
rations or annuities unless the Sioux gave up the Black
Hills. Red Cloud was among the Native delegation that
agreed to the demand, although he later claimed he did
not understand that was what he had done. It's possible he
was being honest because the commissioners were not
interested in explaining the finer points of their demands.
They didn't need to because the nation was in a fighting,
not a talking, mood.

In the years that followed, Red Cloud continued to
demonstrate that he meant it when he declared that he
was a friend of the president. In 1877, he agreed to
search for Crazy Horse and bring him onto the reservation, which he did successfully—Crazy Horse came willingly. Perhaps Red Cloud was also motivated in this
enterprise by the hope that he might have his chieftainship returned. General Crook had taken it from him in
late 1876, when Red Cloud refused to relocate or allow
his people to give up their weapons after the "renegotia-
tion" of the Fort Laramie Treaty. Despite Crook's action,
the Oglala continued to look upon Red Cloud as their
chief. When authorities killed Crazy Horse in September
1877, Red Cloud advised calm among his people. It was
an act that allowed him to reassume his position as chief
in the eyes of the government.

In late 1878, after another meeting with the president in
Washington, Red Cloud moved his people north to the
reservation at Pine Ridge, which would serve as his home
for the rest of his life. He didn't want to go there, but it was
clear that his choices no longer included resisting the
demands of the government. His people desperately needed

supplies, and it was the chief's responsibility to see that these were provided. Because the supplies would not be delivered to the old Red Cloud Agency on the White River, the relocation to Pine Ridge Agency was necessary. All was not tranquil at the new location, however, because Red Cloud clashed with the Indian agent, Dr. Valentine McGillycuddy. (Indian agents were government representatives who wielded considerable power on the reservations.) Like most agents, McGillycuddy was intent on replacing Native culture with that of the white man. This meant religion, education (both of which Red Cloud accepted) but, most of all, farming and the ethics of individual ownership and responsibility that went along with it. Red Cloud objected to these latter points.

"Father, the Great Mystery did not make us to work. He made us to hunt and fish. He gave us great prairies and hills and covered them with buffalo, deer and antelope. He filled rivers and streams with fish. The white man can work if he wants to, but the Great Mystery did not make us to work," he asserted. "The white man owes us a living for the lands he has taken from us."

When officials in Washington ignored Red Cloud's requests to have McGillycuddy replaced, the Oglala chief threatened to kill him. Nothing came of the threat, but everyone at the Pine Ridge Reservation was on edge through 1882. To relieve the tension, the government investigated the mounting claims against McGillycuddy. It was discovered that he was funneling money earmarked for the Oglala into his own pockets. The report was not acted on, however, because the Indian Bureau decided that it was more important that reservation Natives learn to respect and obey the Indian agent rather than question his authority.

Red Cloud refused to let the matter rest. In 1885, he heard there was a new president elected and, after counciling

with his headmen, he again went to Washington. He spoke
to President Cleveland as an equal, one chief to another.

"My people have been treated very bad. Our agent is
a bad man," asserted Red Cloud. "He steals from us, abuses
us and has sent all the good white men out of the country
and put bad men in their places. I want a new agent."

McGillycuddy was called to Washington. Despite the
recent investigation, the government was not convinced
that he had improperly administered the reserve. However,
it was sensitive to increasing criticism from the public that
the Natives were being poorly treated. And there remained
the lingering fear that Red Cloud might well return to the
warpath. McGillycuddy was replaced. Perhaps his victory
on this matter, which further cemented his position as
leader among the Oglala, persuaded Red Cloud to more
actively support government policy with regards to the
Sioux. In 1889 he signed the Sioux Bill, which divided and
reduced the size of the Great Sioux Reservation, declaring
that it was in the best interest of his people—money
accrued from the sale of the lands was to go into a Native
trust fund. He did, however, voice concerns that the government had not met previous treaty obligations.

There were more troubles with the coming of the new
decade. In 1890 the Ghost Dance, a new religious ceremony, arrived from the West. Advocates of the dance suggested that it would facilitate the emergence of a time and
place with no whites, only Natives, including the dead, living off a bountiful land as they once did. Initially, Red
Cloud was ambivalent about the dance. He held deep
respect for Native ways and only advanced age had forced
him to give up participating in the Sun Dance. However,
he had become a proponent of Catholicism (although he
never converted), and he was also concerned that the Ghost
Dance might foment violence. Although his health had

failed in recent years, Red Cloud used his influence to persuade his people to reject the dance. His position did not
go unnoticed by his enemies.

American officials were opposed to the Ghost Dance
because it gave the Natives a reason to gather in large
numbers and to reinvigorate their cultures. At best this
meant passive resistance to the government's plan to assimilate the Natives to white ways; at worst it meant
ongoing encounters with Natives on the warpath. Acting
on false rumors that Sitting Bull would participate in
a great Ghost Dance ceremony, General Nelson Miles
issued orders for his arrest. Sitting Bull was killed in the
arrest attempt. Then the army set out to arrest Big Foot,
a Miniconjou Sioux chief, who was also an alleged proponent of the Ghost Dance. He escaped, but he was arrested
within months. In December, some 350 of his exhausted
band were ordered to disarm and return to their reservation. While camped at Wounded Knee Creek, a medicine
man named Yellow Bird began to chant, dance and
implore the warriors not to give up their weapons. A shot
was fired. When the rifles finally fell silent, 150 Sioux were
dead and another 50 wounded. The Seventh Cavalry,
which had failed so miserably at the Battle of the Little
Bighorn, lost 29 men and suffered another 33 injuries.

A Brulé band was camped near the scene of the battle,
and when they heard the gunshots, they painted for war and
rode to investigate. They arrived too late to be of assistance.
Led by Two Strike, who was no ally of the whites, the band
fled north to join thousands of other Sioux. Along the way,
Two Strike captured Red Cloud, whom he resented because
of his efforts to make peace with the whites. Red Cloud was
caught between desperate, hostile Sioux and a determined
army. He believed his safety was best assured if he escaped
the Brulé camp. On a stormy January night, his daughter led

Red Cloud, taken while in his 60s, holding a sacred pipe with a red catlinite bowl and an ash or sumac wooden stem.

the ailing and now blind chief through a heavy snow-storm to a nearby agency. The Sioux eventually surren-dered, with assurances that they would be allowed to send a delegation to Washington to discuss their treat-ment. Red Cloud did not accompany them, for he had lost too much support.

Red Cloud had aspired to leadership and had reached a height that few Sioux ever had, but he was never again to enjoy that lofty position. He continued to take part in council occasionally and he traveled one final time to Washington in 1897. No one listened to what he had to say.

In July 1903, he formally abdicated his chieftainship in favor of his son Jack, but it meant nothing because neither the Sioux nor the government recognized it. During the ceremony, Red Cloud gave his farewell address to his people. It was a moving speech, somewhat more reflective than his orations of old, but filled with the same fighting spirit.

> *I was born a Lakota (Sioux) and I shall die a Lakota! Before the white man came to our country, the Lakota were a free people. They made their own laws and governed themselves as it seemed good to them. The priests and ministers tell us that we lived wickedly when we lived before the white man came among us. Whose fault was this? We lived right as we were taught was right! Shall we be punished for this? I am not sure that what these people tell me is true.*
>
> *As a child I was taught the Taku Wakan were powerful beings who could do strange things. This was taught me by the wise men and the shamans. They taught me that I could gain their favor by being kind to my people and brave before my enemies; by telling the truth and living straight; by fighting for my people and their hunting grounds.*
>
> *When the Lakota believed these things they were happy and they died satisfied. What more than this can that which the white man offer us give?*

Apparently, the whites could give nothing that matched the life his people had once enjoyed. He grew old with his wife Pretty Owl in the two-story frame house the government had provided for him at Pine Ridge. Red Cloud died of natural causes on December 10, 1909. He was buried in a Catholic cemetery with the full rites of that religion.

CHAPTER FIVE

Sequoyah

Cherokee, 1763–1843

JUST SOUTH OF THE TENNESSEE RIVER in the shadow of the Appalachian Mountains rested the Cherokee village of Willstown. It was populated mostly by refugees, Cherokees who had fled their settlements along the Little Tennessee River during the conflicts with the Americans a generation before in the 1770s and 1780s. A spring day some 40 years later found one of the village's longtime residents anxious to leave. His name was Sequoyah and he didn't want to travel far, just far enough to be alone. He slipped into the nearby woods and, in an isolated location, built a small cabin. There he spent many days in seclusion. Some saw Sequoyah's behavior as odd because Cherokees weren't so inclined to solitude. But Sequoyah was an unusual man. He was a thinker and he needed the peace and quiet so that he could work on a project that had dominated his thoughts for many years. He wanted to unlock the mystery of the white man's talking leaves and to share its power with his own people.

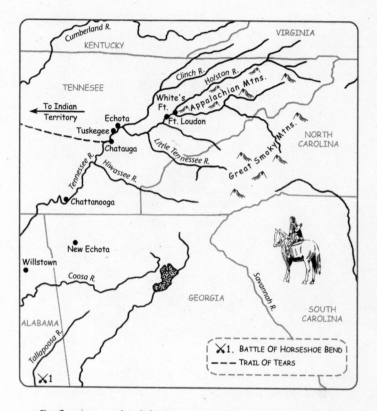

Reflecting on his life, Sequoyah sometimes thought that his path had been directed to this place long before. He could not remember a time when he was not drawing. As a child, he used whatever material he could find to scratch out representations of the world around him. His mother, Wuhteh, often found bark or flat stones that Sequoyah had marked with a piece of charred wood or a knife. Sometimes soft ground and a long stick were enough to occupy him for a morning. In his 20s he became a blacksmith for a similar reason. It was not until he was in his 30s that he realized his creativity might be turned to a greater purpose. The idea first came to him around 1800. Sequoyah remembered the day well; it was one not easily forgotten.

Sequoyah with his syllabary in a portrait by Robert Lindneux.
President James Monroe gave him the medal shown.

"Look!" said Sequoyah's friend. He held a strange object before him. It was not much bigger than an open hand and perhaps as thick as a stout piece of ash. He laid it on the ground and, like the wings of a bird in flight, it opened. Inside were many thin parts, each covered with dark markings.

"It was taken from the white prisoner," said the friend.

"It is the talking leaves," observed Sequoyah. "I have seen them before, though never so many together. The white men use it to communicate over distances and between people," he added.

Sequoyah's friend held the book at arm's length and began to speak words that Sequoyah knew to be a magical incantation.

"What are you doing?" asked Sequoyah.

"I want to know what the talking leaves say. I am trying to make them speak," he replied.

"The white men are not witches, and the talking leaves are not the work of magic," chuckled Sequoyah. "They were invented by the white men and are no more mysterious than their rifles and knifes. A Cherokee could do the same."

"Ha," laughed his companion. "If that is so, then do it."

Sequoyah traced figures on the ground before him.

"What do you see?"

"A hunter, an eye, a deer and mountains."

"What does it mean?"

His friend was silent for a moment.

"A hunter sees a deer in the mountains!"

"The talking leaves are no more than that."

In the years that had passed since that encounter, Sequoyah had often thought of the talking leaves. What a thing it would be if the Cherokee had their own talking leaves! They could write their stories, record their events, talk over great distances and even talk to their children's children all in the words of their own language! They would not have to depend on the white man's invention and not have to lose their own language in the process. But Sequoyah knew that the talking leaves were more than simple pictures. Eventually he had abandoned the idea of illustrations to represent words. There were simply too many things to draw, and pictures could only represent the thing itself; they were not well suited to reveal anything about it. It was one thing to draw a deer and a mountain, but how could he draw "the deer was seen yesterday" or "I will hunt for the deer when I have finished repairing my bow"?

No matter what he tried, Sequoyah could find no way for pictures to qualify statements, no way to express "graceful" or "favorite" or any of a thousand other words. Besides, it required skill to draw such things effectively, and he knew that few shared his talent.

As Sequoyah sat in his cabin, he picked up a book given to him by a teacher at the nearby mission school at Spring Place. While Sequoyah was not an advocate of white education for Cherokee children (he opposed most white influences on his people), he had visited the school several times. On each occasion, he sat at the back of the classroom, thumbing through the books full of talking leaves. Aware of his interest, the teacher had given him a copy of a spelling text. Sequoyah practiced drawing the markings. It was not difficult and he mastered them quickly. But as he flipped through the book, he knew that the white man's markings would not work well with the Cherokee language because their markings made far too many words.

He put the book down and, with a sigh, took out his pipe and filled the bowl. He lit it and took a few rapid drags. Through the small cloud of rising smoke, he looked to the scattered piles of pages he had written on and the stacks of bark he used when he had no blank paper, which was often. Each was covered with symbols, a new approach he'd adopted. The symbols didn't look like anything but were meant to represent ideas. He had invented over a thousand such symbols, so many that he often forgot what they meant when he studied them. And there still weren't enough to express every object and idea. While talking to others, he heard words and thoughts that he had not yet considered and for which he had no symbol. Suddenly, in the midst of a conversation, he would be reflecting on an appropriate representation for a new word, ignoring the speaker. People noticed that he was ignoring other things as well: his family, his work and his responsibilities. Sequoyah was behaving as he had when he used to drink. He seemed to be in another world, and his friends were worried.

Among those concerned was his wife, Sally Benge. She did not need others to tell her that Sequoyah was no longer working in his smithy, that their farm was overrun with weeds and briars or that their children wondered what occupied their father. But she heard people talk about such things. She also heard more troubling rumors. Some suggested that Sequoyah's suspicious behavior, the long periods he spent alone in the forest, indicated that he was a witch. It was a serious charge. The Cherokee were strong believers in magic. Those who used their power for good were respected because they helped to heal others and protect them from enemies. But witches used their powers for evil and could cause others to act in ways the witches wanted. In seclusion they committed monstrous acts that might include killing and cannibalism. Witches were to be avoided and, if they were caught, death was the only appropriate punishment.

Sally asked Sequoyah's friends to go and speak with her husband about his behavior, but their efforts were to no avail. Sequoyah always turned back to his work, ignoring what his friends had to say. Sally was frustrated. She didn't know why her husband acted as he did. The man Sequoyah had become was not the one she had married. Sally thought of leaving him. It was an easy enough matter; divorce was not frowned upon among the Cherokee. She decided against that, but she was determined not to continue living her life in this way.

Each day Sally grew to hate the place where Sequoyah disappeared to more and more. The solitary cabin in the woods began to consume her thoughts. Then a solution came to her. She would burn the cabin down! With nowhere to go and with his precious markings destroyed, Sequoyah would see what a fool he had been. Sally made plans with her friends. They waited for her signal that Sequoyah was not in the cabin and then they set fire to it. Sequoyah saw the smoke and he hurried towards it, only to discover that the fire had already devoured most of his cabin.

Years of work turned to ashes before his eyes. Strangely, Sequoyah was not upset. Instead, the flames brought a measure of relief. He had long sensed that symbols could never be the Cherokee's talking leaves. They were too numerous, too complicated. It was as if a great weight had been lifted from his shoulders.

Sequoyah was granted a fresh start and he was determined that it would be put to good use. Had anyone been nearby, they would have heard him state simply, "Well, now I must do it again."

~~~~

Wuhteh stepped from the long, wood-framed, clay-walled dwelling that was her summer home. As always, her eyes were drawn to the Cherokee Hills (Great Smoky Mountains) to the east. She often wondered about what lay hidden beneath the bluish mist that blanketed the mountain peaks. She suspected that such a wonderful place must surely be home to powerful spirits. The thought was fleeting, however, for there was work to be done. She called to her son.

"Sequoyah! Come, we go to the fields."

The young boy, not yet 10, was seated in the shade behind the nearby smaller, circular sweathouse that also served as their winter home. He was lost in the drawing that was slowly taking form on the piece of bark that rested in his lap. He dipped his finger into the bowl of crushed raspberries that lay on the ground beside him. He withdrew the finger and placed it on the bark, using his fingernail to add delicate features to a bird's wing.

"Sequoyah!"

He heard this time and jumped with a start, tipping the bowl over. He held on to the piece of bark, however, and scampered out from behind the sweathouse.

"Here I am, mother," he answered. "Look at what I've drawn."

"A bird!" she smiled, looking at the bark. "I don't know that I've seen a prettier one in the trees. And that is such a nice shade of red; though I see from your face that all the juice did not make it to the bark!"

Sequoyah laughed and wiped the berry juice from his lips. He knew the drawing wasn't that good, but he appreciated his mother's words. A smile from Wuhteh meant the world to Sequoyah. The two were close. He had no siblings and his father, who was believed to be either Nathaniel Gist (a Virginia soldier) or George Gist (a Dutch trader), had abandoned them soon after his birth in the early 1760s.* While the absence of a father was probably painful for Sequoyah, its impact upon his upbringing was minimal. Among the Cherokee, children belonged to their mother's family, so a boy's maternal uncles had a greater role in raising him than did his father. Wuhteh belonged to the Paint clan, one of seven Cherokee clans, and her brothers and brothers-in-law—Doublehead, John Jolly, Old Tassel, Pumpkin Boy and Tahlonteskee—were among the most important of the local Cherokee.

---

* The year of Sequoyah's birth is uncertain. It is usually given as either 1763 or 1773. This biography uses 1763.

"We must go to the fields and tend to the crops,"
Wuhteh repeated.

Farming was an important part of the Cherokee economy and it was the women's domain. Everyone seeded
and harvested, but while men hunted, traded and constructed buildings, women tended the fields. Children
might lend a hand, but all knew farming to be the
women's responsibility. They grew pumpkins, beans, sun-
flowers, tobacco and, most importantly, corn. On this
occasion, Wuhteh was particularly interested in checking
on the corn. It was late September, and the Green Corn
Ceremony, one of the most important of the annual
Cherokee celebrations, was rapidly approaching.

As they walked along the carefully laid out paths that
crisscrossed the small village of Tuskegee, Wuhteh was
careful not to move too quickly. One of Sequoyah's legs
was weak and misshapen, and she did not want to tire
him.* The condition presented certain limitations, but
even at a young age Sequoyah was determined not to surrender to them. He accepted the fact that he could not
run, but otherwise life was mostly normal. He helped his
mother plow the fields, and already his uncles Doublehead

---

* Sequoyah's condition is the subject of debate and uncertainty. One
translation of his name is "Pig's Foot" suggesting that the affliction may
have been with him since birth. Some argue that he was injured in
childhood, but others point out that Sequoyah, in his 20s, served as one
of the Cherokee warriors under Andrew Jackson. His service might suggest an accident later in life. However, it has been also noted that the
Cherokee were mounted warriors, thereby rendering Sequoyah's lameness less relevant. Still others suggest that his condition was the result of
a white man's disease, perhaps polio. In an 1845 biography, the *Cherokee
Advocate* described his lameness as a "hydroarthric trouble of the knee
joint, commonly called 'white swelling.'" Most agree that Sequoyah had
a bad leg in his childhood, a position accepted in this biography.

and Pumpkin Boy, both successful warriors, were teaching him hunting skills.

Wuhteh's house was on the outskirts of Tuskegee, so the pair had to walk through the community to reach the fields. They passed by the village grain storehouse and adjacent small community gardens that served as sources of ready food for visitors and the needy. The storehouse was large, but it was dwarfed by the great circular town house farther down the path. The town house was the place where matters important to the community were discussed, and it was large enough to accommodate all the villagers. Women had a voice in governing the community, however, the elders and the village's two chiefs made most decisions. The White Chief (sometimes called the Most Beloved Man or, occasionally, the Most Beloved Woman) gave advice on farming, lawmaking and disputes, and the Red Chief gave counsel in matters of war. Nevertheless, consensus was always important in decision-making so, as a result, the chiefs' powers were limited. Near the town house was a large field that was used for feasts, ceremonies and celebrations. After passing several dwellings like their own, Wuhteh and Sequoyah finally found themselves on the path that led to the fields.

The short walk to the fields took them along a stretch of the Little Tennessee River. They passed through a shady stand of chestnut trees, and when they emerged from its shelter they could see the tall corn in the distance.

"It won't be long now, will it mother?" asked Sequoyah.

Wuhteh knew that he was asking about the Green Corn Ceremony because the boy had spoken of little else during the past few days.

"The corn is nearly ripe," she replied. "Any day now, the messenger will arrive with news of it."

No one was allowed to eat the growing corn before the ceremony. What had been stored had been long since eaten or had lost much of its flavor so anticipation of the harvest was great.

When they arrived at the field, Wuhteh sat down near the river. She always took a break before starting the work to allow Sequoyah a chance to rest. Sequoyah sat next to her.

"Mother, tell me the story of Corn-Mother."

As with most Native cultures, stories were the mainstay of Cherokee life. They reminded everyone that the past was alive in the present. Usually the old men of the village told the stories, but Wuhteh enjoyed telling them as much as Sequoyah loved listening to them. She had told him of Corn-Mother before, but a Cherokee could not hear the story of the origin of corn too many times.

"There was once a grandmother who had two grandsons," began Wuhteh. "Those boys loved to hunt and they were good at it. One day, as they prepared bows and arrows for the day's hunt, their grandmother spoke to them.

"'I see you are going hunting. When you return we will have a delicious meal. I will cook the deer that you bring back and I will add to it something called corn. You will like it,' she assured them.

"The young men did not know what this corn was. They had never even heard the word before. While the men hunted, they wondered what it could be. When they returned with the venison, they were eager to eat grandmother's new food. They entered the lodge and saw the pot bubbling over the fire pit. They looked into it and saw the corn, although they did not know what it was.

"'That is corn,' said Grandmother.

"When the meat was cooked, they sat down and ate. The young men loved the corn and told their grandmother that she had prepared a wonderful meal. She smiled happily and told them they would eat it again the next day. As promised, when the pair returned from their hunt the next evening, the corn was cooked and waiting for them.

"'Truly, Grandmother,' said one of the grandsons, 'this is the best meal I have ever had.' His brother nodded in agreement.

"'It is good to hear you say so,' she answered, her face alight with pleasure. 'We will eat it again.'

"The next day the brothers prepared for their hunt. But they found it difficult to concentrate on what they were doing. They could think only of the corn.

"'Where does Grandmother get this corn?' asked one of them.

"The other shook his head. 'I do not know. Perhaps if one of us watched while she prepared to cook, we might discover her secret.'

"They agreed and so one of them hid behind the smokehouse. Soon Grandmother came out of the lodge carrying a large tray. She entered the smokehouse. The young man found a peephole in the building and looked in. His grandmother placed the tray under her feet. Then she hit herself on her ribs," said Wuhteh, as she tapped her own sides. "With each strike, corn fell from every part of her body. She continued until the tray was full. Then she returned to her house and began to cook the corn.

"The young man ran to tell his brother what he had seen. After he had told his story, both were disgusted. The pair agreed that they would not eat corn again. Grandmother was disappointed to find that her grandsons left their corn untouched at the evening meal.

"'What's wrong? There is plenty of food. Don't you like me?' she asked.

"'Of course, Grandmother,' replied one of the boys. 'We are just tired.'

"'I think that you don't like me. Or perhaps you don't eat because you learned something somewhere.'

"Grandmother knew they had discovered her secret," explained Wuhteh, "and that very night she fell ill. She went to her bed and called her grandsons to her side.

"'I am going to die,' said Grandmother. 'Listen carefully to what I say. When you bury me, build a large fence around me. Something will grow up from the grave. It will be tall and have a flower at the top. On the lower part will be tassels and inside them will be ears of corn covered with corn silk. Leave the ears alone and take care of the plant,' she directed. 'When the ears are dry and white with the shuck dry and crisp and the silk dark brown, you will harvest the corn.'

"'Take the kernels off the cob and store them. In the spring plant the kernels two apiece in small holes. You will grow many more ears of corn. You can roast it, boil it or grind it into meal.'

"'I will be the Corn-Mother,' she revealed, 'and corn will have its origin in me.'

"The brothers did as they were told and, in the fall, they gathered the few ears from the single plant that grew from their grandmother's grave. Later that year one of the brothers took a wife. When he took her to his home, he explained that they would plant the corn. They hoed a great field and planted the kernels. They harvested plenty of corn. Everybody in the world soon had some. The corn had its beginning in a human being, a woman, and the young couple had much to eat," concluded Wuhteh.

"Do you think the grandson should have spied on his grandmother?" asked Sequoyah.

Always questions, always curious, thought Wuhteh.

"Some things not meant to be shared," she replied. "Grandmother died because of what her grandson did. But she was not bitter. She had used her power to help the Cherokee. When there is corn and land on which to grow it, there is great happiness," she reflected. "All prosper in such a place."

And it was true; the Cherokee had long prospered. While they had migrated from the upper Ohio Valley, by Sequoyah's time they had long called the mountains and valleys of the southern Appalachian Mountains home. They called them-selves *Ani-Yun'wiya*, meaning "principal people." The word "Cherokee" is either a Choctaw word, meaning "people of the caves" or a Creek word, meaning "people of different speech." In the early 1700s, they were the largest southeast-ern Native tribe. There were as many as 20,000 Cherokee who lived in 60 villages and controlled 40,000 square miles of territory in the present-day states of North and South Carolina, Virginia, Tennessee, Georgia, Kentucky and Alabama. However, a decimating smallpox epidemic in the 1740s reduced their numbers by thousands.

Most Cherokee villages were located on rivers and streams where adjacent fertile plains could be used for farming. Sequoyah's village of Tuskegee was one such vil-lage, located a few miles west of the main Cherokee town of Echota (in present-day southeastern Tennessee). Perhaps Tuskegee was an average-sized village of about 400 Cherokee. It may well have consisted of more than one set-tlement because the term village was used to indicate a political body. While they shared cultural and economic bonds, Cherokee villages were independent. Historically, there was no broad decision-making body that could direct or coordinate the action of all Cherokee. For many genera-tions, tribal members were well served by local bodies who discussed and resolved matters in the town house.

However, traditional ways began to change in the mid-18th century, when white incursion demanded a more united response from the Cherokee. Initial contact with the white man brought no hint of the approaching radical changes to Cherokee life. From the early 1600s they traded with the colonists of the coastal British colonies. The trade benefited the Cherokee because the tools and implements they acquired eased many of their labor-intensive activities. By the end of the century, however, Cherokee-white relations soured. Land-hungry settlers were launching unprovoked attacks against Cherokee villages, and traders were capturing individual Cherokee to sell as slaves in the West Indies. Some Cherokee complained formally to Governor Moore of South Carolina, but little came of it. In the face of colonial disinterest, the Cherokee concluded that the most effective way to deal with the white settlers was to link the villages in a more formal confederacy, allowing for unified action. A tribal council similar to the model of the village council was created, and in the 1720s, the Cherokee chose a principal chief to represent them all.

Throughout the mid-century, the frontier violence of the French and Indian War provided the setting for life west of the Appalachian Mountains. The Cherokee allied with the British during the lengthy war, but that relationship changed in 1760 when a party of Virginians attacked a band of Cherokee. The Virginians justified their actions by claiming that the Natives were stealing their horses. The tribal council, increasingly dominated by warriors who were versed in the ways of warfare and were qualified to address it, decided to attack white settlements. Led by Chief Oconostota, designated the principal Cherokee war chief, the Cherokee War lasted two years, until 1762. Although they enjoyed some success, including the capture of Fort Loudon in the Great Valley of the Appalachians, the Cherokee eventually surrendered. They were forced to cede large tracts of traditional Cherokee eastern and northern lands and to pledge their support to the British yet again. As a result, there was peace until the outbreak of the American Revolution.

Sequoyah was a child during this peaceful interlude. He knew little of war and he enjoyed many peaceful days with his mother tending the crops, just as they did on this day. When the sun approached the western horizon, their work completed, the pair returned to their lodge. A few days later a messenger from the town council appeared to inform his mother that it was time to gather in the village to celebrate the Green Corn Ceremony. As was tradition, Wuhteh extinguished the fire in the lodge before she and Sequoyah hurried to the field that was used for celebrations. All of the villagers came as well as a few visitors. Everyone participated in the ceremony.

Once all were together, they made their way to the river. Everyone stepped into the water seven times, after which ritual markings were scratched on their bodies. Sequoyah tried hard not to wince as his uncle dragged a sharp bone tip along his skin, leaving thin trails of blood in its wake. When everyone was marked, they drank the medicine that was to protect them from the illness believed to be associated with eating green corn. Finally, a shaman sacrificed seven ears of green corn in a sacred fire burning in the town house. As he did this, he offered prayers to speed the growth of the corn and to prevent illness. These rituals served to purify the Cherokee and, once completed, the dancing, singing and feasting began.

The men initiated the dancing, and Sequoyah watched as some 20 of them shuffled in a circle. At intervals they fired their rifles in succession to imitate thunder. At the end of the morning they stopped and ate. In the afternoon the

women danced to the rhythm of a drum. As they made
their way around the dance ground, they sang. Later in the
day the men and women shared the dance ground,
although they performed separately. When the dancing was
finished, there was a feast. Nightfall saw more dancing and
feasting, as well as storytelling and merrymaking.

Wuhteh and Sequoyah returned to their home early the
next morning exhausted but content and carrying a torch
lit by the sacred communal fire in the town house. It would
be used to ignite the fire in their own dwelling, an important symbol of renewal. Even at his young age, Sequoyah
sensed that the sharing of the fire was important. The sharing of the fire, the ceremony as a whole, symbolized a col-
lective commitment to the important values of harmony,
generosity and cooperation that linked the Cherokee.

With the completion of the Green Corn Ceremony, the
more mundane rhythms of life reasserted themselves.
Sequoyah practiced the hunting skills that his uncle taught
him. The blowgun was especially popular among young
Cherokee boys. Sequoyah quickly mastered the technique
of fashioning a blowgun from a hollow reed and trimming
twigs to use as darts. Spurred on by the men and women in
the community, who always praised those who returned
with game, the boys spent long hours in the forest honing
their skills with the simple but effective instrument. Pots
often filled with squirrels and rabbits were the measure of
their success.

Occasionally Sequoyah's uncle Pumpkin Boy joined him
on his journeys into the woods. The trained senses of the
older man gave a more purposeful direction to Sequoyah's
education; he learned to listen to the birds, to see the signs of
the animals and to know their ways. While Pumpkin Boy
might point out such things, it was up to Sequoyah to master
an understanding of them. He needed little encouragement

to go into the forest alone because Sequoyah enjoyed the solitude. Alone, he could devote his attention to looking, listening and reflecting. Eventually such habits became second nature, as they did for most Cherokee.

Sequoyah also kept busy tending the animals that his mother raised. Raising domestic farm animals was a relatively new practice in Cherokee villages, one likely copied from the white settlers. Some Cherokee, particularly young warriors, were opposed to the animals for that very reason. They wanted to distance themselves from the doings of the white man, especially after the Cherokee War. But since women mostly raised the animals, the men didn't interfere too much, although few ever accepted cattle, "the white man's deer" as the Cherokee called them. Wuhteh had some milk cows as well as pigs and chickens and a small herd of wild horses. The animals fed Wuhteh's family and community and were also used for trade with the increasing number of whites in the region. Wuhteh appreciated Sequoyah's help with the care of the animals, especially when he turned his ingenuity to his work. On one occasion, he surprised his mother by building a shelter over the river, so that stored milk and cream could be kept cool.

One important experience of Cherokee youth that Sequoyah missed out on was *ahnehjah*, the ball play. Similar to lacrosse, ball play participants used three-foot long hickory sticks with small pouches on the ends to throw a deerskin-covered ball through a goal. But the ball play was more than a simple game. The skilled athletes who were chosen to participate trained and fasted for lengthy periods before a match, and endured hundreds of bloody ritual scratches. That was but small suffering compared to the pain and sacrifice that came with actually playing the game. Competitors fought with the determination of warriors. As contests were usually held between villages, great honor was at stake and enthusiastic onlookers made large wagers on the outcomes. Even prayers were deemed appropriate for such occasions.

Before each game the players spoke in unison: "Grant me such strength in the contest that my enemy may be of no weight in my hands, that I may be able to toss him into the air or dash him to the earth."

Although he longed to join in the ball play, Sequoyah's bad leg kept him from participating. He knew that if he were to become a hero like those who excelled in the game, he would have to find another path.

But it would not be found in Tuskegee. In 1763 the French and Indian War ended with the Treaty of Paris and Britain triumphant. By year's end, the governors of Virginia, Georgia, North Carolina and South Carolina made peace treaties with the southeastern Native tribes. Peace triggered dramatic changes for the Natives. No longer concerned about frontier violence, once-hesitant settlers from the coastal colonies migrated inland in increasing numbers. Despite a 1763 royal proclamation that forbade the purchase of Native lands west of the watershed of the Atlantic Ocean, the Cherokee was one of several tribes that found it necessary to cede such lands to the pressing immigrants. It seemed the best option. Once the settlers had moved on to traditional Native lands, it would be difficult to remove them. Treaties brought some financial return and security to the Natives, and they also helped avoid conflict. The Cherokee, however, did not yield the land on which they had settled, and they tried to keep a buffer between themselves and the newcomers. Nevertheless, by 1775, they had sold most of their traditional homelands and their hunting territory north of the Cumberland River and east of the Savannah River.

Not all the Cherokee supported land cession, especially many of the warriors. However, they were preoccupied with ongoing conflicts with other Native tribes. In the late 1760s, fighting was renewed with the Iroquois confederacy to the north. Theirs was a long-standing conflict that reached back a century. Around 1770 it was finally brought to a close. A few years later an Iroquois peace delegation arrived at Echota to strengthen the bonds of peace. Sequoyah was one of many Cherokee who gathered in the great town house for the meeting. He watched with interest as the Iroquois representative gave the village chief, his uncle Old Tassel, a wampum belt as a symbol of friendship. He listened as the meaning of the patterns of shells on the belt was explained. The experience might have been his first exposure to an unspoken form of Native communication. Perhaps it was at that moment that the seeds of his later work were first sown.

Treaty with the Iroquois, however, did not mean peace for the Cherokee. In the early 1770s the Cherokee were at war with the Chickasaws and other western tribes. Intertribal hostility was brought mostly to a close with the outbreak of the American Revolution in 1775. Initially, the Cherokee were neutral during that dispute, but their impartiality did not last. Hoping that their neutrality might be looked upon favorably by the colonists, they pressured American officials to repudiate some of the more recent land sales. Their request was refused. Not long after the Cherokee received the reply, a delegation of the Iroquois confederacy visited Echota. It was led by the Shawnee chief Cornstalk, an opponent of white incursion. They came to encourage the Cherokee to join with them and their British allies against the colonists. Persuaded by British promises that assured protection against white expansion and gifts of British arms and supplies, the Cherokee agreed. By July 1776, 600 warriors were raiding

Tennessee settlements north to the Cumberland River. The southern colonies responded in force by rapidly organizing companies of frontier militia. In August 1776, 2000 men under the command of Colonel William Christian joined with several hundred men from North Carolina and made for the Cherokee settlements along the Little Tennessee River.

Wuhteh and Sequoyah were in the fields on a platform banging pans to scare away birds intent on eating the young corn. Above the clanging they could hear the shouts of an approaching runner before they could see him.

"Hurry! Back to the village and collect your belongings! The soldiers approach!"

Wuhteh was surprised. She had known for many weeks that the white soldiers were attacking Cherokee towns in the region. That much had been revealed by village leaders at an important meeting in the town house. She thought, however, that they had made peace. She was correct. Cherokee headmen had met with Colonel Christian and appealed for peace. They had no alternative. Most of the warriors were engaged in distant battles, and the villages were left unprotected and easily razed by the soldiers. Christian agreed to cease hostilities under certain conditions, including the cession of five million acres of land and that the Cherokee abandon claims to disputed territory occupied by Tennessee settlers. However, he was determined to attack Tuskegee because the community had tortured, burned and killed a young boy taken from the white settlement of Chatauga. The Cherokee justified those actions because they had lost lives in the attack on Chatauga. Cherokee law maintained that a loss of life must be repaid with the life of the killer or one of his people.

No one wanted to abandon Tuskegee, but everyone was aware of the fate that awaited the reluctant. Unsuccessful warriors faced death and scalping. Women and children left alive would be sold as slaves. Wuhteh and Sequoyah hurried back to their lodge, took what they could gather quickly and slipped into the forest. The sweat on their bodies was just evaporating in the cool shadow of the trees when they heard the gunfire of the approaching soldiers. Afraid, the pair pushed deeper into the forest. They were sitting and resting when Sequoyah pointed to a small patch of sky visible through the tangled branches of trees.

"Look, mother!"

"Smoke. I could smell it."

"But why are the clouds of gray so great? Even the largest fire in the town house paints only a thin band across the sky."

"There is much smoke because the fire is large. They have set the crops afire, Sequoyah," she sighed.

The crops! Sequoyah found it difficult to believe that they could do such a thing.

"But it is our food."

"That is why they burn it."

Sequoyah thought for a moment.

"There will be no Green Corn Ceremony this year," he stated.

"Many things will be different this year," agreed his mother.

The next morning Sequoyah learned that his mother was right. They returned to their village only to find it destroyed. What wasn't burned had been trampled by the animals, which had been stampeded. Few animals remained, and most of those that did were carcasses. Stunned villagers gathered at the remnants of the town house. All agreed that it was necessary to relocate. Some wanted to move as far away from the white settlers as possible, where they might live in peace. Others, including Sequoyah's uncles Doublehead and Tahlonteskee, wanted to remain nearby and join with other

tribes, particularly the Chickamauga, to fight the soldiers.
Wuhteh shared the view of the majority who wanted
peace. Before year's end, Sequoyah found himself in the
Cherokee village of Willstown north of the Coosa River,
near the western border of traditional Cherokee territory
(in present-day Alabama).

Sequoyah and Wuhteh were able to piece their lives
back together in Willstown. It was far from the advancing
edge of white settlement, so mother and son turned the
distance to their advantage by opening a trading establishment. The two had sometimes traded in Tuskegee, but the
business was a more important part of their livelihood in
Willstown. The white man's supplies—from rifles to hoes
to cloth—were in high demand by the Cherokee, and the
operation enjoyed a modest success. Much of the work fell
on Sequoyah's shoulders and he became a skilled trader.

Sequoyah discovered that he was often among the first
to hear news brought by the hunters who usually stopped
to barter their furs upon first arriving in Willstown.
During the American Revolution, the news was rarely
good. In 1779, the pro-war faction of the Cherokee that
had remained in the north was dealt a major blow. When
reports indicated that 300 warriors were advancing on settlements in North Carolina, volunteer forces from that
colony launched a surprise attack on defenseless Native
villages. The Natives regrouped and built a new settlement
farther downstream. They continued to raid throughout
the duration of the revolution (usually supported and
encouraged by the British), but the need for braves to
defend the villages ensured that war parties were small in
number and that they caused little damage.

Perhaps what white settlers thought to be reduced violence was an indication that it was safe to resume migrat-
ing west. In the fall of 1782, Old Tassel of Echota, leader

of the pro-peace faction of the Cherokee, sent word to the governors of North Carolina and Virginia that the settlers were within a day's walk of Cherokee villages. He asked them to respect the agreed-upon boundary and have their people move, but nothing came of the request until 1785. In November of that year, the Cherokee signed the Treaty of Hopewell. No land was ceded, and borders were reaffirmed. The treaty made certain that the Natives recognized United States' sovereignty and it provided for the punishment of Natives and white men who broke the law. But it wasn't long before both sides were ignoring the treaty and the raiding of settlements was again commonplace.

Sequoyah heard of these developments, often before they were addressed in the town house. For the most part, the renewed raiding was of fleeting concern because it occurred far from Willstown. But events would take a pro-foundly personal turn in 1788.

Sequoyah was packing pelts for storage when a Cherokee hunter arrived to trade. Sequoyah walked to the packhorse burdened with furs.

"Thick pelts," he said as he pulled his fingers along one.

"Winter was cold in the hills," the hunter replied.

"You've come a long way to trade, brother," observed Sequoyah, who knew that the hills referred to were to the north, where he used to live.

"It is no longer safe to trade there. Even hunters face danger."

Sequoyah looked up from the furs.

"Soldiers attacked Echota," he explained. "Most fled, but Old Tassel remained. It is said that his dead body was found with the white flag of truce beside him."

Sequoyah's shoulders sagged. His uncle, the voice for peace among the Cherokee, was dead. Even the white settlers and officials condemned the murder because they recognized

Old Tassel's desire and efforts to maintain harmony on the
frontier. The Cherokee were infuriated, and the pro-war
faction used the opportunity to reassert itself. Sequoyah's
other uncles, Doublehead, Tahlonteskee and Pumpkin Boy,
joined with the Chickamaugans in an intense renewal of
raiding.

In 1791, the American government sought to put an
end to frontier violence. At White's Fort (Knoxville) on the
Holston River, President George Washington's representatives proposed "perpetual peace" between the new nation
and the Cherokee. The resulting Treaty of Holston recognized Cherokee boundary claims, prohibited the entry of
settlers onto Cherokee land and assured the Natives that
lawbreakers would be punished. Finally, government officials pledged to civilize the Cherokee, to teach them skills
considered necessary for their participation in the new
society.

All Cherokee did not agree to the treaty and some kept
on raiding. There was justification, even by an American
measuring stick. Settlers continued to squat on Cherokee
land. But in 1792, the resisting Cherokee were dealt a major
blow when the war chief Dragging Canoe died of an apparent heart attack. For nearly 20 years he had been one of the
most vocal supporters of armed resistance against the newcomers. In 1794, all opposition was finally crushed, when
soldiers marched on the Chickamaugan towns. The subsequent Treaty of Tellico Blockhouse made later that year
ended the long hostility between the Americans and the
Cherokee, although there remained a bitterness between
them and a division within the Cherokee ranks about the
desirability of peace.

In 1796 the government of the United States appointed
Benjamin Hawkins as Indian agent. It directed Hawkins to
ensure the civilization of the Cherokee. He was pleased

when he saw that the Natives were rapidly adapting to the new ways. They were farming and raising domestic animals, just as their white counterparts. Perhaps he might have been surprised to learn that the Cherokee had been farming for generations. Hawkins did promote new livelihoods, however, those that American officials considered important to Cherokee well being. Carpenters, blacksmiths and wheelwrights were brought into Willstown as instructors and that is how Sequoyah learned the skills of a blacksmith.

While Sequoyah's responsibilities had him forging metal items, such as hoes and bits for bridles, his interests drew him to silversmithing. The hills surrounding Willstown were rich with the metal, so he had a ready supply. Long and determined practice eventually made him more skilled than his instructor. Sequoyah discovered that his creations were in high demand and that a good living could be made fashioning jewelry and utensils. But silversmithing did present a problem. Once an item was sold, there was no way to prove that it was his. It was a matter of concern because, as an artist, he depended on word of mouth to attract customers. He wanted potential buyers who saw his silver work to know that it was his. And he was proud of his efforts. He wanted to be sure that there would be no doubt about what was his work.

But how could he ensure this? Perhaps it was a chance conversation with his friend Charles Hicks, a mixed-blood Cherokee who worked as an interpreter for the new Indian agent Return Meigs, that provided a solution. Hicks was educated in the ways of the talking leaves, as the Cherokee referred to the white man's writing. Hicks showed Sequoyah how to write both his Cherokee and English names (George Guess or Gist). Thereafter, Sequoyah marked his silver work with his name. But he did not find it quite satisfactory. Sequoyah didn't like using the white man's language, probably because he didn't really like the white man. Sequoyah particularly opposed the Moravian missionaries who had arrived as part of the United States' civilizing mission. He had no interest in the white language or their religion and in this he was not alone. His uncle Doublehead, who had emerged as one of the most important Cherokee chiefs, was also a staunch opponent. However, the Moravians had been invited by a consensus of the Cherokee tribal council, most of whom believed that the strength of the white man was linked in some way to their God.

Sequoyah's success as a silversmith and less so as a trader gave him a certain reputation, which was important because he was unable to distinguish himself on the warpath as was expected of young Cherokee men. And, while he wasn't wealthy, it was clear that he could support a family. In the early 1800s, he settled on Utiyu for his wife. A bridal price of horses and robes was agreed to, an arrangement likely made by one of Sequoyah's uncles. On the selected day, Sequoyah took the animals to Utiyu's lodge and staked one outside the entrance. When she untied the animal and led it to her family's herd, it indicated that she was prepared to take care of her suitor's belongings and that the proposal was accepted. While tradition dictated that the husband take up residence in his wife's community, Sequoyah and Utiyu remained at Willstown, perhaps because of Wuhteh's dependence upon Sequoyah. Wuhteh, however, did not come to know her daughter-in-law well, as some months after the marriage, Wuhteh died.

Sequoyah took his mother's death hard. Even as he participated in the prescribed rituals of mourning, few realized the depth of his grief. Reserve was expected and respected among the Cherokee, and Sequoyah kept his feelings to himself. Nevertheless, his pain surfaced in a most destructive way.

Sequoyah turned to alcohol, *nawohti* as the Cherokee called
it. As a trader, Sequoyah had easy access to *nawohti*. In his
mother's absence, he could trade as he saw fit and, increasingly, trade involved *nawohti*. Few disliked Sequoyah, and his
storytelling ability had already made him especially popular
in Willstown, but once word spread that he was willing to
share *nawohti* with visitors and customers, he rarely found
himself alone. Sequoyah, however, did not drink for com-
panionship; he drank to forget.

Still, it felt good to bring laughter to others, even if he
couldn't remember the next day what he'd said that was
so funny. But there was a price to be paid for those feelings. The effects of drinking slipped into other parts of
Sequoyah's life. His trading suffered and he abandoned his
silversmithing. He ignored his wife and perhaps a child
who may have been born by this time (the pair eventually
had three children). Self-discipline was very important
among the Cherokee and without it, Sequoyah developed
a new and unenviable reputation in the village. Sequoyah,
who had shown great promise, could not even meet his
family responsibilities. Talented or not, many lost respect
for him.

It is not known how long Sequoyah lived under the
foggy and destructive influence of *nawohti* or, indeed, how
he overcame it. Perhaps it had to do with an illness he suffered. In a fever, he slipped between delirium and unconsciousness; even the healing rituals and medicines of the
shaman and rest in the sweathouse had little effect.
Sequoyah recovered but the experience may well have
been life altering. Like most Natives, Sequoyah saw life as
a journey. What one did was not a statement about whether
the person was good or bad. It was more a reflection about
where one was on the journey and an indication of what
had to be learned if the journey was to continue. Those

who refused to learn from experience might expect to find their path overgrown and impassable. Sequoyah's journey had revealed a great deal to him about the importance of hope and the possibility of continuing in difficult circumstances. He did just that, and within a few years, he was no longer drinking. He also turned away from trading, perhaps to avoid the temptation of *nawohti*, and he returned to blacksmithing. He started with nothing, constructing his own forge and bellows and making his own tools, but with hard work came success.

While Sequoyah was struggling along his life path, the Cherokee nation was also experiencing more change. In 1803, President Thomas Jefferson authorized the Louisiana Purchase. For $23 million the United States acquired approximately 900,000 square miles of western territory from France, a vast tract of land between the Mississippi River and the Rocky Mountains that stretched from the Gulf of Mexico to the border of present-day Canada. Following that purchase, the United States adopted a new policy towards the Natives. Rather than make the expensive and uncertain effort to civilize them, the government decided to buy Native lands and move them west to its newly acquired territory. Among the Cherokee, the government discovered that it had a most willing partner in Chief Doublehead. While he had long opposed a white presence in traditional Cherokee territory, he had come to realize that any resistance was likely futile. He had fought his battles; he would cede land and perhaps move west; but he would do it to his own advantage.

Urged on by Indian agent Colonel Return Meigs, by 1805, Doublehead and some allied chiefs had sold land in North Carolina, Tennessee and Georgia. With each sale, Doublehead accumulated goods, cash and title to valuable pieces of land at the mouths of the Clinch and the Hiwassee rivers. Eventually, however, he overstepped his authority. In December 1806, he ceded a large tract of land without the consent of the Cherokee tribal council. Many were angry, especially those who had already adjusted to the white presence, including the leaders of the younger generation who were slowly coming to power. Most of them had embraced farming full-time and they operated large spreads, often worked by slaves. They did not want to see their land ceded and be forced to move only to start again. The young chiefs decided to kill Doublehead. The action was justified by Cherokee law, which permitted such punishment for one who sold Cherokee land without tribal consent. Three men, led by Chief Major Ridge (The Ridge), assassinated Doublehead in June 1807. Many were already incensed by Doublehead's behavior, which included beating his pregnant wife to death and eating a captive taken during the American Revolution, so few tears were shed upon his death.

It was not the end of the matter, however. Indian agent Meigs was under the direction of the secretary of war in Washington to continue his efforts to get the Cherokee to trade what remained of their traditional lands for territory west of the Mississippi River. By this time, government officials became aware of the rift within the Cherokee tribe. Those in the north had adapted to the white economy of farming, while those farther south remained committed to a more traditional hunting lifestyle. The problem for the southern Cherokee was the depletion of game. Meigs used the scarcity of game to his advantage, by pointing out that the western lands were rich in animals. Sequoyah's uncles Tahlonteskee and John Jolly were among those chiefs who saw the sense in Miegs's proposal and agreed with it. In 1809 these chiefs tried to convince the Cherokee tribal council that the Cherokee should move west. Younger chiefs, mostly from the north and again led by The Ridge, refused to move and they usurped the power of the older leaders. The loss of power meant little because the older chiefs were prepared to move. In 1810, Tahlonteskee and his followers traveled to Arkansas, where they became known as the Western Cherokee, while a smaller number migrated to Texas.

The Eastern Cherokee, those who remained on the traditional lands mostly in Georgia, decided that there would be no more land sales. But they could not maintain their stand for long. The Western Cherokee discovered that they had moved to the traditional land of another Native tribe, the Osage. They raised the issue with government officials who informed them that nothing could be done to assist them unless the Eastern Cherokee ceded more territory. In 1817, the Eastern Cherokee resolved the matter by agreeing to cede land in Georgia and Tennessee. In return, the Western Cherokee were granted an additional tract of land.

The Eastern Cherokee, aware that their future lay in living near the settlers, also decided to try to adopt to white ways. Few continued to hunt. Most farmed, selling their crops rather than using them solely to provide for community needs. Sequoyah, who had remained in Willstown, did not agree with the rush towards assimilation. He knew that many had accepted the changes, such as cotton crops, spinning wheels, looms. He could see the women's cotton dresses and children attending the missionary schools. He also knew that many benefited from adopting white ways as their wood-frame houses and the large farms suggested.

But others lived in poverty. When Sequoyah considered the influence of white men on his people, he found little that was good. They had destroyed settlements and taken land. They had introduced liquor, disease, Christianity and education, all of which undermined traditional Cherokee

ways. Sequoyah held fast to the old ways. He believed in
harmony with nature and communal responsibility. He
thought cooperation was as important as individual acquisi-
tiveness. He wanted to keep the land and the language that
gave meaning to life. Sequoyah did not doubt that prosperity was desirable, but he was not willing to sacrifice what
he considered to be Cherokee to achieve it.

But Sequoyah would not fight for it. Around 1810, the
Shawnee chief Tecumseh visited the Cherokee. He had
a reputation as a powerful leader, and councils were
arranged to allow him to speak wherever he traveled. The
Cherokee listened as Tecumseh outlined his vision of
a Native confederacy. He said that he had allied with
many of the northern tribes and that he would soon go
west to gain support there. Tecumseh spoke of a dish with
one spoon, the notion that Native lands were the trust of
all Natives and that no one tribe or band should cede territory without the agreement of all Natives. He advocated
the rejection of white ways and a return to traditional
Native practices. He foresaw a time when Natives could
live again as they once did. All that was needed was unity
and a willingness to join with the British, who promised
them such a future.

The charismatic Tecumseh impressed many and had the
Indian agents worried. Hawkins and Meigs worked to
undermine the appeal of Tecumseh's message by promising increased annuities and cash. They need not have
offered so much, at least to the Cherokee. The Ridge, the
most prominent of the Cherokee chiefs by this time,
rejected Tecumseh's overtures. As with an increasing number of Cherokee leaders, The Ridge was a mixed-blood,
married to a white woman, and had adopted white ways:
he owned a plantation-like home worked by slaves, sent
his children to missionary school and operated a profitable

ferry. Little in Tecumseh's message appealed to him or, apparently, to many Eastern Cherokee.

Some southeastern tribes did respond to Tecumseh's message, including the Red Stick faction of the Creeks, who were neighbors of the Cherokee. When the War of 1812 erupted, these bands allied with the British against the Americans. On an international level, the War of 1812 was an effort by the United States to assert its sovereignty. Britain was otherwise engaged in a war against Napoleon, and the outcome was uncertain. To improve their chances of success, the British searched American ships and pressed American sailors into military service on British ships patrolling the Atlantic. Furthermore, the strong British navy prevented American ships from trading with European countries. The War of 1812 was something of a continuation of the American Revolution, and the United States was determined that it would come through the war without any doubt about its nationhood.

Many Natives, however, saw the War of 1812 as an opportunity to resist white encroachment on their traditional lands and to recoup the losses of the past half-century. They had reason to believe they might enjoy success. The British promised them ammunition and assistance. They further assured the Natives that they supported the Native cause for an exclusive homeland, a pledge they promised not to abandon. Thousands joined Tecumseh, who organized the Native confederacy to fight with the British. The Cherokee did not join Tecumseh, but led by The Ridge, they joined the United States Army and fought in what became known as the Creek War under Andrew Jackson, commander of the Southwestern troops.

Sequoyah supported The Ridge in the alliance with the U.S., himself enlisting in October 1813. It might have been the only time he served his people as a warrior. Although he

was accepted as a man in his village, the usual route to manhood was to prove oneself in battle. Sequoyah may have
longed for the opportunity to prove himself in the traditional
way. Perhaps he supported the alliance for just that reason.
Little is known of Sequoyah's activities during the Creek War,
but they must have been limited because of his bad leg. He
did participate in the Battle of Horseshoe Bend, the decisive
encounter of the Creek War. Fought in March 1814 along
the Tallapoosa River in present-day Alabama, the Battle of
Horseshoe Bend saw Jackson's 2000 men defeat 1000 Creek
warriors, killing more than 800 Creeks in the battle. Jackson
lost 49 soldiers and 23 warriors. Sequoyah watched as the
Cherokee and other Native victors took scalps; perhaps he
even took one himself. But he had to turn away from the
grisly activities of the soldiers who skinned the dead Creeks
so they could make belts and reins as trophies of their victory.

Within a year, Sequoyah returned to Willstown. His
journey took him through razed Cherokee villages and past
burned cornfields. He was surprised because he had not
heard of enemy attacks along the Tennessee River. Surprise
turned to confusion when he learned that Cherokee allies
had caused the damage. American soldiers returning to
their eastern settlements had terrorized Natives they found
along their route. The Cherokee could not comprehend
why the Americans would treat the Cherokee so. Perhaps it
was a misunderstanding. Surely Jackson could clear up the
matter. The Cherokee appealed to him for an explanation
and for justice. At the very least, supplies and stock should
be provided to replace those destroyed. Apparently Jackson
had already forgotten about the Cherokee assistance during
the Creek War. He denied their allegations and turned
a deaf ear to their demands.

Sequoyah had gone to fight in the War of 1812 a single
man. At some point and for unknown reasons, he had

divorced Utiyu. Soon after returning to Willstown, he took a new wife. Sally Benge (or Waters) was a Cherokee from a prominent family, which was important given the time. Many Cherokee leaders were marrying white women, which Sequoyah saw as evidence of the white man's growing influence among his people. It was a trend he did not like, and his marriage was undoubtedly a statement to that effect. It seems he had little other reason to marry because immediately after they were wed, he built the isolated cabin in the forest. There he spent most of his time alone, working on the talking leaves. He had first thought about the project more than a decade before, and his renewed interest was probably a result of contact with the white soldiers during the war. He would have seen their books and letters and noticed how these items often gave comfort to men who were hundreds of miles away from family members. How wonderful was this writing!

Sally did not share his enthusiasm. While she may have been attracted to Sequoyah because of his creative talents, she did not think much of him using his abilities in such a strange undertaking. Sequoyah would have agreed that his project was a strange one, without apparent connection to the Cherokee world. But he was confident that its success would mean great things for his people, not the least of which would be an ability to maintain their traditional practices. Stories and customs could be shared and passed on without relying on the language of the white people, who sought to destroy Cherokee ways. The talking leaves soon consumed Sequoyah.

Day after day, he sat in his paper- and bark-filled cabin, smoking his pipe and reflecting on the symbols he thought might serve as the Cherokee talking leaves. It was a struggle, because the symbols he had developed were proving unsatisfactory—too many and too complicated. Then, one day, he no longer had to grapple with the symbols. Sally and her friends burned down his cabin, and the work of a decade or more was suddenly turned to ashes. But Sequoyah saw the fire as an opportunity, allowing him to move on unburdened by failed ideas.

Sequoyah did not return to the talking leaves immediately because other pressing matters were facing the Cherokee. The United States government was again demanding land. In the years following the War of 1812, government pressure forced the Cherokee to cede more and more land. The most significant concession occurred in 1817. Indian agent Meigs discovered that the old arguments to encourage Cherokee cessions were no longer effective. When he pointed out that they would be able to live near their relatives and hunt in lands rich with game, frustrated Cherokee noted that the government and missionaries had told them to turn their rifles into plows and to farm rather than hunt. In the summer, Andrew Jackson arrived determined to address the situation.

Given the Cherokees' assistance to Jackson during the Creek War, they might have expected him to support their claims. But it quickly became clear that the American war hero was no friend to the Natives. Jackson was raised on the Tennessee frontier and he shared the frontiersmen's desire that the Natives be removed from their traditional lands. To that end, he employed whatever tactics he deemed necessary to force the Cherokee to relocate. He bribed some leaders to accept the proposed treaty and threatened others with the cancellation of promised annuities for past cessions. It was also alleged that the Cherokee had not given up enough land to compensate for the tracts given to the Western Cherokee and that Eastern Cherokee land might be seized to redress the balance. Jackson forwarded the Treaty of July 8, 1817, to Washington, although the majority of Cherokee present opposed it. Sixty-seven chiefs even signed a letter protesting the land swap and emigration to Arkansas. But President Monroe wanted the lands in Georgia and Tennessee, so he approved the treaty.

Sequoyah was present at the negotiations and marked the treaty as George Guess, but there is no evidence that he accepted bribes or was intimidated by Jackson's maneuvers. He had other concerns. In early 1817, a new missionary body had taken up work among the Cherokee. The Brainard Mission, a joint effort of the Congregational and Presbyterian churches, was determined to accelerate the civilization process. The missionaries were less concerned with economic transitions than they were with cultural ones. In their minds, the Cherokee religion and language were the greatest obstacles to civilization and salvation. It was a belief that struck at the heart of what Sequoyah considered most important. Their culture and language made the Cherokee who they were; to lose them was to become something other than Cherokee. When Sequoyah learned that a branch of the Brainard Mission was to open in Willstown in 1818, he decided that it was time to move west, away from the corrosive influence of the white man and his teachings. In February 1818, he joined with 331 other Cherokee, including his uncle, Chief John Jolly, and made for the settlements of the Western Cherokee in Arkansas. For the time being, his family (he would eventually have four children with Sally) remained behind.

Life among the Western Cherokee suited Sequoyah. Far from white settlements, they were not influenced as much by white ways as their eastern relatives. Many continued to hunt and they farmed on communal fields. Sequoyah's thoughts turned again to the talking leaves. In the West, his fellow villagers were less interested in his preoccupation than those in Georgia had been. He spent time alone, in thought, without concern for the opinion of others.

One day, not many months after his arrival, Sequoyah sat chewing on his pipe stem. He followed the trails of smoke as they floated towards the roof of his cabin. He watched the shapes form in the curling bluish-gray wisps. Try as he might, he could not get the old idea of the symbols out of his head. His eyes fell on a drip slowly leaking from the ceiling. It was raining and he became aware of its pounding rhythm on his cabin. The sound of the rain, the same sound, never changing. Suddenly it came to him. Sounds! Words had sounds! He spoke aloud, no longer trying to picture the words, but rather listening to them. He fumbled for bark and charcoal and began noting the different sounds he heard in what he said. Many pieces of bark later and unable to think of new words, he excitedly left his cabin to seek others so that they might talk to him.

"Speak! Speak!" he implored as he scratched markings on palm-sized pieces of bark.

People looked strangely at Sequoyah, but he did not notice. More words! More sounds! The mystery of the Cherokee talking leaves evaporated as the early morning fog over the river. The answer was finally clear to him and, within a month, he had invented a written Cherokee language.

Sequoyah's system was a syllabary. Rather than use letters, like an alphabet, it employed syllables. He discerned 85 basic sounds in the Cherokee language (which he later expanded to 86 and thereafter modified to a more simple form for printing) and created a symbol for each sound. These became the building blocks for his written language. To make his work more presentable, Sequoyah purchased a quill and paper from a trader and carefully marked the symbols on the page.

His work completed, he set out on a new task. He had to convince his people of the value of his invention. It was not easy. Writing had no place in the Cherokee tradition

Cherokee Alphabet.

D a	R e	T i	δ o	O u	i v
S ga O ka	F go	y gi	A go	J gu	E gv
V ha	P ho	θ hi	F ho	Γ hu	W hv
W la	C le	P li	G lo	M lu	A lv
Ꮙ ma	O me	H mi	3 mo	y mu	
O na t hna G nah	A ne	h ni	Z no	A nu	O nv
T qua	W que	P qui	V quo	W quu	E quv
U sa W s	4 se	b si	ᴸ so	E su	R sv
L da W ta	S de T te	Ꮷ di Ꮩ ti	A do	S du	P dv
S dla L tla	L tle	C tli	Ꮳ tlo	Ꮨ tlu	P tlv
G tsa	V tse	Ir tsi	K tso	J tsu	C tsv
G wa	W we	O wi	C wo	D wu	6 wv
W ya	B ye	Ꭹ yi	h yo	G yu	B yv

Sounds represented by Vowels

a, as a in *father*, or short as a in *rival*. o, as aw in *law*, or short as o in *not*.
e, as a in *hate*, or short as e in *met*. u, as oo in *fool*, or short as u in *pull*.
i, as i in *pique*, or short as i in *pit*. v, as u in *but*, nasalized.

Consonant Sounds

g nearly as in English, but approaching to k. d nearly as in English, but approaching
to t. h k l m n q s t w y as in English. Syllables beginning with g except Ꮪ have sometimes the
power of k. A, S, D, C, are sometimes sounded to, tu, tv, and Syllables written with tl except Ꮮ
sometimes vary to dl.

The written Cherokee language invented by Sequoyah. Known as Sequoyan, it is sometimes referred to as the Cherokee alphabet, although it is properly called a syllabary because it uses syllables rather than letters. Sequoyah completed the syllabary in 1821 and it quickly spread "through the [Cherokee] nation like fire among the leaves," as one missionary put it. Sequoyah hoped that his syllabary could unite the Cherokee and protect their traditional ways. He was pleased to witness the creation of the *Cherokee Phoenix*, a newspaper written partly in Sequoyan, which raised awareness of Cherokee issues. Sequoyah died before A'yunini, a mid-19th-century Cherokee medicine man, used Sequoyan to compile a vast catalogue of the history, stories and songs of his people. Sequoyan continues to be used today.

and few imagined its value. Most were simply not interested, and some raised the possibility again that Sequoyah was practicing bad magic. Sequoyah, however, was a patient man. He did not stop showing others his syllabary until a friend finally listened to what he had to say. His friend learned the symbols quickly and, with that, news of the invention spread. It was as if an obstructing log had been removed from a stream. Soon all the Cherokee in his village were discussing Sequoyah's talking leaves.

Sequoyah believed that the syllabary held great value for his people, especially because it allowed them to be educated and to communicate in their own language. His problem, however, was that most Cherokee still lived in the East. Many had already accepted English as the language they must learn, and Sequoyah knew that it would not be an easy matter to convince them otherwise. He also realized that, even if they were open to the syllabary, they might not be anxious to listen to the man who brought it to them. His past behavior, seen as strange by many, offensive by some, and his unpopular decision to sign the 1817 treaty would be remembered. Still, Sequoyah recognized that he must try and, in 1821, he returned to Willstown.

He carried with him letters written by Western Cherokee, who had quickly mastered the uncomplicated syllabary. These letters were to be read to their eastern relatives and friends. Also traveling with him was his daughter Ahyokah. She and the rest of Sequoyah's family had moved west to be with him some time after his arrival. Sequoyah had taught Ahyokah, who was only five years old, his syllabary. He thought her presence might work to his advantage in persuading others that his invention was both real and simple.

The meeting with the headmen and Eastern Cherokee priests did not unfold as Sequoyah had hoped. When

Sequoyah outlined his project, the response of the priests, who used their powers for the benefit of the community, was immediate and forceful.

"This is magic! It has been long suspected that you are a witch. Now you bring us evidence of it in these markings. It is bad magic."

"Wait," cried Sequoyah. "Let me read to you the messages sent by the Western Cherokee."

Sequoyah took one of the pages from a bundle and read it aloud. Before he was finished, he was interrupted by one of the priests.

"A story memorized! Or worse, a story told by using magic. If it is magic, and we cannot know that it isn't, everyone knows the punishment. Sequoyah the witch must be killed!"

Finally Ahgeelee (George Lowery), the chief, spoke.

"The priest is right, but we *cannot* know that Sequoyah uses magic. He will not be killed until we are certain."

Ahgeelee turned to Sequoyah.

"You say that your daughter knows these symbols."

"As well as I," replied Sequoyah.

"Let us separate father and daughter," directed Ahgeelee. "Then we will send messages between them. If they speak what we have told them, we will know there is something to this syllabary."

"We will speak your words," replied Sequoyah confidently.

The test was conducted and it unfolded as Sequoyah had predicted. But his critics were not silenced.

"Sequoyah has taught his daughter well," agreed one of the priests, "but how do we know that he has not taught her the ways of a witch? I still say it is magic."

"My friends have difficulty believing their ears and eyes," said Sequoyah. "It is understandable because what I bring has not been heard before. But it is not magic, good

Ahgeelee (George Lowrey) was Sequoyah's friend and relative
and a respected leader of the Eastern Cherokee.

or bad. I bring symbols marked on a page. What must I do
to convince you?"

"You will teach the warriors," announced Ahgeelee.
"If your invention can be mastered by a five-year-old,
then warriors should easily meet the challenge."

"Yes," agreed Sequoyah. "It will be so."

And it was. In a week, Sequoyah taught the warriors his
syllabary. They could communicate with it as well as its inventor. Ahgeelee then called the headmen and priests together.

They created messages and had them delivered under the strictest of conditions. Each one was accurately read.

"It is as Sequoyah has claimed," declared the chief. "There can be no doubt. The papers can talk!"

So impressed were those gathered, including the priests, that they asked Sequoyah to teach them his syllabary. The great numbers who were suddenly interested in learning written Cherokee were daunting. But Sequoyah didn't need to be concerned about instruction. The strength of the syllabary was its simplicity. When one mastered it, he or she could easily teach it to another. The skill was passed among the Eastern Cherokee with great enthusiasm.

In 1824, a missionary reported, "The knowledge of Mr. Guess's Alphabet is spreading through the nation like fire among the leaves."

Within months, over half the adult Cherokee population knew the syllabary, a rate of literacy higher than any other nation at the time. So grateful were the Cherokee that in 1825 tribal officials presented Sequoyah with a silver medal. It was inscribed, "Presented to George Gist by the General Council of the Cherokee Nation, for his ingenuity in The Invention of the Cherokee Alphabet, 1825." A pair of crossed pipes and a portrait of Sequoyah were engraved under the inscription.

The General Council of the Cherokee Nation was a new body, one that eventually replaced the old tribal council. It was created in 1820 and intentionally modeled on the United States government. The Cherokee were divided into eight districts, each sending four elected representatives to the national legislature in New Echota (near present-day Calhoun, Georgia), a modern town modeled on eastern American cities. The legislature was divided into upper and lower houses making laws and establishing courts to oversee their fair implementation. The General Council was the creation of the new generation of Cherokee leaders, those opposed to the corrupt land sales of the previous decade. The most important leaders were mixed-blood Cherokees, John Ridge (son of The Ridge) and John Ross. They were proponents of assimilation and thus determined to demonstrate to American officials that the Cherokee would make good neighbors for white settlers. The General Council was meant to be a visible indicator of Cherokee progress towards civilization.

Another important marker on that road was the creation of the Convention of the Cherokee Nation, ratified in 1827. The constitution provoked considerable debate. Many Cherokee thought that the document was meant to enhance the position of the chiefs. They noted that John Ross had written most of it and that it allowed him, as the Principal Chief, to veto decisions of the General Council. But the greater debate swirled around the written language of the constitution. The General Council decided that the document would be written in English, the official language of the Cherokee nation. Such a decision was understandable given the chiefs' desire to use the document as proof of their increasingly civilized ways. Others, however, argued that the constitution should be written in Sequoyan, as the syllabary came to be known. For a few months it seemed as if there might be a rebellion over the issue. In the end, the General Council would not relent. The constitution was written in English. Sequoyah would not be honored with anything more than a medal.

The medal was important to Sequoyah and he wore it often. When he finally received it in 1832 (he had returned to his home among the Western Cherokee), it came with a message from Ross: "The present generation have already experienced the great benefits of your incomparable system." Perhaps Ross was sincere, but Sequoyah remained disappointed in the decision of the General Council regarding the language of the constitution. He believed that the ability of the Cherokee to record their ideas in their own words would be a great unifying force, one that was all the more important since the tribe had been divided some years earlier. Nonetheless, he took great satisfaction in seeing that his invention was used in other ways.

Sequoyah's efforts had long been inspired by visions of a day when the Cherokee would not be forced to sacrifice their identity in order to participate in the changing society. He was not opposed to education that might allow his people to adapt, but he resisted the intense assimilation of the missionaries. Sequoyan derailed a significant part of the missionary efforts. Rather than fight the popularity of written Cherokee, the missionaries soon decided to translate the Bible into Sequoyan. The change in missionary practice eliminated the need to learn English. Concerns about the teaching of English eroding the Cherokee language were no longer heard.

Perhaps more thrilling for Sequoyah was the appearance in early 1828 of the newspaper the *Cherokee Phoenix*. In 1825 the General Council issued a request for donations to purchase a press and types in both Sequoyan and English. Elias Boudinot (Cherokee name, Gallegina) publicized the campaign. Boudinot was The Ridge's nephew, and he had been well educated at a mission school in New England. Many responded to his well-calculated appeal focusing on Cherokee progress. The necessary money was raised quickly. The press was set up in New Echota, and its first publication was a hymnal. It was also used to print the General Council's laws and other informational pamphlets, but its best-known publication was the *Cherokee Phoenix*.

Cherokee Phoenix was actually the English name on the masthead. The translation of the Sequoyan name, also on

Masthead of the first issue of the *Cherokee Phoenix*. The Sequoyan name translates as "Cherokee will-rise-again."

the masthead, was "Cherokee will-rise-again." Boudinot thought it was important that the *Cherokee Phoenix* be written in both languages because he envisioned it influencing both Cherokee and English-speaking readers. It did. The *Cherokee Phoenix* was divided into Sequoyan (about a third) and English. The newspaper enjoyed a readership that extended into Europe, but it was not written for white men.

As Boudinot wrote in the first issue, "The great and sole motive in establishing this paper is the benefit of the Cherokees." With it they could share their stories and concerns and educate others on the state of affairs among their people. The *Cherokee Phoenix* was the first Native newspaper ever printed and a great triumph made possible by Sequoyah's invention.

Sequoyah's reputation soared among the Cherokee, especially those in the West. In 1828 he was selected as one of nine delegates who traveled to Washington to seek redress for unfulfilled treaty obligations, notably regarding boundaries and payments due for their western migration. Sequoyah soon discovered that his reputation was not limited to his own people. Journalists sought him for interviews; a prominent artist, Charles Bird King, painted his portrait; and President John Quincy Adams gave him a medal. But when

it came to treaty negotiations, Sequoyah and the other
Cherokee discovered that restitution was not what government officials contemplated. They asked Cherokee to move
even farther west, to Indian Territory (present-day Oklahoma)
and promised that it would be their permanent home. In May,
Sequoyah signed the treaty, which also awarded him $500 in
recognition for his invention. There is no record of his justification for approving the treaty, but if he remained true to
form, he was likely pleased about distancing his people from
the white settlers and their influence.

This treaty, however, was not popular among many of
the Cherokee. The Eastern Cherokee claimed that the
delegates had no right to sign it, while many Western
Cherokee were not enthusiastic about tearing up roots
that had been growing for only a decade. Nevertheless,
Sequoyah's influence and the respect his people had for
him undoubtedly tempered their anger and, in 1829, he
and thousands of Cherokee set out for Indian Territory.
Sometimes called the Old Settlers, they established their
new capital at Tahlonteskee and settled into lives more like
their traditional ways.

Sequoyah built his cabin near present-day Sallisaw, settled
down with his family and began farming. He also operated
a salt spring, which had been given to him by government
negotiators in return for one he had owned. But he derived
his greatest pleasure from teaching Sequoyan to many
Cherokee. He used the stories and traditions of old as his
tools, and seeing them written in his syllabary surely brought
a great measure of contentment.

While Sequoyah was adjusting to life in Indian Territory,
the Eastern Cherokee were facing their greatest challenge
yet. In 1829 Andrew Jackson assumed the presidency of the
United States. He had never been a friend to the Natives
and, as an avowed expansionist, he was long a supporter of

western settlers and of their unfettered western movement.
He saw the southeastern tribes as obstacles to American
progress and he wanted them relocated. There was great
support for this, particularly in Georgia, where, in 1828,
gold was discovered in the southeastern portion of
Cherokee territory. State officials wanted control of the
territory so that they could reap the financial benefits of
the rush. They pushed the government in Washington to
act on a promissory letter, known as the Georgia Compact,
that was signed in 1802. At that time the state had agreed
to cede to Washington its claims to territory west of its
then boundary and, in return, the federal government had
agreed to extinguish Native claims within the state's limits.
This included Cherokee territory in the north.

Over the years, officials in Washington had made efforts
to have the Cherokee cede the disputed territory, but they
were unsuccessful. In May 1830, President Jackson pushed
the Indian Removal Bill through the United States
Congress. The bill called for the relocation of 60,000 southeastern Natives of the Five Civilized Tribes—Cherokee,
Chickasaw, Choctaw, Creek and Seminole—to land west of
the Mississippi River. The victory was hardly unanimous.
Many prominent Americans, including William Wirt, a past
attorney general, and Senator Daniel Webster opposed the
bill. Jeremiah Evarts, a founder of the American Board of
Commissioners for Foreign Missions, wrote a series of arti-
cles denouncing the oppression of the Native peoples.

Jackson, however, had his own reasons that were popular with southerners, if not the Natives who he argued
were the main beneficiaries of removal. "It will separate
the Indians from immediate contact with settlements of
whites; free them from the power of the States; enable
them to pursue happiness in their own way, under their
own rude institutions and perhaps cause them gradually,

under the protection of the government and, through the influence of good counsels, to cast off their savage habits, and become an interesting, civilized and Christian community."

Taking their cue from Jackson, who informed the Cherokee that Washington was powerless to help them in opposing any actions that Georgia might take against them, state officials adopted measures to exercise jurisdiction over the Cherokee. The Cherokee tried to bolster their own claims to sovereignty through the courts, but in 1831 they were dealt a severe blow when the United States Supreme Court declared in *Cherokee Nation v. Georgia* that the Cherokee Nation was not a sovereign nation, but indeed fell under the jurisdiction of Georgia. The Cherokee received a more favorable judgment in 1832, in *Worcester v. Georgia*, when the Supreme Court decreed that the Cherokee could make their own laws. Georgians were shocked to learn that they could not impose state laws on the Cherokee, and government officials thumbed their noses at the decision. Later that year, Jackson made his position abundantly clear. He would not enforce United States treaties made with the southeastern tribes if they conflicted with the interests of Georgia. As for the unfortunate legal judgment, he suggested that since the Supreme Court had made the decision, it should enforce it.

Georgia increased its pressure on the Eastern Cherokee by holding a lottery for Native lands. Officials pointed out that the other four of the Five Civilized Tribes had signed treaties of removal. Jackson appointed Benjamin Curry as Superintendent of the Removal of Cherokees to hasten the process. Promises were made to those who would move, and those who wouldn't faced violence from angry settlers. In 1834, state officials closed down the *Cherokee Phoenix* because it opposed relocation. Resigned to their fate, some Cherokee began to move West.

John Ross, who continued as the Cherokee Principal Chief, would not agree to the removal. Some Cherokee were as upset as American officials with his obstinacy. In December 1835, a small group, led by John Ridge and Elias Boudinot (who had resigned his editorship in 1832 because he could no longer oppose the removal), signed the Treaty of New Echota with Washington. The Treaty Party, as the group was called, ceded all Cherokee land east of the Mississippi River for western lands and $5 million. Boudinot was a realist. He had come to accept that the treaty was in the best interests of the Cherokee, but he expected that one day he would die for his decision, with good reason. The treaty did not represent the wishes of the majority of the Cherokee. It hardly represented the majority of all Americans; it passed the United States Senate by only one vote.

Ross was determined to have the decision reversed. He collected a petition signed by 16,000 Cherokee. It was ignored. He went on speaking trips to gain white support for the Cherokee cause. It was not enough. In April 1838, under a threat of war from Georgia, President Martin van Buren ordered Major General Winfield Scott to remove the Eastern Cherokee.

Scott had 7000 men at New Echota a month later when he issued orders to the Cherokee to emigrate or be hunted down. Some 2000 left, including the supporters of the Treaty Party. The remainder were gathered together by Scott's troops and, at gunpoint, forced into hastily constructed stockades. The captives were not allowed to retrieve or pack goods; their homes were pillaged and their livestock taken by heartless opportunists. By early June, 17,000 Cherokee were imprisoned. Many wondered how they had arrived at this point. Hadn't they made every effort to adjust to white ways, to make themselves good neighbors? It was not enough because the settlers wanted their land, not their goodwill. Many Cherokee would pay for the miscalculation with their lives on the Trail of Tears, as the forced removal came to be called.

Throughout mid-June 1838 the army marched three parties of Cherokee detainees west. They endured oppressive heat and uncommon drought. Hundreds escaped to avoid the sickness that swept through the camps and the deaths that often followed. The second group, which departed on June 15, reported that three to five Cherokee died each day and sometimes as many as seven. The suffering was such that John Ross appealed to General Scott to allow the remainder of his people to depart in the fall. Scott agreed and set the Cherokee free from the stockades on their word that they would emigrate peacefully on the appointed date. In October, Ross divided the Cherokee into 13 detachments, each the responsibility of a different chief and, over the weeks that followed, they moved west.

In January 1839, the *New York Observer* printed an item sent to them by a man who had happened upon one of the Cherokee parties in Kentucky.

> *On Tuesday evening, we fell in with a detachment of the poor Cherokee Indians…about 1100…60 wagons, 600 horses and perhaps 40 pairs of oxen….The sick and the feeble were carried on wagons—about as comfortable for traveling as a New England ox-cart with a covering over it—a great many ride on horseback and multitudes go on foot (even aged females, apparently ready to drop into the grave, were traveling with heavy burdens attached to their backs) on the sometimes frozen ground, and sometimes muddy streets, with no covering for their feet except what nature had given them….We learned from inhabitants on the road…they buried 14 or 15 at every stopping place*

and they made a journey of 10 miles per day only on an average....One fact to my own mind seemed a lesson indeed to the American Nation, that is they will not travel on the Sabbath...they must stop, and not merely stop— they must worship the Great Spirit too....Some cast a downcast dejected look bordering upon the appearance of despair, others a wild frantic appearance as if about to burst the chains of nature and pounce like a tiger upon their enemies....One lady passed on in her hack with her husband, apparently with as much refinement as any of the mothers of New England; and she was a mother too and her youngest child of about three years old was sick in her arms, and all she could do was to make it comfortable as circumstances would permit...she could only carry her dying child in her arms a few miles farther, and then she must stop in a stranger-land and consign her much loved babe to the cold ground, and that too without pomp or ceremony, and pass on with the multitude....When I read in the President's message that he was happy to inform the Senate that the Cherokees were peaceably and without reluctance removed—and remember it was on the third day of December when not one of the detachments had reached their destination...I wished the President could have been there that very day in Kentucky with myself, and have seen the comfort and willingness with which the Cherokees were making their journey.

The observer could have been describing any of the western-bound Cherokee detachments. What he didn't mention was the poor treatment given them along the route by traders, men who were more interested in making money than in relieving misery. The last of the detachments arrived in Indian Territory in late March. By then the Trail of Tears had taken the lives of 4000 Cherokee.

Robert Lindneux's 1942 painting of the Cherokee Trail of Tears. Some 4000 Cherokee died on the forced march.

The arrival of the Eastern Cherokee brought together many who had not seen each other for years, but the joy of the initial reunion was short lived. At a council meeting called by the Western Cherokee chiefs in June 1839 to welcome the newcomers, tempers flared. Sequoyah, now a chief among his people, was present. The Western Cherokee were surprised to hear John Ross demand that a new government be established, in line with the one used by the Eastern Cherokee. This entailed a dramatic change. Those in Indian Territory had a system of government more reflective of past practices. It elected chiefs, council members and police and was without a written constitution. The Western Cherokee chiefs suggested that the Eastern Cherokee should simply accept what was in place. Ross argued that as the Eastern Cherokee were in the majority, their wishes should be granted.

Sequoyah thought it would be a good idea to have a written constitution, and he tried to bridge the opposing factions. Before that could be achieved, however, a violent outbreak rocked the Cherokee nation. In late June, John Ridge, his father The Ridge and Elias Boudinot, three leaders of the Treaty Party, were assassinated by unknown assailants who most likely blamed the trio for the forced relocation and the hardships that accompanied it. Perhaps the deaths of those hated by so many helped to facilitate the reunion of the Western and Eastern Cherokee. On July 1, 1839, 2000 Cherokee met at the Illinois Camp Ground. Most were Eastern Cherokee, and Sequoyah represented those Western Cherokee present, serving as their temporary president. Ever the conciliator and determined to do what he considered best for all Cherokee, Sequoyah made an appeal to the Western Cherokee to attend the council, noting that the Cherokee shared common interests.

He wrote to them in Sequoyan, "These people are here in great multitudes and they are perfectly friendly towards us....we have no doubt but we can have all things amicably and satisfactorily settled."

It was enough to bring one chief into the fold. The council continued with its business, and on July 12, drafted an Act of Union, declaring that the Eastern and Western Cherokee were henceforth "one body politic, under the style and title of the Cherokee Nation." Ahgeelee signed the document on behalf of the Eastern Cherokee. Before Sequoyah signed the document for the Western Cherokee, he spoke to the assembly.

"It has been many years since Western and Eastern Cherokee have stood side by side in council. As tragic as the

Trail of Tears was, the forced emigration of our people has resulted in bringing together again the two branches of the ancient Cherokee family. We may thank the Great Spirit for that. It is important that the two branches unite to create a government adapted to their present condition and providing equally for the protection of each individual in the enjoyment of his rights."

Two months later, Sequoyah signed the new constitution of the Cherokee Nation that he had helped to create.

Sequoyah's popularity had not waned since his emigration and he had visitors regularly. The writer John Howard Payne was one such visitor sometime in the mid 1830s, and he described the man, now in his seventies.

"Guess had a turban of roses and posies upon a white ground girding his venerable gray hairs; a long dark blue robe, bordered around the lower edge and the cuffs, with black; a blue and white minutely checked calico tunic under it, confined with an Indian beaded belt, which sustained a large wooden handled knife, in a rough leathern sheathe; the tunic open on the breast and its collar apart, with a twisted handkerchief flung around his neck and gathered within the bosom of his tunic. He wore plain buckskin leggings; and one of a deeper chocolate hue than the other. One of his legs [is] lame and shrunken. His moccasins were ornamented buckskin. He had a long dusky white bag of sumac with him and a long Indian pipe, and smoked incessantly, replenishing his pipe from his bag. His air was altogether what we picture ourselves of an old Greek philosopher. He talked and gesticulated very gracefully; his voice alternately swelling; and then sinking to a whisper; and his eyes firing up and then its wild flashes subsiding into a gentle and most benignant smile."

The picture was one of contentment, but Sequoyah had a last goal he longed to achieve. Although representatives of the Western and Eastern Cherokee had united to form the Cherokee Nation, Sequoyah knew it to be incomplete. In 1819, at the invitation of a representative of the Spanish government, some 60 Cherokee families had emigrated to the Sabine River in Texas, then Spanish territory. After the successful Mexican Revolution in 1821, the Cherokee found themselves subject to new masters. The governor of Texas, however, decreed that the Cherokee would be permitted to remain along the Sabine River and would be treated as Hispano-Americans with the full rights enjoyed by such peoples. Despite negotiations, however, Mexican authorities never gave them title to their land. In 1835 the Texas Revolution for independence from Mexico erupted. Recognizing that the Cherokee had several hundred warriors, and desiring that they remain peaceful, the Texas provisional government declared that the promised boundaries of Cherokee territory would be recognized. With the success of the revolution, the Cherokee were no longer considered a threat, and Texan officials labeled them intruding Natives. In July 1839, soldiers were dispatched to force the Cherokee from their homes. One hundred Natives died in the resistance. Their fate was sealed, however, and they left. Some immigrated to Indian Territory while others went to Mexico.

It was the Mexican Cherokee that Sequoyah wanted to find. He wanted to teach them his syllabary and thereby unite them with the Cherokee Nation. He set out in 1842, accompanied by 10 others, including his son Teesee. After days of travel, Sequoyah fell ill. Fortunately, they came upon a friendly Comanche village, where the chief Ootillka offered them food and lodging.

As he rested, Sequoyah spoke to his companions, "My friends, we are a long way from our homes. I am very sick and may long remain so before I recover. Tomorrow, therefore, I wish you all to return home, except my son Teesee and my friend Worm."

It was agreed, and some weeks later, the trio continued on their journey where further misadventure awaited. One night their horses were stolen. The aged Sequoyah could not walk any distance, so he directed Teesee and Worm to find him a safe hiding place while they went to Mexico in search of horses. They found a cave near a river, and after leaving him a supply of honey and venison, the two set out on their mission.

Days passed. Sequoyah wrote in his journal, but even that did not speed the slow journey of the sun as it traveled across the sky. On the twelfth day, the skies opened up with a great rainstorm and the cave started to flood. He climbed out of it and spent the stormy night without shelter. The next day the rain subsided. He slipped back into the cave only to find all his belongings had been swept away. Sequoyah wrote a note describing what had happened and left it near the cave. Then he began to walk downstream, towards Mexico.

He had not gone far when he came upon a small party of Delaware. They were willing to take him to their village, but Sequoyah was determined to reach his goal. They gave him a horse and some food and he continued on his way to Mexico. Meanwhile, Teesee and Worm had been successful. They had come upon a Cherokee named Standing Rock, who informed them that a Cherokee village was nearby. The pair visited the village and they were able to recruit some of the locals to join them on their journey back to Sequoyah. All were concerned when they saw, near the cave, the telltale footprints of a man who walked with a limp and used a stick. They were relieved when they saw that the footprints disappeared to be replaced by the tracks of a horse. Soon after, they found Sequoyah. Overjoyed, they returned to the Cherokee village.

While there, Sequoyah fell ill. The events of the previous months had proven too strenuous. But Sequoyah had found the Mexican Cherokee and perhaps he was even able to teach them his syllabary. He never returned to Indian Territory. In August 1843 he was discovered, alone in his lodge, dead. He was buried in the Mexican town of San Fernando.

CHAPTER SIX

Louis Riel

~~~

Métis, 1844–1885

LOUIS RIEL PULLED THE REINS of his horse tight and brought it to a stop. He stepped from the cutter and walked the short distance to the local hotel in Pembina, a Métis settlement just south of the Canada-United States border. As he entered the lobby, his eyes fell on Ambroise Lepine and Joseph Dubuc, good friends and close allies during the days of the Red River Resistance, some 10 years before.

"My friends, it is so good to see you!" smiled Riel, as they embraced.

"And you! You look well," replied Lepine.

"I have had time to…relax."

"We have heard of your months at the asylum. Imagine them believing that Louis Riel was insane!" laughed Lepine.

"Surely it was a punishment for your actions," added Dubuc. "The Canadians will not forget nor forgive."

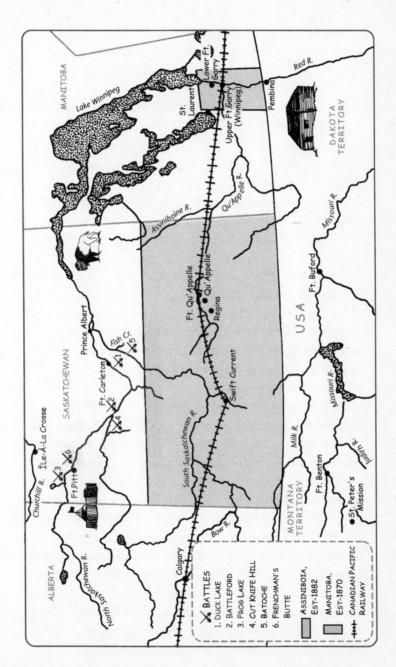

BATTLES
1. DUCK LAKE
2. BATTLEFORD
3. FROG LAKE
4. CUT KNIFE HILL
5. BATOCHE
6. FRENCHMAN'S BUTTE

ASSINIBOIA, EST-1882

MANITOBA, EST-1870

CANADIAN PACIFIC RAILWAY

Riel nodded and sighed with relief. He did not know how his friends would take his recent hospitalization. Together they found a table and sat down to talk.

"Tell me of Red River," said Riel.

"The news is not good!" replied Dubuc. "Settlers from Ontario arrive in greater numbers every day. The Métis' political power erodes. Soon the English Protestants will make the laws! We worked so hard to protect our peoples' language and culture, and now it seems it was for nothing."

"But the Manitoba Act guarantees Métis rights!" objected Riel.

"They will change what they can and ignore what they cannot."

"Not that it will matter much to the Métis," added Lepine. "They move west in greater numbers each day. The lands promised by the Dominion government have not been delivered. In frustration many have chosen to take the money instead. Others have sold to speculators, sometimes after they have been liquored up."

"So they have given up?"

"No, they move to open lands, free from the persecution of the English, where they might again live as their fathers did."

"Something must be done!" stated Riel. "Bold measures must be taken." But on this day, he had nothing to suggest.

The friends met often to discuss the situation, but eventually unemployment forced Riel to leave Pembina. He traveled south and joined a Métis camp on Beaver Creek, just north of the Missouri River. It was raw country, a new frontier for the almost 40-year-old Riel. For the first time since childhood, he lived as the Métis had traditionally, a life dependent on the rhythm of the buffalo hunts and the spoils they provided. Life was exciting, as the stories of his childhood became real. For the first time in many years

Louis Riel, taken at age 29 about three years after he had led the successful Red River Rebellion.

Riel felt at peace. In 1881, he married a young Métis, Marguerite Monet, and by 1883 they had two children, a boy and a girl.

Riel was also exposed to Native culture in an intense way. The buffalo had all but disappeared from the western prairies, and Natives—Blackfoot, Sioux, Cree—were drawn to the few remaining herds below the Missouri. Not so

long ago, the Natives were enemies of the Métis, but the
onslaught of white culture, and the hunger, poverty and
disease that came in its wake, had done much to diminish
intertribal hostility. While reflecting on white injustices,
a seed took root in Riel's thoughts. Perhaps the Natives
would join the Métis in a great Native alliance to throw off
their oppressors and control the West.

The possibility energized Riel. He made overtures to
several Native leaders, including the powerful Blackfoot
chief Crowfoot.

"The Sioux and the Cree have pledged to join the
Métis in our fight against the white man," Riel informed
him. "With the support of the Blackfoot, it will be an easy
matter to take control of the North-West Territories. Once
we are in possession of their forts, I will proclaim a provisional government, as in Red River."

"The name Riel is well respected among our people,"
admitted Crowfoot. He remembered the Métis success of
1869–70, the time when a Native-led resistance forced the
government to come to dictated terms. "But I have given
my word to the Red Coats, who are my friends, and to the
Grandmother. I have made treaty and I will not fight."

Riel had in his hand a copy of the Cree treaty with the
white man. He threw it on the ground and trampled it.

"The Indians deserve better!" he barked. "I am sending
out runners to take word to Indian chiefs and half-breed
leaders of a great council that we will have in Montana. We
will plan our attack. We will take back our land!"

But the proposed council did not take place. The memory of Native warfare on northern plains remained vivid for
Americans, and officials were suspicious of any effort to fan
the flames of Native resistance. When they learned of Riel's
plans, the government representatives on reservations,
known as Indian agents, were directed to confine their

charges to the reservations. Soldiers turned away other Natives they encountered north of the Missouri River. Riel resigned himself to supporting his family. In 1883, he became an American citizen, and later that year he settled in St. Peter's, just west of the Judith River in Montana, where he took a position teaching Métis children. Although he was a good teacher and the job allowed him to provide for his family, Riel was bored and felt unfulfilled. His responsibilities were a far cry from those he had shouldered in Red River. The thought of days past quickened his pulse, but there was no outlet for his energy in St. Peter's.

He was attending Mass, one of the few activities that consoled him, when word came of visitors from Canada. His heart raced as he recognized Gabriel Dumont, a friend from Red River.

"Gabriel," said Riel, "you bring news of Red River?"

"I no longer live there," replied Dumont. "I moved west to Saskatchewan, to be free of the domineering English."

"I have heard that it's difficult to be Métis in Red River."

"It is difficult to be a Métis anywhere!" boomed Dumont. "The settlers will not stop in Red River. They come to the Saskatchewan valley. They ignore us and take our lands. A railroad is being built across the land. Even more settlers will come. We complain to the government, but they pretend we are not there. The buffalo are gone. It doesn't look good," he admitted, shaking his head. "We have traveled 700 miles to meet with you. We must fight for our rights. Louis Riel, you must return with us!" implored Dumont.

Riel paused. His people needed him. So did his wife and children. Was his mission in the North-West complete?

"I will give you my answer tomorrow," replied Riel.

In the summer of 1851, Jean-Louis Riel glanced at the setting sun and laid his shovel against a Red River cart. He pulled a dirty handkerchief from his pocket and mopped the sweat from his brow. For weeks now, he had been digging a canal from the Rivière a la Graisse that would provide water for his mill, which would card wool and grind grain. He had been a miller in his youth in Québec and believed he could put the experience to good use in the growing community of Red River. Perhaps he might enjoy enough success to become a merchant and free himself from the back of a plough. Why not? He had the education and the desire and, in 1851, it seemed that many things were possible for a determined Métis. But he had done enough work for one day. He took the path back to his whitewashed log cabin. As he was walking, night fell; he could see the occasional spark thrown from chimneys in the nearby community of St. Boniface. Reaching his house, he took a quick look at his small herd of livestock, scraped the mud off his boots and threw open the door. Sara, three years old, ran to him. He took her in his arms and danced her around the table.

"A song, Julie! Sing us a song!" he begged his wife. She smiled, but not enough to light up her face, and said nothing. Perhaps it was the recent deaths of two of their children or her deeply held religious convictions, but she was not given to displays of frivolity. So, Jean-Louis hummed his own tune. Eventually he sat on a bench and, with Sara on his knee, caught his breath.

"Where is Louis?" he asked.

"At Grandpère Baptiste's," she replied. Jean-Baptiste Lagimodiere was her father. He had lived in Red River since 1816, only four years after the colony's inception. He prospered, and by 1849 he owned 100 head of cattle, an extensive transportation business and the largest farm in

St. Boniface. Grandpère Baptiste was a model of success that was to shape young Louis's belief in what the people of his community could achieve. "He will be home soon. He knows that tomorrow is his first confession and he must prepare."

The family was eating the evening meal when Louis returned, his face flushed from running. He sat next to his father at the table.

"Not out causing trouble, boy? Nothing more to tell the priest tomorrow?" suggested his father as he ruffled the boy's mop of hair.

"Jean-Louis! It is not to joke about," interrupted Julie, as she rubbed the cross that hung around her neck.

"Hardly," he agreed readily.

"Besides, such a thing would not cross his mind," she added. Neither parent doubted that.

"I was at Grandpère Baptiste's, father. He told me of the Sayer Trial, of your important role in it. Tell me the story."

"It was a great blow struck by the Métis, the day we threw off the shackles of the Hudson's Bay Company," smiled Jean-Louis, who easily slipped into the story he had not yet tired of telling. The Sayer Trial was a proud moment for the Métis, a significant marker in their growth as a people.

The Métis were a mixed-blood people, often called half-breeds during this time. Anyone with a Native-white heritage was a half-breed, but the Métis were mostly of a French-Native (Cree, Chipewyan, Assiniboine) heritage and could trace their ancestry to the operations of the North West Company (NWC), a fur-trading operation active in the late 18th and early 19th centuries. Headquartered in Montreal, the NWC used a system of trade that saw employees go to the Native communities to collect furs. Over time, these traders, known as wintering partners, formed relationships with Native women. These relationships were called *a la façon du pays*, meaning "according to the customs of the country." The arrangement was beneficial to both parties because the wintering partners learned the ways of the woods from Native women while the Native peoples assured themselves of regular trading partners. The children of these relationships, sometimes called *bois-brûlés* (burnt wood) because of their dark complexion, were usually raised with their mother's people.

With the merger of the Hudson's Bay Company (HBC) and the NWC in 1821, the old practices of the NWC disappeared and the *bois-brûlés* found themselves increasingly dependent on the supplies and employment offered by trading posts. Many of them concluded that a future subject to the vagaries of trading-post life was unappealing, so they decided to break away. Most moved west to the Plains and east to Red River, a settlement in southwestern Manitoba populated by retired HBC employees, country born (a specific term for the mixed-blood offspring of HBC employees and Natives) and Scots brought over by Lord Selkirk in the early 1800s. It was primarily the experiences of the *bois-brûlés* in Red River that led to the evolution of the Métis people. Over time they developed distinctive economic and cultural practices. They provisioned fur traders for their economic sustenance, and it was this role that led them to become buffalo hunters. They practiced Roman Catholicism and spoke a French-Cree patois.

Louis Riel was of these people. His grandfather, Jean-Baptiste Riel, left Québec to work for the NWC around the turn of the 19th century. By 1809 he was living at the NWC post at Île-à-la Crosse, on the Upper Churchill River. In 1812, he married Marguerite Boucher, a Métis. Riel traced his Native heritage to this marriage, but it was more than bloodlines that made Riel Métis. The Métis dominated the Red River community of his childhood.

Before he entered school at seven, Riel could speak Cree as if it was his first language. Perhaps more important, however, were the inclinations of his father, Jean-Louis, who was committed to the idea of Métis nationalism and actively participated in the Métis community. Louis had a great respect and deep love for his father and readily assimilated his views.

"The Hudson's Bay Company tried to choke the life from the Métis in the years following the great merger," continued Jean-Louis, pausing to put a spoonful of stew into his mouth. "They had a monopoly. We could not go to any other competitor to improve the prices we received for our furs. All that changed in 1844, when Kittson opened his American Fur Company post at Pembina. The Métis quickly began selling their furs in Pembina, where they received better prices. The Hudson's Bay Company did not like that. What, do they think we are stupid?" he snorted.

"In 1849 they arrested Guillaume Sayer and two others, charging them with trading their furs in violation of the Company's charter. They wanted to tell us how to run our lives! We'd have none of it. A committee…"

"Led by yourself, father!" interjected Louis.

"Yes," smiled Jean-Louis, chewing on a piece of bread, "led by myself, rounded up all the Métis we could find and surrounded the courthouse. There must have been 300, all shouting to let the prisoners go free. They say that Sayer was found guilty of trading in violation of the company's monopoly, but one of the jurors himself came to the door and shouted…"

"Le commerce est libre! Vive la liberté!" called Louis.

"Just that," nodded Jean-Louis. "After that, we had no problem with the Hudson's Bay Company," he smiled. "We showed them that they could not trample on us, that we were a nation capable of making our own laws."

Sayer had actually been found guilty, but the jury had also recommended mercy because of Sayer's belief that his activities were legal. The leading Hudson's Bay Company representative in the region agreed with the judge's decision not to punish Sayer. The enthusiastic juror had misinterpreted the verdict and concluded Sayer was innocent. The judge realized there was no way to convince the gathered Métis otherwise, and from that point on, the HBC lost its monopoly. Trade was free, and the Métis had their own efforts to thank for it.

"Tomorrow is your first confession, Louis. Are you prepared?" asked his father. He need not have asked. Louis first words were "Jesus, Joseph and Mary" and, even at this young age, no one doubted his faith.

"I have met often with Father Bermond," he replied. "Mother and I have prayed for guidance."

"Tonight we will say a rosary," added his mother.

Louis later remembered that his "first years were perfumed with the sweetest scents of faith....Family prayers, the rosary, were always in my eyes and ears. And they are as much a part of my nature as the air I breathe."

It was his mother, Julie, who shaped his deep religious convictions, which is not to diminish the influence of his father, who had once trained to be a priest with the Oblates of Mary Immaculate. Julie's commitment was unfailing. She attended Mass daily, held herself rigorously to all religious obligations and could often be found praying. Before her marriage, she considered a religious life, but she chose not to because of a vision she experienced in her early 20s. She saw an old man surrounded by flames, who commanded her to follow her parents' wishes. Julie believed it was the voice of God and, since her parents wished her to marry, she did so. Louis Riel was nurtured at an early age by his father's Métis nationalism and his mother's Roman Catholicism, and these emerged as the two pillars of his life. It would have been so for any Métis, though perhaps, Louis's experiences were more intense.

Louis received his first lessons at the knees of his educated parents. Just as indelible, however, were the lessons he learned away from his books, immersed in the culture of his people. He often fell asleep listening contentedly to the fiddles and songs of the Métis. Other times, sleep did not come so easily when he thought of the passionate words of his father that he heard at a rally. He spent long hours watching the great trains of Red River carts bound for adventure on the Plains. Stories of adventure were of particular interest to young Louis, and he was a willing audience of anyone who would tell of his people's struggles against the HBC, their battles with the Sioux or the great buffalo hunts.

Such stories were told less frequently in the years following Louis's first confession. In 1851, his parents sent him to a school run by nuns, the Grey Sisters, in St. Boniface. Like the other students, Louis lived at the impressive three-story school. It was the first time he had been separated from his parents, but his family soon moved close when the Red River flooded and washed away their house. They were granted permission to live at the Bishop's house in St. Boniface. By 1855, Louis had new teachers. The Christian Brothers had moved into the community and accepted responsibility for the male students. They provided a classical education, one that espoused a virtuous life rooted in Catholicism.

Louis was an eager pupil and willingly took to the religious precepts. He considered his first communion in 1857 particularly noteworthy because it "opened to me the road of my aspirations towards God." Father Taché, a teacher at the school (later a bishop), must have sensed something of

this because he identified the boy as a possible candidate
for the priesthood. Most boys in Red River completed
their education by age 13. Taché's decision meant that
Louis's education would continue, a step that opened
many doors for him, including that of the bishopric
library. He enjoyed many hours there. Louis also learned
Latin, at which he excelled. In the spring of 1858, Taché
announced that Louis was to be given a full scholarship
(provided by a wealthy Québec* family) to attend one of
the best colleges in Québec, the Collège de Montréal. The
understanding was that he would train to become a priest
and then return to Red River.

Julie was disappointed to see her son leave because she
knew that it would be many years before she saw him
again. Yet she took consolation in the fact that he was giving his life to God. And he would not be alone because he
had relatives in Montreal. Still, Louis's departure was a sad
one since he had to leave without saying goodbye to his
father. Jean-Louis was somewhere between Red River and
Montreal, having traveled east months previously to buy
machinery for his mill. Following a solemn blessing by
a priest on the steps of St. Boniface Cathedral, the boys
(two other scholarship winners accompanied Louis) joined
a train of Red River carts heading for Québec via
Minnesota. Once in St. Paul, their journey would take them
to Wisconsin by steamboat down the Mississippi River,
where they would catch a train bound for Chicago and,
eventually, Montreal. It was along the Mississippi River that

---

* During Riel's life what would become the provinces of Québec and
Ontario were known by a variety of names. For simplicity's sake, only
Québec and Ontario will be used.

the small party unexpectedly encountered Jean-Louis on his return home.

"Louis! What are you doing here?" exclaimed his father in disbelief.

Louis explained the momentous events of the previous weeks.

"Ahh, it is good," replied his father, after a moment of reflection. "Our people need leaders who are educated. And a priest! To serve God, there is no greater calling. I am proud of you, my son."

A call came from the ferry, signaling its imminent departure. Jean-Louis embraced his son. "Learn well, and do not forget what is important!" With that, the two parted company.

What a sight was Montreal! Riel's new home boasted over 90,000 inhabitants and they were enjoying an economic boom, evident in the frenzied construction of railroads, bridges and buildings. Riel had seen nothing like it. The scholarships were for different schools, so the boys parted after their arrival. Riel was taken to the Collège de Montreal, run by the Gentlemen of St. Sulpice. The Sulpicians enjoyed a history in Montreal that stretched back more than 200 years. Their educational efforts commenced just after the British Conquest in the 1760s. While they trained young men for the priesthood, they also promoted French culture and language, an important responsibility since severing ties from France. The education designed to achieve these goals had changed little over the century. The Sulpicians emphasized the classics, and students graduated with a fine grasp of Greece, Rome and philosophy, as well as the Catholic faith.

The Collège de Montreal and its practices had gone almost unchanged since the beginning. The school was an uninspiring, four-story stone building with a mostly dirt enclosure that served as a recreation area. Contact with the outside was frowned upon; newspapers were forbidden because they were considered to be a corrupting influence. It was just as well, since the imposed routine left the seminarians with little time free. Daily Mass, lessons, study and prayers, all done under the ever-watchful eye of a priest, ensured that idleness had little opportunity to exercise undue influence. Regular exams, drills and corporal punishment also sharpened the seminarians' focus.

It took Riel time to adjust to his new regimen. He performed poorly during the first year of his studies, but by his second year he was more fully adjusted and aware of what was expected. His grades regularly placed him near the top of his class. The priests were also impressed by his conduct. It was noted, however, that he had an independent turn of mind, and both instructors and classmates were often frustrated by his refusal to accept views he did not share. But Riel was popular among them and he made friends easily. Perhaps it was the mystique Riel carried with him. He was Métis, reared at the frontier's edge; he had stories of Blackfoot and Sioux, buffalo and the Great Plains, and a ready willingness to share them.

Riel's storytelling sometimes took a metaphorical turn expressed in poetry and fables. Religious themes dominated his writings, which were often reflections on God's wrath and His protection of the virtuous. Occasionally, his compositions revealed a nationalistic sentiment, suggestive, even at his young age, of his concerns about the plight of the Métis.

Riel enjoyed six successful years studying at the Collège de Montreal, but in early 1864 tragic news arrived from Red River that was to cause him to reconsider his future at the institution. Riel's father had died unexpectedly, and the young man slipped into what many saw as an unusually deep depression. His despair was worsened by the priests' suggestion that he not write home until he had regained some measure of composure. Those close to him thought that his recovery took a long time.

His uncle in Montreal, John Lee, later remembered, "That death caused him extraordinary sorrow....it had so touched his heart that he was inconsolable. I perceived then that this profound sorrow was affecting his brain and that he was delirious. That was obvious in his exaggerations and religious eccentricities; for he threw himself into excesses of piety and spoke on religious matters in language, which I found unreasonable....Afterwards he remained very melancholic; I observed that to last about a year or a year and a half, after which he became his old self again."

However, his grades hardly suffered, and Riel himself believed that he "became his old self" long before a year had passed. The priests at the college were less certain and noted that he was restless, rebellious and unstable. They began to wonder whether he was a good candidate for the priesthood after all.

Evidently, Riel shared their concern. By the end of 1864, he decided to quit the Collège de Montreal. He did so in March 1865, four months short of obtaining his degree. He never defended his decision to abandon the priesthood, but it is not difficult to find plausible reasons. As the eldest son, Riel felt a responsibility for his family. The duties and income of a priest would have limited his ability to take care of them. Riel had also come to find the restrictive rules of the college burdensome, even smothering. His father had abandoned the priesthood and had become active in the Métis cause for self-determination. Riel held no other person in greater esteem, so perhaps he saw his father's path as appropriate for himself.

Riel's first challenge was to find employment. While a seminarian, he had listened to a speech given by George-Étienne Cartier, himself an alumnus of the Collège de Montreal. Cartier was a major figure in colonial politics and Riel was as impressed by his bearing as he was his inspirational words. He wrote to Cartier several times seeking assistance in finding a position but received no response. Eventually Riel found work as a law clerk. His new employer, Rodolphe Laflamme, was an ardent Québec nationalist who opposed both the power of the Catholic Church and the proposed confederation of the British colonies, which had dominated political discussion for the previous few years. It was an awkward environment for the young Métis, particularly because of the pervasive anti-clerical sentiment. It did, however, give him ample opportunity to sharpen his debating skills.

And it wasn't just at the law office where Riel was exposed to the important topics of the day. Free from the restraints of the Collège, his evenings were occupied with visits to popular pubs and restaurants where the future of Québec dominated discussion. The world of political debate was familiar to Riel, who had often witnessed his father and other Métis leaders give impassioned speeches. But back then he was an observer who understood little of the discussion. As a young man in his 20s, he entered the fray as a participant and he took to it with enthusiasm.

Riel also found another love in Montreal, Marie Julie Guernon. Her family were neighbors of his uncle. It took some convincing on his part for Marie to accept his hand in marriage, since she feared her parents' reaction to the proposed betrothal. Nevertheless, in June 1866, she accepted and a marriage contract was drawn up without her parents' knowledge. The Guernons were livid when they discovered their daughter's intent, as Riel discovered when he went to her father, Joseph, to plead his case.

"You wish to marry my daughter? Do you think I'd agree to give her hand to a man who failed at his education?"

"It was not a failure, but a choice!" replied Riel. "A religious life was not for me."

"Well, a poor choice then, especially as my family is concerned! Better you were a priest. Then there would be no talk of this marriage nonsense. What prospects do you have as a law clerk? The position won't provide for a wife, let alone a family!" he raged.

"You are correct," admitted Riel. "The income is low. But our love will dull the pains that might accompany want. We will not come to you for money. You know that the marriage contract states that there is no need for a dowry," Riel reminded him.

"I would willingly give one to the right man. You are not him!" snapped Guernon. "Go back to your people in the West!" he advised. "If you remain in Montreal, stay away from my daughter."

Marie was spirited off to a secret location and, although Riel made an effort to win her parents over, his heart was not in it. In the months since he had left the Collège de Montreal his thoughts had turned more often to Red River. While his future as a lawyer held promise, it did not interest him. He had a poet's nature, one given more to imagination and romance than was appropriate in the legal profession. He decided that it was time to return home.

It was the better part of two years before he actually arrived home. For a time he resided in Chicago, where he joined an expatriate French Canadian community. While there, his nationalistic and romantic tendencies sharpened. Riel lived with Louis Frechette, a friend of Laflamme, who shared much of the lawyer's philosophy. Frechette was the owner of a radical French-language newspaper whose clientele were supporters of a Québec unfettered by any

English master. Frechette was also a poet of some repute and Riel enjoyed the opportunity to write his verse in a supportive community. However, he could not make a living writing verse, so he moved to St. Paul. He held a variety of uninspiring jobs there, the most steady of which was as a clerk at a dry goods store. But he earned a wage and that was what mattered because Riel did not want to return home empty-handed. Finally, on July 28, 1868 he arrived back in St. Boniface. Riel was 24 years old. He had been away from Red River for 11 years. Much had changed in that time, not the least of which was the young man himself.

During the years 1867–68, the community was suffering from the results of a series of droughts that had stretched back a half dozen years. Locusts descended in great numbers, devouring what little grew. The agricultural collapse was compounded by the failure of the buffalo hunt. Locals faced the very real threat of famine. Government grants helped the situation, but most valuable were the public relief campaigns. Donations came from Canada (where a growing number of the settlers had relatives) and Great Britain (where the Hudson's Bay Company was headquartered). A significant amount of relief also came from the United States, understandable given Red River's new relationship with its southern neighbor.

Red River was no longer the isolated community it had once been. Firm economic ties were established with the American trading centers of St. Paul and Pembina. Such links were a matter of geographic reality and convenience since the imposing Canadian Shield to the east had deterred efforts to construct a viable trade and travel route into Ontario. The political face of this trading relationship was a groundswell of support for the United States' annexation of Red River. The few advocates of this idea included many of the descendants of the original settlers of Red River. Some in Minnesota were also vocal supporters of annexation, not the least of whom was the local senator, Alexander Ramsay.

Most Métis opposed the idea, but the proposal was most vocally countered by a group of settlers new to Red River. Led by an Ontario-born pharmacist, Dr. John Schultz, the Canadian Party advocated confederation with the newly created Dominion of Canada (some of Britain's North American colonies had united in 1867). Known as Canadian expansionists, many of these settlers had emigrated west, harboring the belief that they were in the vanguard of the British Empire. Concentrated in the growing community of Winnipeg (just northwest of St. Boniface), the Canadian expansionists represented about 1 in 10 of Red River's population. They considered confederation as both desirable and inevitable. The first step in achieving this was to throw off the yoke of the Hudson's Bay Company rule.

The Canadian government was also negotiating to remove the HBC thorn, though it was not motivated by the outcry of western loyalists. The government wanted possession of HBC territories so that it could control the vast resources of the northwestern part of the continent. Given the expansionist tendencies of Americans to the south, there was also some urgency. The Canadian government and the Hudson's Bay Company finally reached an agreement in 1869. For £300,000, the government purchased Rupert's Land (the drainage basin of the Hudson's Bay), a piece of land about 10 times the size of the then Dominion. Canada had its western hinterland.

Or so it thought. The long-time residents of Red River were alarmed at the turn of events. Unsure about what the new relationship would mean for them, they were worried when the Canadian expansionists proposed answers. The expansionists controlled the local newspaper, the *Nor'Wester*, and in it they promoted their vision of the North-West

Territories. The *Nor'Wester* claimed that the future of the
West lay in immigration. Its editorials were directed at
farmers in Ontario, who were reminded of the glowing
agricultural reports written by the recent Palliser and
Dawson expeditions. But those who came from Ontario
were English Protestants and, if the expansionists were
any indication, racists. The prevailing sentiment among
them was that the Métis were lazy and dirty (the French
and the Catholics were little better), who could only
interfere with the development of the North-West
Territories. The sooner the immigrants outnumbered the
Métis, the better. Until that blessed time, the expansionists advised government officials to delay implementing
any form of democratic self-government in the region.
The expansionists knew that the dominant Métis population would fill most of the elected positions, an outcome
they wished to avoid.

Amidst this rapid change, the Métis were mostly content
to live as they had traditionally. While there was a dawning
realization that the buffalo might not continue to be their
main source of sustenance, the transition to farming was not
difficult, especially since most had farmed small plots for
many years. The Métis also enjoyed a harmonious relationship with the other settlers of Red River. Though they had
unique cultures, spoke different languages and practiced
a variety of religions, the long-standing residents of Red
River got along well enough. Suddenly, this new group of
Canadian expansionists wanted to change all that. The Métis
(and others in the community) looked to the expected flood
of farmers from Ontario and saw it washing away peaceful
relations and the rights of the locals.

It seemed as if the Dominion government was supporting
the wishes of the Canadian expansionists. The government
had, after all, purchased Red River without consulting the

locals. Bishop Taché would later write that the residents considered that *they*, the people, had been sold, which was an intolerable idea. Some argued that justice demanded the government pay those who lived on the land and not some distant landlord (the Hudson's Bay Company). Now there was talk of imposing a government on the people. Rumor had it that a territorial governor would soon be dispatched, and doubtless he would draw his government appointees from the expansionists.

More than rumors suggested it was the government's desire to open the West to immigrants. In the fall of 1869, work crews arrived to build a road east that would connect Red River with the Lake of the Woods (and thus Ontario). Government officials were quick to argue that the road would give easy access to rations in times of need. However, those employed to construct the road hardly eased Métis fears. Many were from Ontario, and most shared the racist perspective of the Canadian expansionists. Some in the work crew were so violent that they had to be fired, including a man named Thomas Scott. The workers also made claims to choice locations along the route. The Métis organized patrols to ensure that no land would be staked in their parishes, and more than once they chased away would-be settlers in the act of marking off a homestead.

To the Métis, bigotry, violence and land grabbing were ominous signs of a clear threat to their traditional way of life. Over the summer of 1869, they began to hold public meetings to address the situation. It was like the old days. Speakers fired impassioned speeches from the stoops of churches and atop crates. Riel was actively involved, as his father might have been in speaking to the Métis wherever they gathered. There are no records of his speeches, but it is not difficult to imagine them, his vision broad and anchored firmly in past Métis triumphs.

Brothers and sisters, these newcomers do not have our interests at heart. The Canadian Party seeks to improve their own position at our expense. They see us as beasts, without rights!

Riel opened a copy of the *Nor'Wester*.

Listen! They call us "indolent and careless. The Native tribes of the country will fall back before the march of a superior intelligence." They know little of our people!

We have seen their like before. Remember the Pemmican Proclamation of 1814? The Governor tried to strike at the foundation of our way of life by forbidding the sale of pemmican and outlawing the buffalo hunt, so that a handful of English colonists might be better fed.

The great Métis leader Cuthbert Grant would have none of that. If the Métis were to survive, he knew that the colonists had to be removed. He did not hesitate. He attacked the Company post that supported the colonists. He met Governor Semple's men at Seven Oaks. He did not want violence and asked the governor to surrender. Instead, there was gunfire. When the dust settled, 21 of Semple's men but only one Métis were dead!

No, the colony was not destroyed and we learned to live together. But the English also learned that the Métis would stand up for their rights! Grant won for us the right to live according to our customs. Today we face the same struggle. Schultz and his ilk need to be taught a lesson! Let us hope it does not involve the bloodshed of years earlier.

He ripped up the *Nor'Wester* and flung it to the ground. Then he led the gathering in the Pierre Falcon song that memorialized the events at Seven Oaks. All joined in heartily.

Ah, would you had seen those Englishmen,
And the bois-brûlés a-chasing them!
One by one we did them destroy
While our bois-brûlés uttered shouts of joy!

"Brothers and sisters," concluded Riel, "we have the memories of our ancestors to respect. We have their actions as our measuring stick. They envisioned a proud future for the Métis. It is our responsibility to ensure it!"

Everyone knew that Riel's father was a man who spoke loudly for Métis rights, but many who listened to Riel were surprised because they remembered him as a young boy. The question remained: Would he do more than speak? Yes. It was at Riel's suggestion that the Métis organize patrols to stop the survey crews from making land claims. In the fall of 1869, he proposed that the Métis form a central committee whose purpose it would be to consider the best way to protest the injustice done to Red River by Canada. Two men from each parish were elected and Riel served as secretary (essentially, the committee's leader).

One of the immediate concerns of the committee was the matter of land ownership. They knew that government surveyors would soon arrive to begin dividing Red River into lots. The standard formula was to partition the land into sections one mile square. However, the Métis homesteads did not match that configuration. Theirs were long rectangular lots that stretched back from the river's edge. More worrisome was the fact that the Métis were without legal title to the land. It had meant little to a people for whom tradition was the rule, but it was unlikely that future settlers would see it thus. The government had promised that documents guaranteeing title would arrive, but there was no sign of them. The Métis were suspicious. On October 11, they gave action to their mistrust of the government.

"Louis!" came the call, "Louis! Come! The surveyors have arrived!"

It was André Nault at Riel's door. André had been tending cattle on Edouard Marion's field when the surveyors began hammering their stakes.

"I told them that they were trespassing," explained Nault, "but they ignored me."

"It is time then," replied Riel. He threw on his coat and the pair mounted their horses. Within an hour they had rounded up 16 Métis and were on their way to Marion's, near St. Vital. Arriving there, they dismounted and surrounded the surveyors.

"You go no farther!" directed Riel. "This land belongs to Monsieur Marion. The Canadian government has no right to make surveys here without the express permission of the people of the settlement."

Riel nodded to a Métis companion. In one great stride, Janvier Ritchot stepped onto the surveyors' chain. The surveyors fled and the opening salvo in what became known as the Red River Resistance was launched.

Later in October the Métis took more dramatic action. Word arrived in Red River that the new lieutenant-governor, William McDougall, was en route to the community. Accompanying him were Captain Donald Cameron, who was to establish a police force in the region, and a handful of men who were to be appointed to McDougall's council. McDougall was slated to take power on December 1, the day that the transfer of the Hudson's Bay Company's lands to Canada became official. In mid-October, Riel called a meeting to address the situation. Many Métis gathered in the house of Abbé Ritchot at St. Norbert to listen to what the young man had to say.

"We must take a stand that cannot be misinterpreted by the Dominion government," declared Riel. "Our families have lived in Red River for more than 50 years. It was not always easy for them, but they conquered all challenges with great courage and strong will. What we enjoy today is a legacy of their efforts.

"We have learned through the press that our land, rights and liberties have been sold to the Canadian government. How can such things be bartered? We have also learned that the Canadian government is set to impose a government on our country. The Métis will have no influence in that government! It will be a band of unscrupulous and irresponsible fellows who will rule over us. They will plunder and eat our subsistence and not once think that it is wrong."

"Everyone is aware of the debt owed to our parents and grandparents," agreed one of the Métis. "But how can we be faithful to their legacy? As you suggest, the deal is done, and the Canadian government is not likely to listen to Métis pleas that our rights be acknowledged."

"My brother speaks with insight," replied Riel. "The government will not listen to us. So we must not use words. Our actions will speak for us. They will ring loud, so loud that the echoes of what we have done will roll east to the hall of that distant government and cause those there to tremble!"

"Louis, you are an artful speaker, but what can we possibly do that will make the government tremble?"

"We will not allow McDougall to enter Red River until Métis' rights are safeguarded."

To identify the rights that needed protection, a National Committee of Métis was organized. Each parish selected two representatives to serve on the body, and once it was established it replaced the earlier central committee. Riel served as the committee's secretary, but everyone knew he directed it.

The Provisional Government of Red River, taken in 1869. Louis Riel sits in the center. His close friend Ambroise Lepine stands third from the right, while William O'Donoghue, who would later initiate a failed attempt at American annexation of Red River, sits on Riel's left. The Provisional Government came out of a National Convention of the English- and French-speaking parishes of Red River. Riel organized the convention in the hope that the community might emerge from it with a unified voice. Convention delegates supported demands for increased local control over the affairs of Red River, particularly as outlined in the List of Rights unveiled in early December 1869. Many of the English-speaking delegates, however, opposed the treatment of William McDougall, the lieutenant-governor in waiting, and they were wary of the armed rebellion that Riel indicated might be necessary to achieve local control. Undaunted, Riel established the Provisional Government without their support.

The creation of the National Committee was something of a coup for Riel. Some Métis did not want to resist the Canadian government—established traders who desired a comfortable transition that would not disrupt business. Others did not think that a conflict with Canada could achieve anything. Throughout the fall, Riel worked tirelessly to bring opponents around to his perspective and, by October, he had won many supporters, including some of the country born and descendants of the original settlers. Their numbers were supplemented in late fall with the arrival of the Métis buffalo hunters and those employed as laborers in the western fur trade. These were the groups from whom Riel drew his greatest support.

The National Committee slipped easily into the mantle of government. Resolutions were adopted that made laws and a military force was established, with the traditions of the buffalo hunt evident in its organization. The soldiers elected captains, and these captains served as the council for the military, just as they would do during a hunt. Each captain had soldiers under his command.

When word arrived that McDougall brought with him crates of rifles to be distributed to government allies (mostly the Canadian expansionists) and used to maintain peace and order in the settlement, the Métis military was put to immediate use. The National Committee directed several of its captains to meet McDougall at the border. They carried with them a letter written by Riel. Others built a barrier along the road from Pembina (thereafter called La Barrière).

McDougall arrived at Pembina on October 30, 1869, where he received Riel's letter. He was a big man, his round facial features hidden behind a generous moustache. But as he read the document, the Métis could see his cheeks become flushed.

GREAT CHIEFS, VOLUME I

> *Sir,*
>
> *The National Committee of the Métis of Red River orders William McDougall not to enter the Territory of the North-West without special permission of the above-mentioned committee.*

"By God!" boomed McDougall. "Who is this collection of half-breeds to tell the representative of the Queen what he may do?" His tirade included many words that sounded most unroyal. He tore up the letter. "Let this *committee* try and keep me off British soil! I'll be moving to the Hudson's Bay Company post!" he declared. The post was a few miles inside the border, but still some distance from the Red River settlement.

The Council of Assiniboia (a legal body established by the HBC and, until McDougall assumed his position and the land transfer was complete, the government in the region) summoned Riel and his associates to appear before it to answer for Métis actions.

"The council hopes that the rumors it has heard about the actions taken against the Honorable William McDougall are without foundation," began Judge John Black, chairman in place of Mactavish, governor of the HBC, and the present legal authority in the region, but one who was also too ill to assume his position.

"The actions have strong foundations, the Métis nation," retorted Riel. "We are perfectly satisfied with the present government and want no other. If another is necessary, we object to any government coming from Canada without our being consulted in the matter. No governor, save one appointed by the Hudson's Bay Company, will be admitted, unless delegates are first sent, with whom we might negotiate the terms and conditions under which we will acknowledge him."

Riel went on to outline Métis grievances. The council meeting deteriorated into a raucous debate, with a frustrated Black suggesting that the Métis actions foretold disastrous consequences.

"Disaster lies in our failure to act!" countered Riel. "We are simply acting in defense of our own liberty. We do so on behalf of all the people of Red River."

As it turned out, McDougall's bravado got him to the HBC post, but no farther. On November 2, a Métis patrol arrived there and ordered him to leave. McDougall produced his commission appointing him as lieutenant-governor, but it didn't change the situation.

"By whose orders do you direct me to leave?" barked McDougall.

"The government's," came the terse reply.

McDougall eyed the horsemen, all well armed and well weathered. Thinking little of the National Committee and confident that he would soon be in Red River, he had previously directed Cameron to proceed to Upper Fort Garry and prepare for the transfer of power, so he was without much support. He decided to return to Pembina.

As he crossed the border, he heard the shout, "You must not return beyond this line!"

McDougall later learned that Cameron had also been humiliated. He found his way to the fort blocked by the barrier, and when he asked them to move it, the Métis laughed.

On the day McDougall skulked back to the United States, Riel and the Métis took Upper Fort Garry in an attack that met no resistance. It was a crucial victory. There had been rumors that the Canadian expansionists planned to take the fort and use it to defend their interests in Red River. It was also strategically situated at the center of Red River, allowing whomever possessed it to control movement within the

community. Most importantly, however, the attack on Upper
Fort Garry demonstrated something of the organization and
determination of the Métis. They had taken the most prominent administrative center in the North-West Territories.

Not everyone in the Red River community supported
the attack on Upper Fort Garry. The English-speaking settlers (who did not include the Canadian expansionists and
amounted to just over a third of the local population)
shuddered at the prospect of armed rebellion. Riel, however, realized that the Métis cause would be much stronger
if he could present their grievances to the Dominion government under the banner of a mostly united Red River.
To that end, he called a meeting of the community's
12 English and 12 French parishes for November 16. His
goal was to implement a provisional government that could
replace the HBC administration. The debate was heated.
The English objected to the Métis' interference with
McDougall while the Métis countered that such action was
necessary to prevent the Canadian expansionists from
strengthening their position. The debate crystallized when
a letter from Governor Mactavish arrived unexpectedly.
Mactavish desired that it be read aloud at the meeting and,
while Riel opposed the idea, he eventually acceded.
Mactavish accused the Métis of committing unlawful acts.
He suggested that good might come out of the meeting if
the Métis laid down their arms and abandoned Upper Fort
Garry immediately. If they decided otherwise, they would
suffer the lawful consequences.

When the letter was read, James Ross, a leading country
born representative and ally of Schultz, declared, "It is clear.
We must recognize that the Métis are engaged in sedition."

An angry Riel took the floor and responded to the
charge.

"If we are rebels, we are rebels against the Company that sold us, and is ready to hand us over, and against a Canada that wants to buy us! We do not rebell against British supremacy, which has still not given its approval for the final transfer of the country....Moreover," he continued, now in full stride, "we are true to our native land. We are protecting it against the dangers that threaten it. We want the people of Red River to be a free people. Let us help one another! We are all brothers and relations....Let us not separate. See what Mr. Mactavish says. He says that out of this meeting and its decision may come incalculable good. Let us unite! The evil that he fears will not take place."

Riel had skillfully hit the notes that appealed to all who were present. The argument roused English sympathies, but those in attendance couldn't agree on a course of action. In the final days of November, a frustrated Riel took matters into his own hands. At a secret meeting, he convinced the Métis delegates to agree to the creation of a provisional government replacing the Council of Assiniboia. On November 24, Métis soldiers entered the local Hudson's Bay Company post and confiscated all its papers. It was a symbolic act that demonstrated the end of the rule of the HBC. The English delegates were stunned at news of the takeover when they arrived at the meeting later on the 24th. Ross demanded to know Riel's plans.

"You know perfectly well what we want. We want what every French parish wants, to form a provisional government for our protection and to negotiate with Canada," declared Riel. "We invite you to join it with all sincerity. This government will be made up equally of French and English; it will be only provisional in nature."

At Ross's request the meeting was adjourned to allow consideration of Riel's proposal. Matters took a more dramatic turn on December 1, which was the day that

McDougall believed his commission was to take effect.
When he attempted to cross the border to take his position,
he was turned back yet again. Unbeknownst to McDougall,
Prime Minister Macdonald had decided that the situation in
Red River was such that he wanted more time to address it.
He had wired London, insisting that the transfer of the
North-West Territories be peaceful. McDougall's proclama-
tion was void. The Métis were also unaware of the develop-
ment; they merely wanted to prevent McDougall's entry.
The North-West Territories remained under the HBC's
control. McDougall eventually returned to Canada, never to
take up his commission.

But even as McDougall tried to enter the North-West
Territories, the National Convention that Riel had proposed in mid-November was in session and busy debating
a proclamation listing the rights of the Red River community. It had been developed by the Métis, but undoubtedly
shaped by Riel. On December 4, a *List of Rights* was made
public.

1. *The people have the right to elect their own
   Legislature.*
2. *That the Legislature have the power to pass all laws
   local to the Territory over the veto of the Executive
   by a two-thirds vote.*
3. *That no act of the Dominion Parliament (local to
   the Territory) be binding on the people until sanc-
   tioned by the Legislature of the Territory.*
4. *That all Sheriffs, Magistrates, Constables, School
   Commissioners, etc., be elected by the people.*
5. *A free Homestead and pre-emption Land Law.*
6. *That a portion of the local lands be appropriated to
   the benefit of Schools, the building of Bridges, Roads
   and Public Buildings.*

7. *That it be guaranteed to connect Winnipeg by Rail with the nearest line of Railroad, within a term of five years; that land grant to be subject to the local legislature.*

8. *That for the term of four years all Military, Civil and Municipal expenses be paid out of the Dominion funds.*

9. *That the Military be composed of the inhabitants now existing in the territory.*

10. *That the English and French languages be common in the Legislature and the Courts, and that all Public Documents and Acts of the Legislature be published in both languages.*

11. *That the Judges of the Supreme Court speak the English and French languages.*

12. *That treaties be concluded and ratified between the Dominion Government and the several tribes of Indians in the Territory to ensure peace on the frontier.*

13. *That we have a fair and full representation in the Canadian Parliament.*

14. *That all privileges, customs and usages existing at the time of transfer be respected.*

The intent of the document was to promote the cultural harmony that existed in Red River, to protect the rights of long-time residents and to ensure that the Dominion government realized that any relationship with them would be conducted on an equal footing.

While many of the non-Métis delegates were upset at the treatment of McDougall and continued to believe that he should be permitted entry as the Queen's representative (which they thought he was), they were pleased with the level-headedness of the demands in the *List of Rights*. Riel remained insistent that McDougall not be

granted entry because he believed that McDougall's presence would strengthen the position of the Canadian
expansionists. They, too, were active during the turmoil of
early December. Many of them had congregated around
Lower Fort Garry, the headquarters of John Dennis, who
had been commissioned by McDougall to suppress the
uprising. Dennis was not yet prepared to fight. Instead,
some 50 of them gathered at Schultz's Winnipeg store,
which stored a shipment of government supplies. They
fortified the location, which was quickly dubbed Fort
Schultz. On December 7, Riel directed the Métis soldiers
to take control of the location. The soldiers arrested several
expansionists who tried to defend the store. The expansionists, Riel's most vocal opponents, were no longer a significant factor. Riel's actions divided convention members
and, on December 7, it dissolved without agreeing on
what to do next.

Riel was not to be dissuaded by fence-sitters or opponents. On December 8, he issued a *Declaration of Métis
Independence* and proclaimed the establishment of a provisional government. Riel, named president, took full control
of Red River. The proclamation finally forced Prime
Minister Macdonald to take action. His vision for Canada
included a North-West Territories that was firmly under the
control of the Dominion government, which would be
responsible for directing the exploitation of its resources. Yet,
there was little Macdonald could do as he watched the situation in Red River deteriorate. He couldn't send in a military
force (which, in any case, would first have to be organized)
because access to the region, even during the best conditions, was difficult. With winter approaching, the community
would be isolated for the next six months. Desperate, he gave
a special commission to Donald A. Smith, directing him to
break Riel's power over Red River.

Smith was the leading Hudson's Bay Company official in Canada, having worked his way up through the company's ranks over many years of hard work. But Riel was suspicious of Smith. The feeling was heightened by demands made by Smith upon his arrival in the settlement. He desired to meet with the community of Red River rather than the provisional government. Riel agreed, but only with Smith's commitment that he would not declare the provisional government to be an act of rebellion. On January 19, more than 1000 gathered in freezing temperatures at Upper Fort Garry to listen to Smith.

"I sincerely hope that my humble efforts may in some measure contribute to bring about peaceably, union and entire accord among all classes of the people of this land," he declared.

Smith addressed the locals' concerns that the Dominion government would treat them poorly, and he effectively eased their worries. But he proposed no course of action that might address the political and cultural concerns of Red River. Sensing an opportunity, Riel jumped in.

"I came here with fears. We are not yet enemies," he said to those gathered, "but we came very near to being so. As soon as we understood each other, we joined in demanding what our English fellow subjects in common with us believe to be our just rights. I am not afraid to say our rights; for we all have rights!" bellowed Riel to the cheering crowd. "We claim no half rights, mind you, but all the rights we are entitled to. Those rights will be set forth by our representatives and, what's more, gentlemen, we will get them."

Riel proposed that a new convention be called to consider the commissioner's words and Smith agreed. It was a mistake on Smith's part. Whatever momentum he had built up at the outdoor meeting was lost during the new convention, where Riel was again firmly in charge. On January 25, an interim provisional government was appointed with Riel as its president. The representatives also adopted a new list of rights (longer, though similar, to December's list) that included a new demand that Red River send delegates to Ottawa to negotiate the community's entry into the Dominion as a province. Riel wanted to give greater authority to the interim government and, in a reasoned and impassioned speech, he proposed that it be made the legal governing body of Red River:

> ...we are yet in a loose, unsatisfactory way. It is now necessary for us to place ourselves in a more suitable position. We must have a more fixed existence before proceeding further. Unquestionably our position can be improved by drawing closer together than at present; and it is equally unquestionable that we ought to be bound together by bonds of friendship and self-interest. Union is our strength. United we command a hearing from Canada, where our rights are to come from, which we can command in no other way.

Cheers erupted from the delegates.

> One of these days, then, manifestly we have to form a Government in order to secure the safety of life and property, and establish a feeling of security in men's minds, and remove a feeling of apprehension which it is not desirable should continue for a moment. How often have we not, on our side, expressed a fear as to the security of property and life. It is our duty to put an end to this, and it will be our glory as well as our duty....Should this Convention separate without coming to an understanding, we leave matters worse than ever; we leave a gap in which all our people might be engulfed, and in the angry waves of the flood which might sweep over the

*Settlement we may find reason for regret, that a wiser course
had not been adopted when it lay in our power.*

Riel had little difficulty convincing the Métis, but the
other delegates were reluctant to take such a bold step, which
might be seen as an affront to the Crown. When Governor
Mactavish advised that a government—*any* government—
would reestablish stability in the settlement, their concerns
evaporated. Before the convention closed on February 10,
the delegates had voted to form a provisional government for
Rupert's Land and the North-West Territories. In subsequent
elections, Riel was elected president.

In the weeks that followed, Riel's relatively unencum-
bered ascent to power took a disastrous turn. At the convention, Riel had agreed to free the Canadian expansionist
prisoners. He would do so only if they agreed to leave the
colony or obey the orders of the new government. Some,
including Schultz and Thomas Scott, would not. Schultz
broke free and returned to Ontario, determined to stir up
protest against Riel. His case was strengthened when news
came of the action taken by the provisional government
against Scott, who held the Métis in utter disdain and gave
voice to his opinion in an endless stream of bigoted comments. The Métis endured his abuse for two months before
he was ordered, perhaps by Riel, to face a military court-
martial for insubordination. He was sentenced to death.
Riel signed the order of execution, declaring that the
action would make Canada respect the Métis. Scott was
executed on March 4, 1870.

Schultz now had a martyr—one associated with the
prominent and staunchly Protestant Orange Order—and he
used it with enthusiasm. His determined efforts inflamed
Ontario's passions against Riel. At the same time, sentiment in
Québec was strongly *for* Riel, who was seen as the protector

Some western political leaders. Clockwise: Governor Morris, Riel, Governor Archibald, Governor McDougall, Dr. Schultz.

of French and Roman Catholic rights in the West. Prime Minister Macdonald, anxious to bring a swift end to the matter, decided on compromise. He would negotiate with the Red River provisional government, and he would send in a military force to ensure peace in the North-West.

For an anxious period, it appeared that the compromise would not be enough to appease Ontario. Three delegates— Abbé Ritchot, Judge John Black and Alfred Scott—left for Ottawa in March to negotiate the terms of confederation. Riel was not among their number because he was aware of the sentiment against him in Ontario, where there was both

a reward for his capture and deafening calls for his execution.
The delegation carried with them the list of rights drawn up
at the convention. It had been modified by Riel to demand
that the North-West be admitted as a province rather than
a territory, that a bilingual lieutenant-governor be appointed
and that there be a general amnesty for all participants in the
resistance. In addition, Bishop Taché included a demand for
separate schools so that each religious denomination could
educate the children of its faith. Ritchot and Scott were
arrested upon arrival as suspected accessories in the murder
of Thomas Scott. Macdonald, who sensed political chaos,
ordered them set free.

Negotiations continued without further difficulties, and
on July 15, 1870, the Manitoba Act was proclaimed, creat-
ing the province of Manitoba. Most of the demands of the
provisional government were met, particularly those that
protected Métis cultural rights. However, Macdonald
insisted that the new province not include all the North-
West Territories, so Manitoba was a mere 100 square miles.
While Métis land rights were protected (including a grant
to unmarried Métis children), they were refused land
grants in large blocks, which would have served to act as
a buffer against new settlement. The agreement also
included amnesty for those who participated in the resistance. Riel had led the Métis to victory.

There remained, however, the troublesome matter of
Macdonald's military force. On May 21, Colonel Garnet
Wolseley left Toronto with the 60th Rifles under his command. Known as the Red River Expedition, Wolseley declared
that his was a mission of peace. The Métis were not so certain.
Riel had pressed for confirmation that he was included in the
general amnesty that was to be given to those in Red River. It
had not been forthcoming. When he learned that Wolseley
had reached Red River, Riel fled to the Métis settlement of

St. Joseph in the United States. Along the way, he stopped at Bishop's Taché's resident to make one last declaration.

"No matter what happens now, the rights of the Métis are assured by the Manitoba Act; that is what I wanted. My mission is finished."

It is well that he fled. The truth was that Wolseley was uninterested in peace, as he revealed in a letter to his wife: "Hope Riel will have bolted, for although I should like to hang him from the highest tree in the place, I have such a horror of rebels and vermin of his kidney, that my treatment of him might not be approved by the civil powers."

Manitoba did not prove an idyllic homeland for the Métis, and the days following its creation brought them many problems. Led by Schultz, who returned to Manitoba in early 1872, the old Canadian expansionists would not forget what the Métis had done. Métis found themselves subject to threats and beatings. Some were killed. The military under Wolseley was mostly sympathetic to Schultz's position, and it turned a blind eye to their lawlessness.

Adams Archibald, the new lieutenant-governor, captured the poisoned atmosphere in a letter to Prime Minister Macdonald. "Unfortunately there is a frightful spirit of bigotry among a small but noisy section of our people....[they] really talk and seem to feel as if the French half-breeds should be wiped off the face of the globe."

The situation was enough to urge Riel to return to Red River, despite an outstanding warrant for his arrest and a reward. Word reached him that the National Committee had been reorganized. The meeting took place in St. Norbert in mid-September 1870, and Riel took control of it with ease. He railed against the "perfidious treachery" and unfulfilled promises of the Dominion government and the insidious treatment of the Métis. Aided by William O'Donoghue, an Irish American and sometime supporter of the Métis cause, Riel drafted a *Memorial and Petition* to be sent to United States President Grant. The hope was that the president would press the Queen for an investigation into Métis grievances and Canadian atrocities. When O'Donoghue, a long-time advocate of American annexation, pushed for the meeting to show its support for annexation, Riel called it to a close.

It was not the end of the matter, however. The meeting authorized O'Donoghue to deliver the document to President Grant. Before he departed, he slipped into it his own demands for American annexation. When Grant proved disinterested in the petition, O'Donoghue turned to the Fenian Brotherhood, an Irish American organization dedicated to the overthrow of British rule in Ireland, which made its case by raiding into Canada. As an organization, the Fenians offered O'Donoghue their prayers only, but he was able to recruit individual members to aid his cause. On October 5, O'Donoghue led his small armed contingent of 35 men from Pembina to the Hudson's Bay Company post just north of the border and captured it, allegedly in the name of the provisional government of Red River. Within hours, American soldiers arrived to defuse the situation. Those unable to flee were arrested. O'Donoghue himself was captured by two Métis and turned over to the Americans. He had depended on Riel's support, but it had not been forthcoming.

Riel was not opposed to any action that might force the government to reconsider the way it treated the Métis, but he was not convinced that a Fenian invasion was the best way to go about it. Instead, he decided to use his influence against the invasion, anticipating that a demonstration of his loyalty might well place the Dominion government under obligation to him. His decision was made easier by his dislike for O'Donoghue and his opposition to Fenian objectives.

Throughout the summer of 1871, despite a lingering illness
first suffered during the winter, he was often in Red River,
speaking at meetings against O'Donoghue's efforts and for
the principles established in the Manitoba Act. The Métis,
who generally shared Riel's stand on the Fenian mission, listened to their leader and refused to participate in
O'Donoghue's planned offensive. Lieutenant-Governor
Archibald was so pleased with Riel's intercessions that he
shook his hand in public! While the act wasn't an indication
that the government felt indebted to Riel, it suggested that
government no longer considered the Métis leader a force
for disruption in the community.

Riel was again feeling comfortable in Red River, but
political considerations would again drive him from his
homeland. The matter had little to do with local politics,
although some officials in the community remained concerned that his presence alone could do much to cause
problems in the community, despite the belief of the lieutenant-governor. The first provincial election had taken
place in late 1870, but Riel did not forward his name as
a candidate (despite Métis desires that he do so). His
decision was greatly influenced by the Québec politician
Cartier, who was a prominent member of Prime Minister
Macdonald's Dominion government. Realizing that a visible Riel would continue to be used as political fodder by
the Dominion government's opponents, Cartier made it
known that he did not want Riel involved in the political
life of the community.

Ultimately it was pressure from the Dominion government that forced Riel to leave Manitoba. Macdonald was
under increasing pressure from Ontario to address the Riel
matter. Sentiment against the Métis leader remained passionate there, where politicians who opposed Macdonald continued to criticize his handling of the affair. As Macdonald and

Cartier anticipated, opponents stoked the fires of Ontarians' anger so as to embarrass the Dominion government. A substantial reward was offered for the arrest and conviction of those involved in Scott's "murder." Macdonald cringed at the thought of Riel on trial, an event that might appease Ontario but would serve to inflame sentiment in Québec. With a Dominion election only months away, the prime minister had to defuse the situation.

An opportunity presented itself in the fall of 1871. Bishop Taché appealed to the Dominion government for word on Riel's amnesty. Macdonald agreed to see him. The meeting was not what Taché expected.

"No government could stand that would endeavor to procure the amnesty," declared Macdonald. "Confederation remains in the gristle and, if the government should fall, its future is in doubt. The Dominion is more important than the inconveniences suffered by Louis Riel. It is best we put fanciful considerations of amnesty out of our mind," continued Macdonald. "How might we persuade Riel to leave the country for a while?"

Taché knew it was useless to continue pressing for Riel's amnesty.

"You must remember that this man is poor; his mother is a widow with four young girls and three young boys, and she has no means of support, especially when her eldest son is away," replied Taché. "He himself has only his labor for his support, and I do not think it is fair to ask him to leave his home without some compensation or some means of traveling."

Taché left Ottawa with $1000. When Taché gave it to Riel, he expressed disappointment. Riel had shown his loyalty to the Dominion government and had hoped for vindication. But, as Taché pointed out, the matter was not about justice. Riel insisted that $1000 would not go far, either in support of his family or for his own needs, so Donald Smith gave Taché a further £600. On February 23, Riel, accompanied by his friend (and close ally on the Métis provisional government) Ambroise Lepine, left for St. Paul, Minnesota.

Riel lived an uncomfortable few months in the United States. He often spotted known allies of Schultz and heard rumors of impending assault; after all, a price remained on his head. He was anxious to return to Red River when word came from Métis leaders requesting that he run in the Dominion election as a member of Parliament. Riel agreed, and by late summer of 1872, he was actively campaigning in his home district of Provencher. While there was little doubt about his victory, it was not to be. In early September, days before the official nomination, Macdonald sent a telegram to Lieutenant-Governor Archibald. Cartier had been defeated in Québec and Macdonald wanted him to run in Manitoba (balloting was staggered across the country at this time). Riel, still respectful of Cartier, withdrew his name. Cartier was elected and Riel awaited compensation; he wanted his amnesty.

But it was not forthcoming. Soon after he was elected, Cartier died and Macdonald, ever mindful of the fragility of Dominion politics, remained obstinate on Riel's amnesty. Cartier's death required a by-election in Provencher. Riel again put his name forward as a candidate. His enemies, who remained mostly the old advocates of Canadian expansion, knew there was no way he could lose the vote, so they set about defeating him by other means. They had a sympathetic magistrate issue a warrant for his arrest. A warrant was also issued for Lepine, who was taken into custody. On hearing of the arrest, Riel went into hiding. He refused even to be there for his nomination meeting, where authorities waited for him. Nonetheless, Riel won his parliamentary seat by acclamation on October 13, 1873.

Immediately following the election, Riel went to Montreal, where his supporters made plans for him to take his seat in the House of Commons. Riel, however, refused to venture into the Canadian capital for fear of arrest. When Macdonald's Conservative government fell because of the Pacific Railway Scandal in early November 1873, he had still not taken his seat. Riel ran in the subsequent election in February 1874 and, despite an opponent, won handily. This time, Riel did not hesitate to go to Ottawa. Remaining cautious, however, he chose a cold March day that allowed him to bundle in heavy clothes, masking his identity. Accompanied by a member of Parliament from Québec, he entered the House of Commons through a side door. His accomplice approached the Clerk of the House and asked him if he would swear in a new member. It was routine business and the clerk did not hesitate. Only when he looked at the name on the register, its ink still wet, did he realize he had sworn in Louis Riel.

Riel hurried away, and despite an order from the House of Commons directing him to take his seat, he would not return to fulfill his responsibilities. He knew that to do so would be to invite arrest. Meanwhile, a motion was raised in the House of Commons (seconded by a new member of Parliament, Riel's nemesis John Schultz) that Riel be expelled from the legislative body. It was pointed out that he was a fugitive from justice and that he was in willful disobedience of an order from the House of Commons. The motion was passed on April 9, 1874.

Riel returned to Montreal and discovered that he was no longer safe even there. In May, he made his way to St. Paul and while there, he was again re-elected in the September 1874 by-election triggered by his expulsion. During these months the matter of the legality of the Métis actions during the winter of 1869–70 was also finally addressed. Ambroise Lepine went to trial in October 1874 for his part in the execution of Thomas Scott. However, the proceedings were about much more than Lepine's involvement in that affair. His trial included a consideration of the legitimacy of the Métis provisional government. It was argued that Scott's execution might be justified if a legitimate government authorized it. The court decided that the Métis government possessed no such authority. Lepine was convicted and sentenced to be hanged.

Alexander Mackenzie, the new Liberal prime minister, found himself in the same unenviable position as had Macdonald. When pressed to give amnesty to Lepine, he declared that it could only be granted by the British government and threw the matter into the lap of Lord Dufferin, the governor general. Though disgusted with the whole affair, Dufferin did what no Canadian politician would: he took a stand. Dufferin agreed that the provisional government had no standing in law, but he was impressed with Riel's loyalty during the Fenian affair, and he placed great stock in the fact that Lieutenant-Governor Archibald had seen fit to shake hands with the Métis leader. He had placed his life in the man's hands, so Dufferin could hardly consider him a felon. Lepine's death sentence was reduced to two years imprisonment and he was stripped of his political rights.

Dufferin presented Mackenzie with the wedge he needed to resolve the whole sordid affair of the Red River Resistance. When the House of Commons met in February 1875, Mackenzie introduced a motion calling for the amnesty of all those involved. He claimed that because the Conservative government had promised an amnesty, it was only just and proper that the matter be acted upon. It was a cunning move that ensured any uproar from English-Protestant Canada would be directed at his political opponents. Riel and Lepine, however, would first have to endure five years of exile. The motion passed easily. Riel accepted the inevitable and settled in the United States.

The next year was a difficult one for Riel. The harsh treatment of the Métis in Manitoba continued and, as the number of immigrants from Ontario increased, many left their homeland and moved west. The homeland he had envisioned, one of equality and opportunity, was being crushed. It weighed heavily on Riel's mind, as did the years of living a secluded life on the run from his enemies. The stresses of the past half dozen years were finally catching up with him, and Riel increasingly turned to his faith for comfort. Slowly his devotion consumed him. The markers were evident as early as December 1874, when he had his first vision.

"...while I was seated on the top of a mountain near Washington," he revealed, "...the same spirit who showed himself to Moses in the midst of the burning cloud appeared to me in the same manner. I was stupefied. I was confused. He said to me, 'Rise up Louis David Riel, you have a mission to fulfil.' Stretching out my hands and bowing my head, I received this heavenly message."

Riel concluded that his mission was not merely to safeguard Métis rights in the West, but also Roman Catholicism. In this he was encouraged by support from Ignace Bourget, Bishop of Montreal. Bourget held that the French were a nation within Canada and that their nationality was defined not only by their culture, language and history, but also by their religion. He feared that the English wanted to assimilate his people, and he believed that the North-West Territories provided a suitable defense against those English desires. Populating the region with French Canadians could secure the future of the French and Catholicism in Canada.

Bourget's philosophy stoked the religious flames in Riel. In July 1875, he wrote to the Bishop. "I come and throw myself humbly at your feet to assure you that I want to spend my life in the dust at God's feet, humble in heart and body."

Bourget's reply confirmed solidly to Riel that his mission was indeed a religious and a righteous one: "...God who has up until the present directed you and assisted you will not abandon you in your most difficult of struggles, for He has given you a mission which you must accomplish step by step [and] with the Grace of God you must persevere on the path that has been laid out for you. That is to say, you must give up everything that is yours; you must wish ardently to serve God and to procure the greatest Glory in the name of God; you must work without ceasing for the honor of religion...."

Newly inspired, Riel immersed himself fully in the Métis/French Canadian cause. He flirted with the idea of American annexation of the North-West Territories, an odd choice given Bourget's vision. However, he received little support from American politicians. On the heels of his failure came news that one of his younger brothers, Meunier (Charles), had died. Within days, Riel was subject to a series of intense religious experiences. By December 1875, he was convinced that God had chosen him as His prophet for the New World. He would lead the Métis into the new millennium. Then came word that President Grant would see him. It seemed as if God was actively preparing his way, but when the pair met in mid-December, Grant was not receptive to the idea of annexation.

Whether it was Grant's rejection or another religious experience, with the arrival of the new year, Riel began referring to himself as the Messiah. He spoke of himself as being part of a trinity that included the Count de Chambord and Don

Carlos, claimants of the thrones in their respective European countries. Friends Riel lived with noted that he was increasingly difficult, sleeping rarely, often crying, howling and praying. No one doubted that he had lost his senses. His hosts could no longer keep him. Finally, a wire was sent to John Lee, Riel's uncle in Montreal. In late January, he came to Keesville, New York, where Riel was living, and took his nephew back to Montreal. Precautions were necessary since Riel was in Canada illegally. His nephew's deteriorating condition meant that Lee could not house him.

When Lee refused to allow Riel to attend Mass because of his illness, Riel declared, "No, I'm not crazy! Never say I'm crazy! I have a mission to perform and I am a prophet...I am sent by God."

In March he was committed to the Hospice of St. Jean Dieu, an insane asylum near Québec City. For a time while at the asylum, he began referring to himself as "Louis David Riel, Prophet, Infallible Pontiff, Priest King." David was not his Christian name; it was the name of the great Israelite leader. But eventually the visions came no more, and Riel came to believe that he might have misinterpreted them in the first place.

He later wrote to Bishop Taché, "I thank God for having humiliated me and for having brought me to understand what human glory is....how vain it is for him who having for a little while captured the attention of men, suddenly feels the hand of God weighing upon him."

Riel was released from St. Jean Dieu on January 29, 1878, as his doctors considered him "more or less" cured. He might remain so, it was suggested, if he avoided political intrigue.

Riel returned to the United States, and by 1879 he was again in Pembina. The town proved a poor choice for one who was directed to stay clear of politics. Old friends

from Red River visited him and he eagerly sought news
of local happenings. He was disappointed by what he
heard. Manitoba was undergoing a rapid transformation.
The population had nearly tripled since 1871, and most
of the immigrants were Protestants from Ontario. The
Métis were outnumbered and losing political power.
Promised land grants had not been forthcoming, so many
Métis had sold their land rights and moved west out of
frustration. The news upset Riel and he declared that
action must be taken but suggested none.

Riel left Pembina and eventually made his way to
a Métis community north of the Missouri River. There he
participated in the buffalo hunts and lived as the Métis
once had. It fired his blood to charge into the herds on
buffalo runners shooting at the shaggy beasts amidst the
dust and noise!

"The buffalo meat," he wrote to his mother, "is a good
remedy because I feel stronger."

But there was competition for the scarce buffalo. Camped
nearby were many Natives, all hungry and anxious to hunt
the animals that had once been the foundation of their way
of life. Seeing the gathered tribes inspired Riel. He knew
that many of them were once enemies, but circumstances
had driven them together. Perhaps they would join the Métis
in an alliance to defeat their white oppressors?

It was not to be. American officials disrupted Riel's proposed meeting of Native chiefs to discuss the matter. Riel
put such ideas behind him, and after living a few years in the
Métis camp, he accepted a job as a school teacher. Less than
a year later, four Métis emissaries arrived asking him to
return to Canada and to take up again the Métis cause in the
North-West Territories. Their leader, Gabriel Dumont,
a prominent Métis who had earned the respect of his people
as captain of many successful buffalo hunts, was persuasive.

There was no reason for Riel not to return since his exile was over, and in his mind lingered the belief that he had unfinished business in Canada.

"The Canadian government owes me a land grant. That much of the Manitoba Act, I hope, hasn't changed. I will return with you to make my claim. While I am there, I will assist my Métis brothers in obtaining their own rights," he pledged to Dumont and the others. "Once I have achieved those things, I will return to Montana, where I will organize the local Métis so that they might obtain their rights also."

Dumont embraced him. The five men left on June 10, 1884.

As they rode off, Riel called to his wife, "I will be back by September!"

Conversations with Dumont on the journey north bolstered Riel's confidence that the Dominion government might well be forced into making concessions since so many Métis felt slighted. Riel listened with interest as Dumont described the situation.

"The Métis have sent many petitions to Ottawa, seeking assurances that the newcomers will not take our land or force us to change our ways. They have gone unanswered."

"Ottawa has long had difficulty hearing," replied Riel.

"It is not only the Métis who have been disappointed by the government," Dumont stated. "Other settlers are angry that the railroad was pulled far to the south. They fear their communities might not survive so far from the transportation route. Some have demanded a representative in the House of Commons who might put forward their grievances."

"They should have political representation. We live in a democracy," observed Riel. "Geography or race do not make us lesser members of the country."

"The Indians are also angry," added Dumont. "The buffalo are gone and they are hungry. The treaties were sup-
posed to guarantee them food, but the government gives
them little and even that is of poor quality. Indian agents
tell them where they may or may not live. They tell them
they must farm. The Indians did not agree to that. Already
they discuss taking up arms against the government."

"I have met with the Cree chief Big Bear in the
Missouri valley," replied Riel. "He shared his vision with
me—an Indian confederacy that links reserves across the
West. I thought it a good vision."

It was a vision that did not need Riel's leadership though
it could benefit from his alliance. Even as the small Métis
party made its way to the Saskatchewan valley, the tribes of
the North-West Territories were participating in a Sun
Dance called by Big Bear near Battleford. The council that
followed the ceremony witnessed history's largest gathering
of Plains chiefs. Listeners were sympathetic to Big Bear's
ideas of an Indian Territory and greater autonomy. His
efforts united the Plains Cree and appealed to the Blackfoot
farther west. A great council of all the Plains people was
proposed for the summer of 1885. Indian Commissioner
Edgar Dewdney convinced Macdonald (who was again
prime minister) that serious trouble was on the horizon, and
he agreed to increase the number of Mounted Police in the
Canadian West.

When Riel and his companions arrived at the
Saskatchewan valley in early July 1884, they were probably unaware of what was transpiring among the Natives.
Knowing that they were restless and intent on acting,
however, surely must have encouraged Riel. The greater
the Dominion government's trouble in the West, the
more likely they were to listen. Riel tackled the problem
with his old enthusiasm. He spoke at gatherings in the

Métis-dominated Batoche-St. Laurent area on the South Saskatchewan River and found himself cheered at every stop. He was even popular at the English settlements of Fort Carlton and Prince Albert on the North Saskatchewan River. Soon individuals were coming to the house of his cousin, Charles Nolin, where Riel was living, to share their concerns.

Clearly, the people held great hope in this man. They envisioned he could do for them what he had done for Red River. But it was not the same man. Already religious fervor was slipping into his thoughts.

He wrote to his brother, "Not long ago, I was a humble schoolmaster on the faraway banks of the Missouri. Here I am today in the ranks of the most popular men in the Saskatchewan. What has brought all this about? You know that it is God. I humble myself to the ground. The Lord has done great things for me. What shall I render to God for the favors he has heaped on me?"

If Riel had again begun to think about his religious mission, the Métis were not concerned. If anything, it increased his influence among them. One priest observed that the Métis considered Riel "a Joshua, a prophet, even a saint."

Bishop Grandin confided to Bishop Taché that the Métis "spoke to me of Riel with an extraordinary enthusiasm. For them he was a saint; I would say rather a kind of God...." The Catholic church became worried and it began to distance itself from Riel, a split that would widen over subsequent months.

By December 1884, the grievances of those in the Saskatchewan valley were given form in a petition that echoed the concerns outlined 15 years earlier in Red River. It also complained about the treatment of Riel in Manitoba. The *Bill of Rights* was endorsed by representatives of the entire community and sent to Ottawa on December 16. In late January, the government acknowledged its receipt and promised a commission to investigate problems in the North-West though Métis grievances were not specifically noted, and there was no mention at all of the *Bill of Rights*. The commission would not, however, negotiate with Riel because he was now an American citizen.

Upon hearing of the reply, Riel sought to abandon the cause. In February, he made plans to return to Montana, but his Métis allies convinced him to remain. Urged on by close associates supportive of armed action, including Nolin, Dumont and Maxime Lepine (brother of Ambroise), Riel finally took the step from which there would be no retreat. In March 1885, from the steps of the church at St. Laurent, he addressed a large crowd and set the North-West Rebellion in motion.

"It is time to adopt a new policy in dealing with the Dominion government, tactics that might prove more promising. Our efforts at peaceful negotiation have achieved nothing! We might expect more if we bare our teeth!" he declared. "It is time to make a show of force. For I have only to lift my finger, and you shall see a vast multitude of nations rushing here who are only awaiting the signal on my part."

Included in this "vast multitude of nations" were the Natives. He had many Native allies in the United States and, since his return, he had met with Native chiefs in Canada. In the summer of 1884, Riel and Big Bear discussed Native grievances. They talked about the treaties and how the Dominion government had acted in bad faith. Both agreed that the Natives needed to fight for better terms. Big Bear asked Riel to help his people once the Métis had secured their rights. Riel knew that a word on his part would bring Big Bear and his allies into the fray. Others knew it too.

Hayter Reed, the Assistant Indian Commissioner, wrote to his superior in January 1885, "Riel's movement has a great deal to do with the demands of the Indians, and there is no possible doubt but that they…are beginning to look up to him as one who will be the means of curing all their ills and obtaining for them all they demand."

But Riel would not bare his teeth or make the call until he had the support of the Catholic church. It was not forthcoming. The church was upset at Riel's criticisms that it was not doing enough to help the Métis cause and that it had sided with the Dominion government. When confronted by Father Fourmond, the parish priest at St. Laurent village, Riel's frustrations were evident.

"How could the church not stand at our side? Priests accompanied us on buffalo hunts, and they lived with us in our prairie camps through long, cold winters! They have always been welcomed in our communities, and our people have been the stronger for it. Our allegiance to the church has never been in doubt," Riel reminded him. "Now the priests have turned on us. They are the spies of the police. Well, the Métis will no longer give their blind obedience to the church," he declared.

Father Fourmond angrily replied, "Any Catholic who proposes rebellion can no longer consider himself a Catholic."

"I am a Catholic and I do not need your approval. Old Rome has fallen!" he shouted. Although Riel wanted the support of the church, he didn't need it. "The Métis listen to me, and I listen to God!"

"You speak blasphemy!" shouted the priest. "You are a heretic!"

Riel ignored the priest's final comment, and later he would even go so far as detaining the more outspoken priests. With his supporters, he urged the Métis to gather at

Batoche, a major Métis settlement along the South
Saskatchewan River. Riel made his way there with about 70
followers, not yet certain about what he would do once
there. Along the way they met a group of Métis who
informed them that the government had finally decided to
address Métis grievances by sending in 500 Mounted Police.

There was some truth to the rumor. Superintendent Lief
Crozier of Fort Carlton (about 25 miles northwest of
Batoche) had wired Indian Commissioner Dewdney that
a rebellion was "liable to break out at any moment." On
March 15, Crozier was authorized to take 100 Mounties into
the troubled area in the Saskatchewan valley, possibly to arrest
Riel, but certainly to investigate the situation. The news
prompted Riel to take action. He had his men detain some
government officials encountered on the trail, and he raided
a store of arms and ammunition, promising later payment.

On March 19, the feast of St. Joseph, the Métis patron
saint, Riel directed his followers to meet at St. Anthony's
Church in Batoche. After the appropriate celebrations,
Riel formed his new provisional government. It was not
the democratic enterprise witnessed in Red River. Riel
nominated the members and those gathered simply signi-
fied their approval with their cheers. Dumont was made
the adjutant general (the captain of the army). Riel called
the new provisional government the *Exovedate*, meaning
"those picked from the flock." Riel took no official position in the *Exovedate;* the Métis prophet was beyond the
need for civic title.

Riel set about consolidating his forces; however, some
Métis opposed armed resistance. One was Charles Nolin
(who had been convinced by a priest to abandon his hard-
line position). The *Exovedate* charged Nolin with treason. He
was convicted and sentenced to death. Riel, however, did not
want the sentence carried out since he hoped an act of

mercy might encourage the church to come to support the Métis actions. Unaware of Riel's reluctance, Nolin agreed to support the resistance in order to save himself. Other objecting Métis were also put on trial, and the effect was to suppress all opposition. On March 20, runners were dispatched to the local Native communities to enlist their support. However, Riel was not convinced it was yet time to bring the Natives into the fray. He feared that they were not likely to be restrained once they agreed to fight, and Riel was not yet convinced that armed resistance was necessary. He believed that Prime Minister Macdonald would submit to Métis demands with only the threat of war. However, under pressure from others in the *Exovedate*, especially Dumont, he agreed to seek out Native support.

The country born were another matter. In the face of Riel's sudden and rebellious acts, their enthusiasm wavered. Without them, Riel believed that the success of his mission was at risk. He could not force the country born to participate, so he set about making a reasoned case for their support. He wrote two letters that were to be read to all country born. He reassured them that the Métis had the support of the Native peoples and he revisited the reasons for the Métis actions—Dominion government indifference, neglect and high-handed treatment—and argued that all residents in the North-West were affected.

"Gentlemen, please do not remain neutral! For the love of God help us to save the Saskatchewan....A strong union between the French and the English half-breeds is the only guarantee that there will be no bloodshed!"

The position was persuasive and the reluctant were reassured. Riel got the answer he hoped for on March 23. A meeting of the country born determined that "the voice of every man was with him [Riel]." If there was no treaty made within 48 hours, they would join with the Métis and fight.

In the end, the situation would not take a turn towards peace. Superintendent Crozier had been in contact with Riel through his emissaries. By early March he was convinced that the Métis would rebel. Intelligence sources informed him that Riel would first strike at Fort Carlton. It was Riel's desire to take the fort because he was convinced the act would force the government to address the concerns held by so many in the Saskatchewan valley and, as Riel put it, to "get our rights." Nevertheless, Crozier hoped to avoid violence. On March 20, when he learned that Riel was willing to meet with him and discuss the situation, he dispatched his emissary to make arrangements. It's possible that Crozier's agent informed Riel that only the surrender of the movement's leaders could avoid bloodshed, but whatever he said enraged Riel. His reply to Crozier left no room for doubt.

> *Major: The Councillors of the Provisional Government of the Saskatchewan have the honor to communicate to you the following conditions of surrender: You will be required to give up completely the situation which the Canadian Government have placed you in, at [Forts] Carlton and Battleford, together with all Government properties.*
>
> *In case of acceptance, you and your men will be set free, on your parole of honor to keep the peace. And those who will choose to leave the country will be furnished with teams and provisions to reach Qu'Appelle.*
>
> *In case of non-acceptance, we intend to attack you tomorrow, when the Lord's Day is over; and to commence a war of extermination upon all those who have shown themselves hostile to our rights.*

Riel would not travel with the message for fear of arrest. His delegates never gave it to Crozier. When they met him, the superintendent told the Métis to disband and return to their homes. Crozier likely never intended to negotiate. He was playing for time, waiting for reinforcements to arrive. But they would not be there before the Métis moved on Fort Carlton.

On March 26, Crozier learned that Gabriel Dumont and a band of 16 men had attacked the store of a suspected Mounted Police spy in Duck Lake (about 10 miles southeast of Fort Carlton). He led a party of 121 men (a combined force of Mounted Police and Prince Albert volunteers) to the site. Riel, unaware that Crozier was making for Duck Lake, was also en route with 120 men. He planned to meet up with Dumont, make for Fort Carlton and surround it. When Riel reached Duck Lake, he was informed that Crozier's men were also on the Fort Carlton-Duck Lake trail. He had the Métis and Natives in the community (some 300) organized for support.

The two forces met outside Duck Lake. Crozier gave the first order to fire. He had an artillery piece trained on the trail, and when he saw that the Métis were slipping out of the target range, he decided not to delay. Unfortunately the artillery piece jammed and proved useless. Riel tried to direct the battle, but his orders were ill-advised and Dumont quickly assumed control.

Riel began encouraging his followers by riding up and down the line, waving a cross he had taken from a church at Duck Lake and shouting, "Reply to the police fire in the name of the Father, the Son and the Holy Ghost!"

It wasn't long before the reinforcements from Duck Lake arrived and, with them, the Métis easily outnumbered the Mounted Police and volunteers. Crozier ordered a retreat, and Riel commanded that they be allowed to go in peace.

"There has been too much blood spilled already," he cried. Twelve under Crozier's command had died along with five Métis.

Gabriel Dumont wanted to ambush the fleeing Mounties, but acceded to Riel's demands that they go unmolested. Dumont fumed. He watched as Métis forces in Batoche grew to some 450 in the days following the victory at Duck Lake. He continued to press Riel to go on the offensive, to carry out his proposed war of extermination, but Riel was confident that delegates from Ottawa would arrive. He hoped it would be soon since he knew that if Dumont commanded it, the Métis would follow him. Dumont was the acknowledged warrior, and in battle his directions would reign supreme.

As sound as Dumont's offensive plan might be (the Métis and their Native allies had a good chance of taking control of the North-West before the Dominion government could properly organize a defense), he would not challenge Riel.

"I yielded to Riel's judgment," he later recalled, "...I had confidence in his faith and his prayers and that God would listen to him."

The Natives would not wait, however, and Riel shouldered some of the responsibility for that. Throughout the spring he was in regular contact with most of the bands in the region. The runners he dispatched actively fomented unrest among the Natives by declaring Riel's desire that they attack the North-West Mounted Police and the forts. Riel's wishes were taken seriously because most of the Natives had great respect for the Métis leader.

On March 30, Cree chief Poundmaker surrounded Battleford. It is not clear that Poundmaker wanted anything to do with rebellion. He had long been an advocate of peace and an ally of the white man, but reserve life had been hard on his people. They were hungry, sick and poor. They rode to Battleford for supplies. Townsfolk suspected the worst and so retreated to the fort, where they watched their town being pillaged.

When Riel learned of their attack, he sent a message urging them on. "Arise. Face the enemy. If you can take Fort Battle[ford], destroy it. Save all the merchandise and provisions, and come and join us....Whatever you do, do for the love of God. Under the protection of Jesus Christ, the Blessed Virgin, St. Joseph and St. John the Baptist, be certain that faith works wonders."

The siege of Battleford was followed by what became known as the Massacre at Frog Lake. Big Bear's band of Cree was suffering from poverty and destitution as much as Poundmaker's band. Big Bear was also under Dominion government pressure to take his people to a reservation, which he was reluctant to do. While he preferred a peaceful solution to the Cree's problems, some in his band, led by the war chief Wandering Spirit, were prepared to fight. Their war readiness was due, at least in part, to the efforts of Riel's agents. The news of events at Duck Lake and Fort Battleford was the spark needed to ignite the Cree and, on April 2, a party of young warriors killed nine white men, including the Indian agent and two priests. They also captured Fort Pitt (a North-West Mounted Police post) and set fire to it.

On hearing of the events, Riel sent tobacco in support and messages counseling against undue violence. "Neither kill nor molest nor ill-treat any persons unnecessarily, but take away arms."

By late April, the Dominion government considered the Métis situation critical. Reports revealed that it was sending in the militia rather than negotiators. The new railroad hurried Major General Frederick Middleton to Fort Qu'Appelle. He had some 3000 soldiers under his command, and combined with the Mounted Police and volunteers, some 5000 were ready to suppress the uprising in the North-West Territories. They would attack from Qu'Appelle, Swift Current and Calgary.

As Dominion government forces grew, the Métis force decreased. Many left Batoche because of inaction. Those who remained—less than 300 and fewer still armed—were pressuring Dumont to fight. But Riel had tied Dumont's hands. He did not want his adjutant general to be engaged in nighttime raids and sallies, Dumont's preferred attack strategy. Riel did not want to further divide the Métis soldiers or to see Dumont killed. However, as morale continued to wane, Dumont took matters into his own hands. He sent word to Poundmaker, Big Bear and the Sioux chief White Cap that he was preparing to ambush Middleton's men who, at 800 strong, were marching north.

When he informed Riel of what he had done, Riel replied, "All right! Do as you wish." Riel had come to realize that negotiation required further demonstration.

Dumont's men attacked Middleton's North-West Field Force on April 24, at Fish Creek, just south of Batoche. Although the Métis were well outnumbered (desertions during the battle had reduced their numbers to just over 50) by late afternoon, the army retreated and camped at a nearby hill. It was more of a stalemate than a Métis victory (two Métis and two Sioux dead, with 11 injured; 10 militia dead, with 44 wounded), but it raised Métis spirits. Dumont wanted to press the advantage, and in this he had the support of his men.

Riel, however, would not agree. "God has told me, no farther than this." Dumont acceded to his leader's wish.

To the west, the other columns of Middleton's forces had mixed results. Lieutenant Colonel William Otter was able to end the siege of Battleford, but when he followed up with an attack on Poundmaker at Cut Knife Hill on

May 2, he was forced to retreat. It was a decisive Cree victory.

Major General Thomas Strange marched from Calgary and met Big Bear at Frenchman's Butte (just east of Fort Pitt) on May 27. Both forces retreated simultaneously. But even a victory by Big Bear would not have helped Riel. A couple of weeks before the Battle at Frenchman's Butte, the Métis resistance had played itself out.

On May 9, Middleton attacked Batoche. It started poorly for the militia perhaps because, as Middleton later conceded, the Métis had chosen well and effectively organized their defensive positions. Middleton commandeered and armed a stern-wheeler. He planned to use it to give defense to his ground troops, but the river offensive was launched before the men were in position. When the militiamen finally arrived, the Métis countered from the network of rifle pits that they had dug in anticipation of the assault. For three more days, the struggle continued with little ground gained or life lost on either side. The Métis, however, were in a tenuous position; their ammunition was running low. Some had already begun using nails as bullets. Others, who sensed the inevitable, had deserted.

On May 12, Middleton moved his men into position for an all-out offensive. Riel, who had spent much of the time during intervening days in prayer, advised Dumont to surrender. Dumont would not. In a final attempt to avoid great bloodshed, Riel tried to contact Middleton and inform him that continued attack would result in the execution of the prisoners (including the Indian agent). The message became irrelevant when the militia stormed the town, apparently without Middleton's authorization. Superior numbers won the day, and by nightfall they took Batoche. The Métis fled for the woods while Dumont continued south to the United States (he would subsequently be pardoned for his actions).

When Riel received word from Middleton that his safety would be guaranteed until the matter was decided by the Dominion government, he surrendered on May 15. Poundmaker (May 26) and Big Bear (July 2) soon joined Riel. Middleton made it clear to the Native leaders that he would not stop fighting until they were defeated. Any desire among the Natives to continue fighting was further diminished as the Dominion government flooded their reservations with rations. Both chiefs would eventually receive three years imprisonment although both would be released before their terms were completed.

A party of 16 soldiers led by Captain George Young escorted Riel to Regina, where he would stand trial on July 20, 1885 on a charge of treason. Support for his cause remained high in Québec, and a Riel Defense Committee was established in his support. Three lawyers defended him (a fourth was subsequently added), but even to them, it was clear that Riel had committed treason. He had but one defense: insanity. But Riel would not agree to that plea. Against his wishes his lawyers began to make a case based on his insanity, so Riel stood in the prisoner's docket and addressed the judge.

"Here I have to defend myself against the accusation of high treason, or I have to consent to an animal life in an asylum. I don't care much about animal life if I am not allowed to carry with it the moral existence of an intellectual being."

Riel wanted the opportunity to justify his actions in a courtroom, but despite his feelings and likely under intense pressure from his lawyers, Riel allowed them to continue on with their chosen defense. Some witnesses spoke in support of his actions, while others addressed what

Louis Riel on trial for treason, July 1885. Originally, Riel's case was to be tried at Winnipeg, but Minister of Justice Alexander Campbell moved it to Regina, where he believed justice would be better served. But not, perhaps, for Riel. The change in jurisdictions meant a jury of six English-speaking Protestants rather than a jury of twelve that would likely have included some French-speaking Catholics. Additionally, Riel's trial was conducted by a magistrate, whose position depended on the goodwill of the government, rather than a judge, whose job security was independent of government whim. Despite the apparent bias, Riel's lawyers hoped that an insanity plea might prevent their client's conviction. Riel, however, rejected an insanity defense because he believed it cast doubt on Métis grievances and actions, and would ultimately undermine the Métis cause. Instead, Riel declared to a packed courthouse "I believe I have done my duty." He was sentenced to die for it.

they could only believe was his madness. Insanity, however, was a difficult defense to make at this time. It was governed by the M'Naghten Rule, which used a very strict and narrow definition of mental illness in court cases. Doctors were brought in to evaluate his state of mind; two of three concluded that he was sane.

Finally, Riel was allowed to speak in his own defense. He began with a prayer for himself and the court, requesting, perhaps with dark humor, that it not be taken as a sign of his insanity. Then, in a most rational manner, he outlined the motivation for his—and the Métis'—actions.

"When I came to the North-West in July, the first of July 1884, I found the Indians suffering. I found the half-breeds eating the rotten pork of the Hudson's Bay Company and getting sick and weak every day. Although a half-breed, and having no pretension to help the whites, I also paid attention to them. I saw they were deprived of responsible government; I saw that they were deprived of their public liberties. I remembered that half-breed meant white and Indian…and I have directed my attention to help the Indians, to help the half-breeds and to help the whites to the best of my ability."

Riel went on to describe some of the efforts that had been undertaken. "We have made petitions…to the Canadian government asking to relieve the condition of the country. We have taken time; we have tried to unite all classes, even if I may speak, all parties. Those who have been in close communication with me know I have suffered, that I have waited for months to bring some of the people of the Saskatchewan to an understanding of certain important points in our petition to the Canadian government, and I have done my duty. I believe I have done my duty."

Riel addressed his alleged insanity, declaring it to be no more than his "wish to leave Rome aside, inasmuch as it is the cause of [historical] division between Catholics and Protestants....I do not wish these evils which exist in Europe to be continued, as much as I can influence it, among the half-breeds. I do not wish that to be repeated in America."

Riel concluded with a heartfelt appeal to the jury. "For 15 years I have been neglecting myself. Even one of the most hard witnesses on me said that with all my vanity, I was never particular to my clothing; yes, because I never had much to buy any clothing....My wife and children are without means while I am working more than any representative in the North-West. Although I am simply a guest in this country— a guest of the half-breeds of the Saskatchewan—although as a simple guest, I worked to better the condition of the people of the Saskatchewan at the risk of my life, to better the condition of the people of the North-West, I have never had any pay. It has always been my hope to have a fair living one day. It will be for you to pronounce—if you say I was right, you can conscientiously acquit me, as I hope through the help of God you will. You will console those who have been 15 years around me only partaking in sufferings. What you will do in justice to me, in justice to my friends, in justice to the North-West, will be rendered a hundred times to you in this world, and to use a sacred expression, life everlasting in the other."

In his direction to the jury, Mr. Justice Richardson asked them to consider whether such things as Riel had done could be permitted. They considered it for just over an hour and returned with a guilty verdict. They also recommended mercy. Richardson rejected the recommendation and, on August 1, sentenced Riel to be hanged on September 18. It was the harshest of the sentences imposed by the court on those Métis who had participated in the rebellion, although eight Natives were also hanged.

The verdict was appealed, but unsuccessfully. Riel's lawyers sought clemency from the Dominion government. Prime Minister Macdonald struggled to find a way out that would appease both English and French Canada. Twice he postponed the execution. He appointed a commission to inquire further into Riel's sanity. They were not to consider whether he suffered from delusions or illusions but to determine whether he knew right from wrong. They concluded that Riel knew the difference and was therefore sane. At the end of the day, Macdonald had to face the simple fact that Riel's treason was undeniable.

On the morning of November 16, Riel wrote a final letter to his mother, "as a son respectful of his duty" and attended Mass that afternoon. He was hanged that evening. The tattered letter of encouragement from Bishop Bourget was later discovered in his pocket. Riel's body lay in state at the St. Boniface Cathedral, and he was later buried beside his father in the cathedral cemetery.

Notes on Sources

AS MUCH AS POSSIBLE, the dialogue in this book is accurate and the accounts described are fictionalized as little as possible

SITTING BULL

Hollihan, Tony. *Sitting Bull in Canada*. Edmonton: Folklore Publishing, 2001.

Utley, Robert. *The Lance and the Shield: The Life and Times of Sitting Bull*. New York: Henry Holt and Co., 1993.

Vestal, Stanley. *Sitting Bull: Champion of the Sioux*. Boston: Houghton Mifflin, 1932.

CHIEF JOSEPH

Chief Joseph. "Chief Joseph's Own Story." *The North American Review*, April 1879.

Lavender, David. *Let Me Be Free: The Nez Perce Tragedy*. New York: HarperCollins, 1992.

Yates, Diana. *Chief Joseph: Thunder Rolling Down from the Mountain*. Staten Island: Ward Hill Press, 1992.

QUANAH PARKER

Fehrenbach, T.R. *Comanches: The Destruction of a People*. New York: Alfred A. Knopf, 1979.

Jackson, Clyde & Grace Jackson. *Quanah Parker: Last of the Comanche Chiefs.* New York: Exposition Press, 1963.

Wallace, Ernest & E. Adamson Hoebel. *The Comanches: Lords of the South Plains.* Norman: University of Oklahoma Press, 1952.

Wilson, Claire. *Quanah Parker: Comanche Chief.* New York: Chelsea House, 1992.

RED CLOUD

Hyde, George. *Red Cloud's Folk: A History of the Oglala Sioux Indians.* 1937. Reprint, Norman: University of Oklahoma Press, 1957.

Larson, Robert. *Red Cloud: Warrior-Statesman of the Lakota Sioux.* Norman: University of Oklahoma Press, 1997.

Olson, James. *Red Cloud and the Sioux Problem.* Lincoln: University of Nebraska Press, 1965.

SEQUOYAH

Gearing, Fred. *Priests and Warriors.* (*Memoir 93*). Menasha, Wisconsin: American Anthropological Association, 1922.

Klausner, Janet. *Sequoyah's Gift: A Portrait of the Cherokee Leader.* New York: HarperCollins, 1993.

Rogers, Mary Evelyn. *A Brief History of the Cherokees, 1540–1906.* Baltimore: Gateway Press, 1986.

Shumate, Jane. *Sequoyah: Inventor of the Cherokee Alphabet.* New York: Chelsea House Publishers, 1994.

LOUIS RIEL

Siggins, Maggie. *Riel: A Life of Revolution.* Toronto: HarperCollins, 1994.

Stanley, George. *Louis Riel.* Toronto: Ryerson Press, 1963.